ALSO BY TIMOTHY GARTON ASH

The Polish Revolution: Solidarity

TIMOTHY GARTON ASH

The Uses of Adversity

Essays on the Fate of Central Europe

GRANTA BOOKS

CAMBRIDGE

in association with
PENGUIN BOOKS

GRANTA BOOKS
44a Hobson Street, Cambridge CB1 1NL

Published in association with the Penguin Group
27 Wrights Lane, London W8 5TZ, England
Viking Penguin Inc., 40 West 23rd Street, New York, NY 10010, USA
Penguin Books Australia Ltd, Ringwood, Victoria, Australia
Penguin Book Canada Ltd, 2801 John Street,
Markham, Ontario, Canada L3R 1B4
Penguin Books (NZ) Ltd, 182–190 Wairau Road,
Auckland 10, New Zealand

Penguin Books Ltd, Registered Offices:
Harmondsworth, Middlesex, England

First Edition

Photoset by Cambridge Photosetting Services
Printed in Great Britain by Richard Clay Ltd

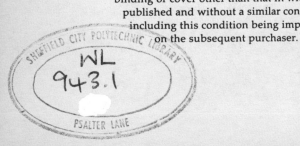

FOR THEM

PREFACE

This book reflects my own interest in ideas rather than armies, cultures rather than economies, nations rather than political systems and, above all, individual men and women rather than amorphous collectivities. By chance—by serendipity—these are also priorities of the debate about Central Europe that for the last five years has wandered across Europe and North America like a brilliant but erratic exile. Most of the main themes of that debate are present in this volume, one way or another, and treated, I hope, with all due scepticism as well as sympathy. For in exploring the once and future Central Europe, I have not closed my eyes to the present reality of Eastern Europe, much as one might sometimes wish to.

> Sweet are the uses of adversity;
> Which, like the toad, ugly and venomous
> Wears yet a jewel in his head;

I have tried to describe both—the ugliness of the body, and the beauty of the jewel.

These essays, sketches, and dispatches are arranged chronologically, with only minor revisions. All bear the marks of their first publication. Most were originally published in the *New York Review of Books* or the *Spectator*. These journals represent two extremes of Anglo-Saxon editing. The *New York Review* is a model of interventionism, offering the writer a marvellous bombardment of criticisms, queries, books, articles, galley proofs, Federal Express deliveries, telexes, faxes, and telephone calls. The *Spectator* is a model of *laissez-faire*. When the telephone rings at, say, midnight on Christmas Eve, my wife at once exclaims 'Bob Silvers' and Bob Silvers of the *New York Review* it generally is, with a suggestion for correcting a dangling modifier on galley ten, or merely a small point about the future of the world. When the telephone rang one day in 1979, albeit at a decent after-lunch hour, I was greatly surprised to find that the caller was Alexander Chancellor, then editor of the *Spectator*. 'Tim, thought you might like to go to Eastern Europe,' said he. Why I might go to Eastern Europe, what I might write, how or when: none of this was mentioned. As a result, the *New York Review* is the *Edinburgh Review* of our time and the *Spectator* is—the *Spectator*.

The other publications in which one of more of these pieces have appeared lie somewhere between these two extremes. Bill Buford's *Granta*, although physically located in Cambridge, England, has a strong vein of New York interventionism. The *New Republic*, although physically located in Washington, America, has more than a touch of English *laissez-faire*. The *TLS* is poised perfectly in the middle, like a rural dean.

I am deeply grateful to those who have edited my work in these journals: to Bob Silvers, Barbara Epstein, and their inexhaustible editorial assistants at the *New York Review*; to successive editors of the *Spectator*, Alexander Chancellor and Charles Moore; to their successive deputies, Peter Ackroyd, Simon Courtauld, Andrew Gimson, and Dominic Lawson; to the production editor, Christopher Howse; and to successive secretaries to the editor, Jenny Naipaul and Julia Mount, around whom the *Spectator*, if it may be said to do anything so enthusiastic, revolves; to the inimitable Bill Buford and his colleagues at *Granta*; to Marty Peretz, Rick Hertzberg, Michael Kinsley, Dorothy Wickenden, and Leon Wieseltier at the *New Republic*; to Jeremy Treglown and Liz Winter at the *TLS*. Piers Spence and Tim Adams of the new Granta Books have given me much practical assistance, often under great pressure. As book publisher as well as magazine editor, Bill Buford has been inimitable, enthusiastic, and wilful. The dust-jacket to this edition, in particular, reflects his sensibility as much as mine.

Beyond this, I must express my gratitude to those who taught me, in Oxford and Berlin, what I know of the historian's craft and to the many acquaintances, colleagues, and friends in academic life, journalism, diplomacy, and politics who have helped me with information, criticism, or advice. I cannot omit to mention two institutions that made the final composition of this volume possible: the Ford Foundation, and particularly its international programme director, Enid Schoettle, and my old and new Oxford college, St Antony's, especially its warden, Ralf Dahrendorf, whose generous support has been intellectual as well as organizational. Caroline Henderson fought valiantly with the typescript. My family gave me endless support and distraction.

My greatest debt, however, is to all those in Poland, Czechoslovakia, Hungary, Austria, and Germany (East and West) who have done what I have merely written about. This book is dedicated to them.

TGA, OXFORD, MAY, 1989

CONTENTS

THE USES OF ADVERSITY

Sketches from
Another Germany

Nostalgia

Nostalgia is not a quality you would normally associate with East Germany. But sitting in Oxford watching brief television flashes from Dresden and East Berlin, I felt a curious pang.

I travelled widely in East Germany in the late 1970s and then, in 1980, I had the rare opportunity to live for nine months in East Berlin. I was there as a postgraduate student from Oxford, researching into the history of Berlin under Hitler. The Humboldt University found me a room in a battered Wilhelmine tenement block in Prenzlauer Berg, an old working-class quarter that was already home to the milieu of attic poets, actors, painters and students from which the recently exiled balladeer Stephan Krawczyk emerged. And the Protestant churches already provided a haven for free expression and honest debate. One local church, I recall, contained an almost Chinese-style 'wall newspaper', with full and fair accounts of the NATO and Warsaw Pact nuclear armouries. The 'peace debate' was just getting under way.

My room had a balcony that seemed in imminent danger of collapse and a huge, dark-wood sideboard. The other room in the flat was occupied by an Angolan taxidermist. Or perhaps I should say *the* Angolan taxidermist, since, so far as I could gather, all the others, being Portuguese, had fled the country after independence. East Germany was giving him further training—a benign form of 'fraternal assistance'. I may, however, have got this quite wrong, for curiously enough, the taxidermist spoke no German and his English was somewhat limited. 'Good night!' he would say every evening before retiring to bed. 'Good night!' he would greet me in the morning. 'Good night!' he would sweetly exclaim if we met at midday.

3

I worked for a time in the Department for Special Research Literature of the old Prussian State Library on Unter den Linden. This department was colloquially known as the poison cupboard, for it contained everything that the state did not want its ordinary subjects to read.

The evening I spent with friends, at the cinema or in the theatre—which was generally excellent, with the added electricity of 'listening between the lines' for covert contemporary allusions. I ate in my splendid local pub, where, since you always had to share a table, you invariably met new people. Once your bona fides as a foreigner had been established, the confidences poured out. Establishing the bona fides was sometimes comical. 'All right, so you say you're a historian,' barked one young worker. 'So tell me: Where was Karl Marx born?' Fortunately, I knew the answer. 'And who was the leader the of the KPD [the German Communist Party] in 1930?' Right again. 'Mmmmmmm, who brought Hitler to power? And'—he could no longer restrain himself—'for f——'s sake don't say the monopoly capitalists.'

Once I went with a Polish friend to the Ballhaus Berlin, a dance hall that (oh shades of Isherwood) still had numbered table telephones. Spotting some pretty girls, we dialled their number. But this was East Berlin, so the telephone didn't work. Returning to my chilly quarters, I would turn on the radio, only to hear the English-language radio station for the American forces in West Berlin announcing the arrival—across the Wall—of Joan Baez: 'So come on, folks. Saturday, 22 March. *Joan Baez hits the Wall!*'

Unreal city. But most inspiring was travel outside Berlin. Unlike the accredited correspondents, I was free to travel wherever I liked in the GDR, without surveillance: an opportunity I used to the full. Few people in Britain realize that East Germany is a beautiful country. Or perhaps I should rephrase that: Few people realize what beautiful country the GDR contains. One might even say what beautiful coun*tries*, for the historic principates and kingdoms of Saxony, Thuringia, the Mark Brandenburg and Mecklenburg are more like countries than counties. All over Eastern Europe, the relative backwardness of socialism has conserved much of what capitalism has destroyed. A dear friend drove me around the Mark Brandenburg with Theodore Fontane's *Wanderungen* in hand, and almost nothing seemed to have changed in a hundred years.

My heart was lost to Thuringia, with its lovely wooded hills (to which Prince Albert always looked back nostalgically), Gothic churches and exquisite small towns. Above all to Weimar, which the grand old lady of East German letters, Anna Seghers, memorably called 'the best and worst place in German history.' Best, for Goethe and Schiller, and perhaps the Weimar of the Bauhaus and the Weimar Republic. Worst, for Buchenwald, which still lurks above the town on the very hillside where Goethe composed his sublime *'Wandrers Nachtlied'*:

> *Der du von dem Himmel bist,*
> *Alles Leid und Schmerzen stillest . . .*

To this day, Goethe's house remains the most delightful and eloquent of writers' homes. Saxony comes a close second to Thuringia in my affections, despite the poor behaviour of the Saxon kings in Poland. One cannot feel too badly about a dynasty whose last representative is said to have abdicated with the immortal words *'Na, Kinder, dann macht Euch Euren Dreck alleene'*—which might inadequately be translated as: 'All right, boys, make the cock-ups on your own.'

But at the heart of Saxony is a gaping wound. The wound is called Dresden. I was there on 13 February, the anniversary of the bombing. 'Are you from *drüben* [i.e., West Germany]?' a middle-aged woman asked me.

'No, I'm English.'

'Ach, why did you do it?'

Not a moment's doubt what 'it' is. I felt the question was justified and that it was fair to put it to me. *Tu quoque* would be no answer at all.

There was a dignified service in the restored Kreuzkirche and a moving performance of Dvořák's *Requiem* in the Kulturpalast. At the end, instead of applauding, the audience stood for a minute's silence. Outside again, at the precise hour when the first bombs were dropped in 1945, the bells of all the surviving churches began to ring: the Hofkirche spoke to the Annenkirche; the Kreuzkirche to the Dreikönigskirche. Most eloquent of all was the Frauenkirche—a mound of silent rubble. But the Germans who gather in the Kreuzkirche now are much more concerned with contemporary

5

lessons: with the demand for an authentic peace and respect for human rights in East as well as West.

At the end of my stay, I was swept away by a mighty Polish river called Solidarność. I subsequently wrote a short book about the GDR for West German readers, in the course of which I compared East Germany somewhat unfavourably with Poland. Some of my closest friends in East Germany told me the comparison was unfair. Re-reading the book today, I think they were right. In Europe's house are many mansions: Let every people seek happiness in its own way. I am sometimes asked if there is an English version of this book. There isn't, and probably won't be. Eight years later, and for English-speaking readers, I would have to write a different book.

The East German authorities, faced, instead of a doctoral thesis about Berlin under Hitler, with a book about the GDR under Honecker—and serialized in *Der Spiegel* to boot—were understandably miffed. (I fear my Oxford supervisor may have had similar feelings.) They summoned a diplomat from the British embassy and protested that this was an appeal to the workers of the GDR to follow the Polish example. With that interesting review, I trust the book made the poison cupboard. I myself certainly made the 'blacklist' of persons not allowed back. When I asked the officer at the Friedrichstrasse underground crossing why he was refusing me entry, he said: 'Giving reasons is not internationally customary.'

(MARCH 1988)

Carmen-Sylva-Strasse

The Carmen-Sylva-Strasse, an evening in spring. Melancholy plaster faces stare down from the crumbling nineteenth-century façades. Along the narrow ravine of the street, the balconies bloom with clothes put out to dry. The neighbours are out too, gossiping, drinking beer from the bottle, shouting lazy insults across the ravine. Children play in the cobbled street. An old man, ragged, unshaven, picks his way among piles of rubbish on the pavement. Somewhere a gramophone pumps dance tunes.

After eight o'clock, when the doors of the apartment houses are locked, the regular twilight chorus. Young men whistle up to the girls waiting for them on the half-lit balconies. From the corner pub, the sound of drunken banter, the occasional row. All the borough is here:

the writer, athlete, soldier, bricklayer, an old gentleman in a frayed grey three-piece suit and bow tie; a bearded lady, seventy at least, whom the waitress addresses as *'junge Frau'*.

Later, around eleven, there is one last rousing 'Hallelujah!,' and a scarcely audible *'Scheisse!'* as a group of drunken youths stagger over the jagged paving stones on their way to bed. Later still the rumble of the last train, its lights momentarily visible as it flies past the end of the street. Then silence, complete, enveloping silence, until the brewers' drays at six in the morning.

I describe a night in the 1980s. But there is nothing here that you could not have seen in 1930. To enter this part of East Berlin is to walk through an etching by Grosz into a story by Isherwood. This *is* Berlin: the Berlin you failed to find in the West. But the appearance deceives.

To begin with, the names have changed. The Carmen-Sylva-Strasse is now called the Erich-Weinert-Strasse, after a second-rate but communist poet. Then, in the morning, you notice that the façades are covered with hundreds of wires, criss-crossing the plaster faces like the creases of old age: aerial wires to pick up Western broadcasts. The old man is not a tramp rummaging for food but a pensioner looking for old bottles, which he sells back to the state at a tiny shop just below my balcony, earning twenty or thirty *pfennigs* a time, to augment his modest pension. In the pub, the workers are grousing about their 'premiums' and the amount that is deducted for what they call *Soli:* 'solidarity donations' for Vietnam or Angola.

In November 1932, in the last election before Hitler came to power, this tough working-class quarter voted overwhelmingly for the Communists. Under the Nazis, the borough was a centre of communist resistance. Even after a fortnight of storm-trooper terror following the Reichstag fire, more than 44,000 voted Communist in the local elections on 12 March, 1933.

Today, the borough is distinguished by its reluctance to vote Communist. According to official figures for the local elections of 20 May, 1979, there were 5,000 abstentions, while 679 votes were cast against the candidates of the 'National Front' (which includes candidates from a number of puppet parties as well as the ruling Socialist Unity Party). To appreciate these figures, it helps to know that in the whole of East Germany, the vote for the National Front was claimed to be 99.82 per cent, with an electoral turn-out of 98.28 per cent. In an East German polling station, a voter presents himself before a board of two or three officials, shows his ID card, and collects a ballot paper. To vote for the National Front, he folds his ballot paper once and drops it, unmarked, into the box. To vote any other way, he has to walk across the room to mark his ballot paper in a voting booth, beside which sits a *Vopo*. A *Vopo* is a 'people's policeman'. The moment the voter steps toward the booth, his name is noted. One independent-minded voter described the few paces to the polling booth as 'the longest walk in my life'. The consequences may include demotion at work or, for a student, expulsion from the university.

'Never in German history', the son of the first president of the Weimar Republic, Friedrich Ebert, declared at an election meeting in East Berlin, 'have the people's representatives been more democratically elected.'

I visited the lowest rank of the people's representatives—my borough councillors—in the bare, unheated backroom of their Club of the National Front on a cold January evening. I asked if they had been elected.

'Yes, of course.'
'By a large majority?'
'Very large.'
'And are you from different parties?'
'No, by chance, we're from the same party.' The Socialist
    Unity Party.

In talking about their duties, they never mention the people who elected them. But they say a great deal about the Plan, a copy of which they present to me. 'The People's Economy Plan for the Borough of Prenzlauer Berg' is an example, in miniature, of the central planning by numbers that was introduced in the Soviet Union in the early 1930s: 'Book-holdings in the libraries are to be increased from 350,000 to 450,000 volumes. The number of borrowings is to be increased to 108.2 per cent.' Not 'People should be encouraged to borrow more books from the public libraries,' but 'The number of borrowings is to be increased to 108.2 per cent.' I pictured the borough librarian at the end of the year, having achieved only 105 per cent of last year's borrowings: 'Excuse me, madam, have you never read the works of Schiller? Only seventy volumes—let me sign them out in your name.'

The Plan concludes with the socialist competition: BEAUTIFY OUR

CAPITAL BERLIN: *MACH MIT* (JOIN IN). I witnessed '*MACH MIT*' in practice when a poster went up in the hall of our apartment house announcing a '*MACH MIT*' action to clear out the winter's rubbish on the following Saturday morning at eleven o'clock. I reported punctually for work. A quarter of an hour passed. Half an hour. Children peered curiously through the broken window-pane of the house door. Nobody, but nobody, *machte mit*. The winter's slush, old cigarette ends, chewing-gum papers remained just where they were.

Here in Prenzlauer Berg I saw what one gifted observer has called 'the counter-revolution of reality'. East Germany clearly is a totalitarian state in the sense that it *aspires* to occupy and direct its citizens' every waking moment. The very idea of free time is suspect to all would-be totalitarian regimes. 'In socialism the contradiction between work and free time, typical of capitalism, is removed,' the official *Small Political Dictionary* explains. Moreover, 'free time must be purposefully and effectively deployed by all members of the socialist community.' Great energy is devoted to this mobilization of the population. Schoolchildren are 'won' for 'activity . . . in the productive sections.' Youths are 'persuaded' to participate in Defence Sport events. Millions turn out for the May Day parade. To this extent the regime does succeed in mobilizing the bodies of its citizens. But even East Germany is rarely able to mobilize their hearts and minds—as it undoubtedly did in the early years of reconstruction, after the misery of wartime destruction.

In my experience, East Germans make the most elaborate arrangements to withdraw from the collective political marketplace into their own unpolitical niches. The split between the public and the private self, official and unofficial language, outward conformity and inward dissent—in short, the double life—is a phenomenon common to all Soviet-bloc countries. The switch from one persona to the other is automatic, even for a fourteen-year-old. This double life naturally implies double standards: I applaud conduct by the state that I would never endorse in private life.

The typical, truly unpolitical East German is one who turns out every year for the demonstration, hangs out his little flag on the national day, and votes in the elections. It is the people who stay away from the polls who are, paradoxically, the political Germans. Thus, the remarkable abstention rate in my borough, Prenzlauer Berg, reflects a long tradition of protest and a certain unbroken

9

working-class pride: 'Why should I take part in a farce?' as one building-worker put it. It also reflects at least a glimmer of the old-fashioned notion that a citizen's public conduct should bear some relation to his private conviction. In this looking-glass world, the non-votes are the votes that count.

Fifty years ago the Carmen-Sylva-Strasse voted in protest for the Communists; today the Erich-Weinert-Strasse votes in protest against them. Fifty years ago the inhabitants had almost no money to buy anything; today there is almost nothing to buy. Fifty years ago they demonstrated on the first of May to express solidarity against the inhuman unemployment created by a capitalist economy. Today they attempt to withdraw from the compulsory May Day demonstrations of *Soli* into the world of private enterprise represented by the allotment garden or the car. Fifty years ago they lived in dreadful insecurity; today, in dreadful security.

(JUNE 1981)

Inner Emigration

Buchenwald looks on to Weimar. Goethe composed one of his greatest poems walking the hillside later chosen for the concentration camp. The smoke from its chimneys blew over the cultured life of wartime Weimar, over the classical theatre, the poetry readings, and the chamber concerts. And the Weimar question—How was this barbarism possible in the heart of a 'civilized' country?—is *the* question of recent German history. Why did Germany's cultured bourgeoisie, the *Bildungsbürgertum*, fail to forestall or resist nazism? How could extermination-camp commandants play Bach in the intervals between supervising the gas chamber? Can we any longer believe that the humanities humanize?

In May 1945, speaking to an American audience about Germany and the Germans, Thomas Mann sought an answer in what he called the 'melancholy story' of German *Innerlichkeit:* From Luther to Goethe, German intellectuals had failed to incorporate the imperative of political and social responsibility into their central notion of what it is to be a civilized person. They raised an artificial barrier between the 'spiritual-artistic' world and the 'political-social' one. They supposed, wrongly, that the inner, spiritual freedom of culture could be divorced from outer, political freedom. In their 'musical-Germanic inwardness and unworldliness,' they neglected the essential, outward, and in the largest sense 'political' obligations of true *Humanität*—of being fully human. It was this fateful legacy that—simplified and hardened beyond anything they could have imagined—led to the acceptance of barbarism in one of the world's most advanced and 'civilized' nations.

Mann's argument has paid the price of its influence, by debasement into cliché, although it has also been refined and extended by George Steiner, among others. It remains a classic statement.

When I went to live in East Germany as a student of history looking, among other things, at the cultural resistance to nazism, I was interested to see if this German cultural tradition—the deliberate cultivation of inward spirituality, the cultured abstinence from political life—survives among today's East German intelligentsia. After all, they too face the challenge of a German dictatorship—though one that does not approach the extremes of Nazi inhumanity. (Buchenwald was used as an internment camp by the Soviets for several years after the war but is now a carefully organized museum.) I found that the tradition persists.

Many of the educated Germans I got to know best live in a classical sort of 'inner emigration' from the totalitarian demands of the Party-state. They nourish themselves on the host of German music (the most mysterious, ambiguous, uncommitted of the arts—the art that Mann chose for his Dr Faustus), on European painting, poetry, and fiction. They love and revere the enigmatic sculptures of Ernst Barlach—products of his own inner emigration in the Third Reich. They drown out the sound of slogans with the music of Bach. Ignoring the state as far as possible, they none the less offer up the required tribute of outward conformity in the university or the workplace. When called upon, they will say and swear things in public that they privately abhor.

Inner emigration is the intellectual form of the double life. Of course, the phenomenon is found in all the unfree societies of Europe today. But it does seem to me that it is more common, more intense, in the unfree part of Germany than in Hungary, Poland, or Czechoslovakia, and this may partly be explained by the special German heritage of *Innerlichkeit*. There is a body of contemporary East German literature that reflects and feeds this 'turning inward'.

in English. Kunze exemplifies the best qualities of East German writing. His language is extraordinarily pure, in sharp and conscious opposition to the poisoned and inflated public language of the state. His short prose pieces are the written equivalent of a Grosz or Hockney drawing, with no single superfluous line. Word-etchings. His subjects have an evident importance—the systematic corruption of youth in East German schools, the 'unpersoning' of writers in Czechoslovakia—and his moral stringency would satisfy the most astringent Leavisite.

Yet since he came to the West in 1977, Kunze's work has ceased to speak to his East German readers. And what is true of Kunze is even more so of his fellow exiles or half-exiles. Why?

Of course, there are practical difficulties. His books are no longer available in East German bookshops, and West German editions have to be smuggled in. Yet, compared with Polish, Czech, or Hungarian writers in exile, the position of the (East) German writer in (half) exile is technically much better. He has all the resources of West German television and radio through which to reach his own people in the East. He has publishers and editors crying out to print his work and thousands of West Germans ready to carry it to their friends and relatives over the border.

The explanation must lie deeper. Although this is treacherous, speculative ground, I do think that, artistically, they miss the challenge of a repressive system. Christa Wolf, who remains domiciled in East Germany, has been heard to remark privately that she doubts if she could work without the *Reibung*—the constant *friction* of a writer's life under communism. Paradoxically, censorship can make a writer's life easier as well as more difficult. The writer's energy is concentrated on one target instead of being dissipated among the thousand subjects that cry out for attention in an open society. His talent is devoted to smuggling his message past the literary border guards, under the cloak of fable or in the false-bottomed suitcase of allegory. These limitations, like the limitation of traditional forms—the sonnet or ballad—can have artistic advantages. And the mere fact of having smuggled his goods past the censor will be applauded by his readers.

Then, suddenly, he can write anything about anything. He experiences the *shock of artistic freedom*. Again, this experience is not confined to East German writers. You have only to look at the disorientation of some Polish writers in 1981. But Polish writers in exile are to a great extent insulated from that shock by a very strong—indeed, overpowering—traditional understanding of their role as moral and political mentors of the nation. The great Polish romantic poets lived in exile yet were called the 'spiritual government' of Poland. Heine notwithstanding, there is no comparable tradition in German literature. Yes, there is the more recent precedent of German literature in emigration during the Third Reich: Thomas Mann's famous 'Where I am, is Germany.' But to raise that precedent is to see the essential differences.

Mann once remarked that the Nazi period was 'a morally good time.' I suppose he meant that the moral choices were then absolutely clear—black was black, white was white—and the moral duty of the writer easy to discern. The present is not (in Mann's ironic sense) 'a morally good time' in Germany. The choices are not clear, and the writer's political and moral task is far from plain. Brecht, for his part, wrote of the 'dark times' when

A talk about trees is almost a crime
Because it implies being silent about so many horrors . . .

But are the 'horrors' of the Honecker regime really such as to demand the concentrated artistic attention of the exiled writer? Many of my friends in East Germany would answer no. Indeed, they would rather talk about trees.

The American exile of Mann and Brecht was at once complete and temporary. They were German writers plunked down on another continent, a foreign culture, waiting to return home. They had no prospect or intention of becoming American writers. The exile of Kunze or Kirsch is at once permanent and incomplete. There is scant prospect of their ever being allowed 'home'. Yet they are still in Germany—German writers living among German readers. Czesław Miłosz or Milan Kundera cannot become a West Polish or West Czechoslovak writer—the notion is meaningless—but East German writers can hope to become West German writers.

Sadly, most of them now seem to be in a peculiar limbo—no longer speaking to their East German reading public, not yet speaking to West Germany. In the East, they could publish nothing but had everything to write about. In the West, they can publish anything but find nothing to write about. None of them speak any more to their own people, as Mann and Miłosz continued to speak to their own peoples from Californian exile. If our criterion of 'rightness' is purely artistic, then it is authors like Christa Wolf and that grand old fox of East German literature Stefan Heym who have made the 'right' decision—to go on *living* in the East, while *publishing* (if need be) in the West. (But our criterion of rightness is not purely artistic.) This is not to endorse the simplistic argument that repression produces good literature. It is just to observe that, so far, this peculiar German *half exile* seems to have crippled rather than inspired some of Germany's best writers.

Writers in Central and Eastern Europe are moral and political authorities in a way that no writer has been in England since George Orwell and Bertrand Russell. But East German writers have been neutralized by emigration—in its inward and outward forms. Emigration, it has been said, is the German form of revolution.

(JULY 1981)

Dr Faust in Schwerin

It is at Schwerin as if the Grand Dukes of Mecklenburg had just departed. The mid-nineteenth-century grand-ducal castle is built on an island 'in my Windsor Castle style', as the architect described it. With its red stone turrets and spirelets, it rather recalls a Victorian sanatorium. But the beautiful necklace of lakes, the glorious and genuine gothic of the cathedral on the other bank, the organic unity of the old town, lend ancient dignity. The town is wonderfully preserved, as if the clocks had stopped at the hour of liberation in May 1945. This was one of the earliest centres of German Christendom, seat of the lords of Mecklenburg ever since, in the twelfth century, they captured the island fastness from heathen Wends. Only the red flag flying from the turret reminds you that Schwerin is no longer the capital of a free state.

Amidst the blowsy pomp of the State Theatre, all gilt and pink stucco bosoms, Goethe's *Faust* is to be performed. The director promises a 'revolutionary' production. According to the programme note, Faust at the end of the play has become the incarnation of the bourgeois employer. Mephistopheles exemplifies the 'devilish life-style' of the bourgeoisie. Goethe 'naturally could not have recognized' that this bourgeois-capitalist social order was only the precondition for a 'third phase' of 'truly free and universally developed individuals.' The fatuous condescension of this last remark prepares me for the worst. It comes. There are four successive Fausts. The last is a bloated parody of a capitalist, with huge cigar, golden chain, and pot belly: Faust as Citizen Kane.

He shouts his lines like a heckler, yet even he cannot entirely spoil Goethe's great motto for a free person in an unfree state:

> Ja! diesem Sinne bin ich ganz ergeben,
> Das ist der Weisheit letzter Schluss:
> Nur der verdient sich Freiheit wie das Leben,
> Der täglich sie erobern muss![1]

Later, together with friends from Berlin, I'm invited to stay with Dr Faust number one, an impressive figure even when he's changed his black robe for blue jeans. He talks interestingly and critically about the production. But as we leave, someone whispers, 'Be careful. Faust works for the *Stasi* . . .' (the *Staatssicherheitsdienst*, that is, the secret police).

As we walk through the deserted streets, I notice Faust's peculiar habit of beginning every sentence with the words *pardon* or *excuse me*. 'Excuse me,' he says, 'I can only offer you the floor to sleep on. Excuse me,' as he pours us large martinis but himself a small beer. The loft apartment is cosy, the candles lit, our glasses filled. 'Not much work at the moment?' he says to my friend, himself an actor. 'Excuse me, I suppose you must be thinking of looking for work in the West?' When my friend is unforthcoming, Dr Faust turns to me and says: 'And you're from the foreign press?'

'Excuse me,' he says. We talk till the cock crows.

The next day we return to Berlin. Dr Faust has a brand new three-room apartment (state owned, of course), an exceptional privilege for a bachelor of his age. It is worth much more than thirty pieces of silver.

'That's our everyday life,' say my friends. 'If we hadn't been warned, we'd have talked about trying to escape to the West.'

[1]Yes! This one thought absorbs me wholly—rife
With wisdom's final lesson, and most true;
He only merits freedom, merits life,
Who daily has to conquer them anew
(Trans. Theodore Martin)

Here was a nice opportunity to compare, as the theatre programme suggested, the classical, humanistic picture of man with the contemporary picture, in this glorious 'third phase' of truly free and universally developed individuals, which Goethe—poor backward benighted Goethe—could never have anticipated.

In East Germany, Mephistopheles may still be working for the devil. But Dr Faust works for the *Stasi*.

(JULY 1981)

Libraries of a Vanished State

$\dfrac{P \qquad à \quad 6}{voulez\text{-}vous \quad 100}$?' wrote Frederick the Great to Voltaire, who smartly replied, '*G a*,' and came to sup at Sanssouci. There the punster-poetaster king, the self-styled 'Philosoph von Sanssouci,' would regale Voltaire, in bad French, with the latest additions to his Royal Library. Alas, he also offered for criticism his own precious verses. 'See,' said Voltaire, 'what a quantity of his filthy linen the king has sent me to wash!' It could not last. Voltaire took a cold farewell and a volume of the king's poetry. At Frankfurt, Prussian agents arrested him, confined him (Macaulay tells us) for twelve days in a wretched hovel, and retrieved the precious volume.

So it was in old Prussia. So it was for the 'Prince-Elector's Library' (*Churfürstliche Bibliothek*), opened in 1661; for the Royal Library, from 1701; and for the Prussian State Library, from 1918. What the state gave with one hand it took away with the other. What it built by its patronage it destroyed by its politics. And so today the Prussian State Library, like Germany itself, is divided between East and West.

In East Berlin, Unter den Linden, stands the original pre-1914 library. A great square slab of grey sandstone with pompous historicist detailing, it was singled out by Hitler in *Mein Kampf* as an example of the kind of architecture he admired. Today, however, your attention is drawn in the cloakroom to *Wladimir Iljitsch Lenin in Berlin und als Leser der Königlichen Bibliothek, der heutigen Deutschen Staatsbibliothek*—'Lenin as reader in the Royal Library, today's German State Library'—a gripping historical romance: hurry, while stocks last. Lenin in hand, you walk past a termagant in the porter's box (*Ausweis, bitte!*), up the gloomy stone staircase, and along ochre-coloured corridors smelling of cheap disinfectant, to the catalogue rooms.

In West Berlin, the Staatsbibliothek Preussischer Kulturbesitz (State Library of Prussian Cultural Property) is a large, gleaming ultramodern building, conceived by the architect Hans Scharoun as a brother to the nearby Philharmonie concert hall. Like the Philharmonie, its outward form is meant to express its inner functions 'organically.' Resolutely and riotously asymmetrical, as if in conscious opposition to the awful symmetry of its East Berlin counterpart, the interior reveals an ascending series of large, light open-plan spaces, all plush carpet and *béton brut*. In the reading rooms, the bookshelves are carefully arranged in small clusters, so as not to spoil the view, and a student can peruse the beautiful people all the way from *Ostasien* to *Osteuropa*. If he or she should tire of reading, books can be borrowed or photocopied at will or used as conversation starters in the elegant canteen, with its fine view of the Berlin Wall.

In the puritan East there are no such distractions. But puritanism extends to the selection of books. Looking through the card catalogues you may stumble on 'Bahro, Rudolf, *Die Alternative: Zur Kritik d. real existierenden Sozialismus,*' or 'Stone, Norman, *The Eastern Front*.' Beside the signature number of the latter it says 'W', beside the former, '= ASF.' 'W' stands for *wissenschaftliche Benutzung*— 'scholarly use,' which means, in practice, only for academic researchers. And 'ASF?' The 'Section for Special Research Literature' (*Abteilung für spezielle Forschungsliteratur*) is a discreet little reading room that contains everything the state considers 'dangerous.' Such rooms are popularly known as *Giftschränke*—'poison cupboards.' Only specially trusted individuals, or already poisoned foreign visitors, are granted access. In its glass-fronted cupboards, the complete *Völkischer Beobachter* stands next to bound rows of *Der Spiegel* and *Stern*; Bahro's *Alternative* next to Hitler's *Mein Kampf*; John Toland's biography of Hitler beside Stefan Heym's novel about East German Stalinism.

When I worked there as a graduate student, dyspeptically turning the pages of Nazi newspapers on grey winter afternoons, an Indian communist professor sat at the next table, forlornly reading the previous week's *Times* (poison, of course). Sometimes we were joined by a senior officer of the Wachregiment—'Feliks

Dzierzynski'—the guard regiment of the ministry for state security. He worked his way steadily through glossy piles of Western military journals, colour magazines, and arms brochures, occasionally licking his lips, knees pressed firmly together, like a middle-aged banker in a porno shop. When I returned to the library this year, as a confessed journalist, I asked one of the library's senior administrators what purpose the ASF classification served. 'Well, I'll give you an example,' he said. 'Just recently we received a book about sexual perversions—and the publishers themselves requested that this should not be made generally available. The ASF is for things like that . . .'

The catalogues in West Berlin hold no such hidden terrors. However, until recently they didn't hold many of their books, either. In one of those mind-jerking absurdities that are Berlin's stock in trade, librarians had to telephone to the State Library in East Berlin to find the signature, and hence the location, of volumes in their stacks in West Berlin—for the old catalogues remained in the old building. Now West Berlin has finished recataloguing the displaced volumes; and the whole of the old alphabetical catalogue—to 1974—should soon be available in microfilm.

It happened like this. When British bombs began to fall on Berlin in 1940, the Prussian State Library decided to evacuate its most valuable holdings to safe storage places across the Reich. By the end of the war, there were twenty-nine evacuation sites, of which six proved to be in territory occupied by the Western Allies and twenty-three in the East. Some 1.7 million volumes 'made their way to West Germany,' as the West Berlin library brochure puts it—nicely suggesting refugees from the Red Army; exhausted old Baedekers in tattered red cloth wheezing through the Harz Mountains, the brothers Grimm pulling their *Nachlass* in a pram, stately von Wilamowitz-Moellendorff with nothing but what he could carry in his appendices . . . Eventually, they made their way, via Marburg and Tübingen, to Hans Scharouns's building in Tiergarten, less than a mile away from their old home on Unter den Linden; and here, for the time being, their *Wanderjahre* would seem to have ended.

East Berlin wants them back. Not content with the 6.5 million or so volumes that remain in Berlin or were returned from Eastern evacuation sites, the 'German State Library' claims the 1.7 million refugees 'illegally detained in West Berlin' as its own citizens. Its own anachronistic title, German State Library, stakes out that claim (for where is the German state?). Its lawyers cite a UN resolution to the effect that artworks should be returned to their pre-war locations. The West Berlin lawyers retort that Germany did not fight Germany and the resolution is therefore inapplicable. Instead, the disputed volumes are held in trust, like all the former 'cultural properties' of the Prussian state, by the *Stiftung Preussischer Kulturbesitz* (Foundation for Prussian Cultural Property). Hence, the almost equally anachronistic title State Library of Prussian Cultural Property. When Germany is reunited, all these double bookings will be sorted out.

Meanwhile, they live in peaceful coexistence. West Berlin has the Gutenberg Bible, the magnificent collection of Oriental manuscripts and, ironically enough, a large holding of East European literature. East Berlin has a fragment of the first Latin Bible, the Prince-Elector's Atlas, and the great bulk of pre-war general and reference books. West Berlin has filled many of its lacunae by acquiring secondhand or facsimile copies and is excellently furnished with post-war reference literature. East Berlin has fallen behind with the latter, because the state cannot afford the necessary hard currency. (Like Frederick the Great, Erich Honecker spends too much on his army.) But East Berlin can borrow its former treasures on interlibrary loan, and despite its legal claims, it scrupulously returns them. West Berlin acts as a centre for the allocation of ISBNs—including those for East Germany. Their rival claims are irreconcilable; but life and scholarship must go on, so Prussia's heirs have found a tenuous *modus vivendi*.

There is, however, one further twist to this Central European family history. It concerns one of the most valuable consignments evacuated during the war—505 crates containing about a quarter of all Mozart's music known to have survived in manuscript, the score of Beethoven's Ninth Symphony, the papers of Alexander von Humboldt, the Varnhagen collection, and much more besides. In 1945 this consignment was known to be stored in a Benedictine monastery at Grüssau, in Upper Silesia. Then it disappeared. For three decades, scholars hunted the length and breadth of Central Europe. (The story of their search is ably told in Nigel Lewis's *Paperchase.*) Then, in the early 1970s, the library's last secret seeped out. The priceless consignment had, it seems, been carried away from that German monastery by the advancing Polish army in 1945—and the Poles had concealed their find from the world. Why?

'After all,' Dr Bernard Vesper, Director General of the West Berlin State Library exclaims, 'they would have been quite justified! If they said in 1945, "We are taking this as reparation for the terrible damage you have done to Poland," no one could have fairly protested.' (Not the kind of remark one heard in East Berlin—where the State Library administrator declined to discuss the matter at all.) Dr Vesper suspects the Poles must have wanted to conceal their find, not from the West, but from the Soviet Union—which made a habit of snapping up the best 'reparations' for itself.

Whatever the reason, it was only in 1977 that the Polish Press Agency (PAP) announced, with its customary frankness, that 'systematic and scrupulous search has recently been rewarded with a successful result.' In May of that year, Edward Gierek flew to East Berlin to sign a treaty of friendship. He took with him seven scores from the 'recently discovered' collection, including *The Magic Flute* and Beethoven's Ninth. '*Alle Menschen werden Brüder!*' explained a headline in the East German Party daily *Neues Deutschland,* as Gierek 'handed back' these masterpieces of socialist humanism. The librarians on Unter den Linden measured up the space for the rest of the hoard. But they are still waiting. Perhaps the Poles were (are?) holding out for the return of Polish national treasures in exchange. Perhaps it was just the dramatic worsening of relations between Poland and the GDR after the emergence of Solidarity. In any case, the rest of the contents of those 505 crates are now open to readers at the Jagiellonian Library, in Kraków, to the delight of many Western scholars and the silent fury of the East Berlin librarians. West Germany has formally advised Poland of its rights and interest in these Prussian relics. Poland may now play off Prussia's heirs against each other. *Alle Menschen werden Brüder,* indeed.

(DECEMBER 1984)

A Tale of Two Germanies

She was dressed much like any other West German girl. But as soon as she spoke I knew she was from the East. The unmistakable accent of Saxony and something about her slightly old-fashioned vocabulary proclaimed that she had grown up *drüben*—on the other side of the Wall. Since the Wall is there to prevent the citizens of the

German Democratic Republic from travelling to the West until they reach the age of retirement, I asked the obvious question: How did she come to be here? Such tales are usually worth hearing. Hers certainly was.

As a student at the Humboldt University in East Berlin, she had decided to specialize in a new field: the study of higher education. 'New?' I exclaimed. Well, she said, new to the university as an academic subject. Since the question of selection for higher education was so politically sensitive, it had previously been handled by the Party schools only. The academic vocabulary of this new discipline was, surprisingly, imported from America rather than the Soviet Union. They started with the principle of economic need. In practice, this is still the guiding principle of East German higher education. The numbers of students for each subject are carefully calculated on the basis of the five-year plan: so many engineers, so many doctors, etc. You may want to study art, but if the state doesn't want artists, there will be no university places in art. It will be suggested that you study electronic engineering, for example, on which the next five-year plan concentrates. At the end of the course you are *legally obliged* to take one of the jobs that the state offers you and stay in it for two or three years (depending on the subject).

The new institute, however, has imported a second concept from America, that of social demand—i.e., what society wants. They were slightly at a loss to know how to reconcile these two principles. This was where Sabine came in. Searching around for an answer, she stumbled upon the works of one Wilhelm von Humboldt, the great Prussian reformer and humanist after whom the university was named. And as she read, with growing fascination, she realized that he had already found the answer some 150 years ago. People, Humboldt wrote, should study what they wanted to study. They should be given a free choice. The purpose of the university was to train minds, not to produce experts. 'If the knife is once sharpened, all kinds of things can be cut with it,' as Herder had said. She wrote this into the concluding part of her doctoral thesis, proposing, in effect, a return to the traditional German idea of a university (an idea subsequently elaborated by J. H. Newman).

Her professor read the thesis with attention. Then he called her in for a chat. 'Basically you are right,' he said, quietly. 'But you must realize that *the time is not yet ripe* for this.' The time not yet ripe!

Perhaps in twenty years the Humboldt University would catch up with Humboldt.

She refused to modify her thesis; he, to pass it as it stood. Her way forward was blocked by her own loyalty to what she believed to be true. She tried to study German literature instead—but, of course, since there was no (Humboldtian) freedom of choice in East Germany, that was not possible. As the pressures on her became greater she made a desperate resolution: She would escape to the West. There, in the free part of Germany, she could study German literature at Tübingen or Göttingen or even the 'Free University' in West Berlin.

Foolishly, she entrusted herself to one of the secret escape organizations, to which she paid a large sum of money. On the appointed day, she waited at the arranged meeting point near the autobahn that carries cars 'in transit' from West Germany to West Berlin. The car duly pulled off the road (a risky business, since the police keep a sharp watch for such incidents) and she was bundled into a special compartment under the back seat. At the border post, vehicles 'in transit' are not searched except on suspicion. To her, as she lay nearly suffocating under the back seat, the car seemed to stand still for far too long. Then the back door was opened and a frontier guard tore up the seat as if he knew exactly what he would find. She was discovered.

'The worst part of what followed was the months of solitary confinement in the State Security Service prison,' she told me. It was not the physical discomfort that was unbearable but the psychological uncertainty. This the *Stasi* cultivated, pulling her out for interrogation at any hour of the day or night. She was tried for attempting to 'flee the Republic' and condemned to three and a half years' imprisonment. She was reluctant to talk even now about the women's prison and the cruelty of the criminals who were deliberately placed in positions of authority over the political prisoners. Nowadays, if your case is known in the West, you can generally hope to be 'bought free' by the West German government after serving approximately half your sentence. But because Sabine was officially held to have been in possession of 'state secrets' (statistics about higher education places!), she was detained for almost the full duration of her sentence. (The nightmare of the political prisoner is to be released *back* into East Germany). Then, at last, came the day when she was called out of prison, given back her own clothes, and driven in an unmarked bus to the frontier.

Now, she thought, she could begin a new life, and now she could practise that educational freedom of choice for which she had suffered so much. But in the West she quickly discovered two things. First, she learned that the driver whom she had paid to smuggle her out had been in the pay of the *Stasi*. This had been proved in a West Berlin court, which had sentenced him to five years' imprisonment. So while she sat in an East German prison, he sat in a West German one.

The second discovery was still more bitter. She soon found that she could not, after all, realize her dream of studying German literature at one of the free German universities. For a start, the West German state would not give her a grant to study a subject different from the one she had studied in the East. Naturally, she had no funds of her own. In the present recession, moreover, and precisely because West Germany has followed the Humboldtian principle of free choice (although it now restricts it through the so-called 'numerus clausus') there are almost no jobs for graduates of German literature. The university towns of the West are pullulating with unemployed Germanists.

So instead she is being financed by the West Berlin city government to train as a civil servant. 'Hardly what I dreamed of.'

(APRIL 1984)

Comrade Brecht

Bertolt Brecht is the most influential German playwright of the twentieth century, but we still have no satisfactory biography of him. Why?

Until recently, when you crossed the Berlin Wall on the way into East Berlin you were confronted with a Perspex tablet on which was written, in red:

> BERTOLT BRECHT:
> Great Carthage
> fought three wars.
> It was still mighty
> after the first,
> still habitable
> after the second.
> It was no longer to be found
> after the third.

This advertisement for the peaceful intentions of the German Democratic Republic was set out as a poem. But it is not a poem. It is the censored remnant of an 'Open Letter to German Artists and Writers' in which (in 1951) Brecht appealed for the peaceful reunification of Germany and, in that cause, for freedom from censorship. When I carried a volume containing this letter into the Friedrichstrasse checkpoint, it was confiscated.

East Germany has turned Brecht into the Berlin Wall of German literature. The class enemy, writes the current head of the Berliner Ensemble, Manfred Wekwerth, must necessarily be a Brecht enemy. For this reason alone, it is understandable that no German scholar, East or West, has yet managed to scale the Wall—to see Brecht steadily and to see him whole. Moreover, partly due to censorship by Brecht's literary executors, a very significant portion of his poetry—

26

including two further Buckow Elegies and four devastating poems about Stalin ('The Honoured Murderer of the People')—was only published in 1982. A major selection of his letters was first published in 1981.

Ronald Hayman therefore begins[1] with two great advantages: his cultural and political distance from the subject and the availability of (we trust) most of the previously unpublished sources. His achievement is to give us the facts of Brecht's life more fully and fairly than any previous biographer. Yet, surprisingly, he does not refer at all to the 1982 supplementary volumes of Brecht's poetry. Moreover, when it comes to the interpretation of German texts or context, his cultural and political distance turns into a grave liability. There are vital dimensions of Brecht's life and work that he simply does not explore, although the territory is now at last accessible and earlier explorers have pointed the way.

Brecht's was a profoundly contrary and elusive (not to say evasive) character. By the age of twenty, the Augsburg attic poet was already a great exploiter: plundering books, friends, and women for his own stimulation and advantage, like the pirate heroes of his exuberant early verses and short stories. Caught between two mistresses, Paula Banholzer and Marianne Zoff, he seriously proposed to appease the latter by 'giving' her his son by the former. Ruthless opportunism would remain a hallmark of his career to the well-known end: enthroned in East Berlin, with a West German publisher, Austrian passport, and Swiss bank account. 'Be good,' he counselled his son Stefan, 'to yourself.' We can soon understand why Auden would remark that Brecht was one of the few people who deserved the death sentence—'In fact I can imagine doing it to him myself.' (Brecht, for his part, would have executed Orwell: 'If necessary I would kill—yes, I would kill him.')

Yet this outrageous literary and sexual pirate exercised an extraordinary charm. When, like his early hero Frank Wedekind, he sang his own ballads in a high, brittle voice, accompanying himself on the guitar, the young Brecht was apparently irresistible. At first hearing, Arnolt Bronnen

---

[1] Ronald Hayman, *Brecht: A Biography* (London: Weidenfeld & Nicolson, 1983).

was overwhelmed with an inexplicable mixture of strong feelings; that he had never previously looked at a human being, that what was happening now would never stop, that 'the heart beating in that small insignificant creature over there is the heart of our age,' and he prayed to Love: 'Give him to me as a friend.'

'All this,' Hayman nicely comments, 'without a word of conversation.' Only in America did the charm fail—for the magic was in his language. In the German-speaking world even his detractors had soon to acknowledge his original poetic gift. 'The monster has talent,' said Thomas Mann sadly. The misquotation of what is probably Brecht's most famous line—"*Erst kommt das Fressen, dann kommt die Moral*" ('First comes the guzzling, then the morality')—is but the crassest example of Hayman's recurrent deafness to the magic of Brecht's German.

The central challenge for the biographer of Brecht, however, must be the relationship between his politics and his art. What were the sources of his commitment to communism? What was the nature of that commitment and how did it change? How did it affect his work, and how does it affect our judgement of it? Here Hayman is at his weakest. It is simply not true, for instance, that in 1924–5 'millions of Germans were adapting to circumstances and suppressing their opinions by joining the Nazi party'—a statement he implausibly links to the theme of *Mann ist Mann*. He entirely misses the significance of Berlin's traumatic May Day 1929, when a virtual civil war broke out between police (controlled by a Social Democratic city government) and Communist demonstrators. This 'Bloody May' galvanized even the young Auden, who was in Berlin at the time, and John Willett has plausibly suggested that this was the moment of definite commitment for Brecht—1929 being the year of the first *Lehrstücke*. Later, Hayman uncritically relays Brecht's wholly lopsided account of the failure of the SPD and KPD to unite against the Nazis. Berlin in the years 1929 to 1932 was a city where writers, like everyone else, could hardly avoid taking sides (as did, in the end, even Thomas Mann—up to a point). This pressing historical context, this sense of a world falling apart, is essential to an understanding of Brecht's politics.

Brecht was unique only in the ferocity of his commitment and the talent that he placed at its service. Having embraced communism, he rushed to spell out its most radical moral implications in *Die Massnahme (The Measures Taken)*:

> What base act would you not commit, to
> Eradicate baseness?
> If, at last, you could change the world, what
> Would you think yourself too good for?
> Who are you?
> Sink into filth
> Embrace the butcher, but
> Change the world: it needs it!

Die Massnahme argues precisely those ethical conclusions from Marxism (from which it is possible to draw other conclusions) and Leninism (from which it is almost impossible to draw other conclusions) that would be used to justify all the atrocities of Stalinism in Brecht's lifetime. It uncannily anticipates the Moscow trials.

It is a remarkable fact that Brecht never explicitly disowned the morality of *The Measures Taken*. 'In 1956,' Hayman reports, 'he told me that I was not entitled to criticize the play's moral values until I had acted as one of the four agitators *and* as a member of the Control Chorus.' He would not, however, allow public performance, because (as he wrote to a would-be producer in the same year) experience had shown that it achieved 'nothing but moral passions (*Affekte*) of a commonly lesser kind' in the audience. To the end of his life he would maintain that *in principle* the end—communism—justified the means—killing, lies, injustice—being used by the governments he supported.

There is abundant evidence that Brecht considered himself, above all, a true and consistent Leninist:

> *Unermüdlich lobt der Denkende*
> *Den Genossen Lenin . . .*

('Tirelessly the thinking man praises/Comrade Lenin') begins one of the previously unpublished poems from *circa* 1930, and goes on to praise Lenin for not being afraid to get his hands dirty. In the same period, he rebuked the revisionist Marxist Karl Korsch for wanting 'to cut the umbilical cord of Leninist ideology and for placing too much faith in the proletariat.' Twenty years later, in the Buckow Elegies, he would contrast the feeble behaviour of East Germany's rulers with the glowing example of Lenin. And in one of four devastating Stalin poems from the last months of his life, we read

Der genialste Schüler Lenins
Hat ihn aufs Maul geschlagen

(Literally: 'Lenin's most brilliant pupil/Has struck him on the mouth.')

As a Leninist, he held, in theory, that the Party must be the ultimate repository of 'scientific' knowledge and final court of appeal. But he never joined the Party. (If there was any evidence that he had, the East German Brechtologists would have given it us by now.) When the KPD, and Moscow, reacted angrily to *Die Massnahme*—because communists don't *say* things like that, not in public anyway—Brecht stuck to his own judgement. Twenty years later, the same story would be repeated (with some Schweikian variations) after the Party criticized the pacifist tendencies of *The Trial of Lucullus*. In practice he always knew better. Party discipline was for everyone else. He was thus a consistently inconsistent Leninist.

But was he a Stalinist? Discussing the Moscow trials with Sidney Hook in New York in the winter of 1935–6, he famously remarked, 'The more innocent they are, the more they deserve to die.' The word that many commentators have found for this remark is *ambivalent*. Hayman follows them. It is not an adequate word. For whichever way one takes the remark, its implications are appalling. If Brecht meant, slyly, that those who were innocent of what they were accused of—namely, plotting against Stalin—deserved to die for *not* plotting against Stalin, if, in other words, he had already understood (on his trip to Moscow in spring 1935?) that Stalin was a mass murderer, why did he continue publicly to endorse Stalin and Stalinism for the next twenty years? If he meant that the 'subjective' guilt or innocence of the accused was wholly irrelevant, because the Party always knew best what would 'objectively' serve the interests of the revolution, then this was a Stalinist remark. If he was just playing with a provocative paradox, then this was a characteristic piece of irresponsible talk. But the irresponsibility is hard to forgive, for this was not—in Orwell's phrase—a kind of playing with fire by people who did not even know that fire was hot. Brecht knew that the fire was hot—and (unlike Auden) went on playing with it.

It is none the less clear from his poems and *Arbeitsjournal*, and from his conversations with Walter Benjamin, that in the period of Scandinavian exile he was deeply troubled by the purges that engulfed his Russian teachers and acquaintances: Meyerhold, Tretyakov, the journalist Michael Kolzov. In 1938 he told Benjamin that there existed a 'justifiable suspicion' about what was happening in Russia. Benjamin records Brecht's thinking: 'Should the suspicion prove correct one day, then it will become necessary to fight the regime, and *publicly*. But, "unfortunately or God be praised, whichever you prefer," the suspicion is not yet a certainty.' For Marxists outside' (the Soviet Union) he confided to his *Arbeitsjournal* in January 1939, 'there follows roughly the attitude of Marx to German Social Democracy, *positiv kritisch.*' In September 1939 he struggled to justify to himself the Nazi-Soviet Non-Aggression Pact and the Soviet invasion of Poland. 'The governments/Write Non-Aggression-Pacts/Little man Write your Will' he had written one year earlier. He certainly did not intend to risk his own neck in the job he was offered at the Moscow Arts Theatre. It was America for him.

When Hitler invaded the Soviet Union, Brecht, like so many others, silenced his doubts with a sigh of relief. In American exile, from 1941 to 1947, he had more immediate political concerns: the struggles against fascism, trying to make a name on Broadway and money in Hollywood, facing the House Committee on Un-American Activities. But when, after failing to secure the theatre he wanted in Switzerland or Austria, he finally settled for East Berlin, he could no longer avoid the problem. Now the Measures were being Taken all around him. The Party begin to demand that he, too, should write to order. His attempts to do so were tragicomically inept. When West German police at the Herrnburg border crossing harassed a group of young communists returning from the East, Brecht sat down to write his dire political cantata *Der Herrnburger Bericht*. A sample verse:

> *Zu Herrnburg hinterm Schlagbaum*
> *Beginnt der Bonner Staat*
> *Bluthunde streichen schnuppernd*
> *Um Fallgrube und Stacheldraht.*

('At Herrnburg behind the turnpike/The Bonn state begins/ Bloodhounds prowl snuffling/ Around fall-pit and barbed wire.') Hayman notes: 'Brecht could not understand why they [the Communist authorities] objected to his carefully calculated condemnation of the West German authorities for blocking freedom of movement between the two halves of Germany.' By early 1953 the Berliner Ensemble was poorly regarded by the Party leadership. Brecht wrote despondently in his *Arbeitsjournal* that reviews did not appear until 'months after the first night.' He had still not been given the Theater am Schiffbauerdamm for which he had all along been angling.

Then came the workers' uprising of 17 June. While workers were being killed by Soviet tanks, Brecht dashed off letters of support to the Party leader, Walter Ulbricht, and the minister-president, Otto Grotewohl. Four days later, *Neues Deutschland* printed the last sentence of his letter to Ulbricht—'I feel the need, in this moment, to express to you my solidarity (*Verbundenheit*) with the Socialist Unity Party of Germany'—as if it were the full text of his message. A chorus of indignation rose from the West. This is perhaps the most controversial moment in Brecht's political career, and mystery has long surrounded what he actually wrote. According to at least two independent sources, the respected Swiss journalist Gody Suter and the German writer Alfred Kantorowicz, this sentence was the censored remnant of a long, subtle and critical epistle—a view accepted by the most sensitive explorer of this minefield, Martin Esslin. Yet, in the 1981 edition of the *Briefe* (published by Suhrkamp, but edited in the Bertolt Brecht Archive in East Berlin), the letter to Ulbricht has only two more sentences:

> History will give the revolutionary impatience of the Socialist Unity Party of Germany its respect. The great discussion with the masses about the tempo of socialist construction will lead to a sifting and securing of socialist achievements.

This seems to me neither subtle nor critical nor long. According to the editorial notes, Ulbricht replied, thanking 'Comrade Brecht' for his 'courageous declaration (*Bekenntnis*) for Peace, Unity, Democracy, and Socialism.' All that in three sentences? Regrettably, here as elsewhere Hayman does not pause for a critical discussion of his sources. He seems to accept the published *Briefe* version, but if so, he has conflated the letter to Ulbricht with that to Grotewohl.

Did Brecht's 'courageous declaration' spring from the depths of his Leninist commitment? Why did he continue publicly to maintain what was essentially a moderate version of the Party line: that the uprising may have begun as a genuine expression of working-class discontent but was soon taken over by 'fascistic and warmongering riff-raff' who brought Berlin to 'the verge of a third world war,' from which it was saved by Soviet tanks? As Hayman perceptively comments, it is hard to assess the extent to which he was telling these lies 'cynically, wanting the Party leaders to reward him with a theatre, or committedly, wanting to counteract the damage done to the communist cause by the new bout of Soviet brutality.' The theatre was, after all, the reason that he had returned to East Berlin. So was it still: 'Sink into filth/Embrace the butcher, but/ Change the world: it needs it!'? Or was it rather: 'Sink into filth/ Embrace the butcher but/ Get your theatre: you need it!'? In March 1954 he at last got the Theater am Schiffbauerdamm.

In these last years there is a growing tension between his public and his private political views. Publicly, he wins favour with the Party leaders by busying himself in the Soviet-led peace campaign. In 1954 he accepts the Stalin Peace Prize and deposits most of the prize money in his Swiss bank account. Privately, he writes 'The Solution'—that devastating epigram on 17 June ('would it not then/ be simpler, for the government/ to dissolve the People and/ elect another?'), and sad, bitter notes about the state of East Germany, with its still nazified people and its Stalinist regime. We can't have democracy, he argues to himself, because if we did, the Nazis would be elected again ... Then, after Khrushchev's revelations to the Twentieth Soviet Party Congress, he writes those four Stalin poems. The most powerful begins:

> The Tsar had spoken to them
> With rifle and whip
> On Bloody Sunday. Then
> Spoke to them with rifle and whip
> Every day of the week, every working day
> The honoured Murderer of the People.

But continues with the clear implication, in the couplet already quoted, that Stalin's conduct was a betrayal of Leninism:

> *Der genialste Schüler Lenins*
> *Hat ihn aufs Maul geschlagen*
> ['Lenin's most brilliant pupil
> has struck him on the mouth'].

He dies in August 1956, just before the cauldron boils over in Poland and Hungary.

Now the biographer should point out that this is, in outline, no unfamiliar path for a communist intellectual and a writer under Communism. The intellectual history of Central and Eastern Europe is littered with such compromises, doubts, and rationalizations. Brecht's is a crooked path when compared with those of Anna Akhmatova, Zbigniew Herbert, or Paul Celan (who rebuked him in four Delphic lines); a relatively straight one when compared with those of German contemporaries like Arnolt Bronnen or Hans Fallada. Perhaps if he had lived longer, he too would have gone West, like so many of his colleagues. Perhaps he would have continued to try to work within the system, in his own Schweikian fashion. He would have been seventy in the Prague Spring.

Apart from its intrinsic interest, Brecht's political life matters for at least two reasons. First, our knowledge of it may affect our reading of his work. This is certainly true of readers in Eastern Europe. In 1980, Polish workers adopted Brecht as a Solidarity poet. 'The Solution' was widely printed on Solidarity posters, alongside poems by Miłosz and Herbert. They were shocked to learn how in fact, on 17 June, Brecht supported the Jaruzelski of his time. Perhaps our knowledge of the man's compromises should not affect our judgement of the work; but in practice it does. We *are* less impressed by a sermon on fidelity if we know the minister for a philanderer, by a call to heroism if we know the writer for a coward.

More important, it is obvious that Brecht's politics crucially affect the work itself—although generally not in the way that Brecht intended. In fact there is a yawning gulf, not only between the qualities of the life and the work, but also between Brecht's intentions and his achievement, between his writing and his own interpretation of it. Isaiah Berlin's famous image of Tolstoy—the fox striving to be a hedgehog—is supremely applicable to Brecht. From the moment of his commitment to communism, his art displays this constant tension between his naturally 'foxy', pessimistic, individualistic view of human nature and the relentlessly optimistic, collectivist, monistic 'hedgehog' philosophy in which he attempted to contain it.

Now it can be argued that the nihilistic author of *Baal* could not have developed without some faith, that his early anarchic talent benefited hugely from the intellectual discipline of Marxism, and that, as Esslin writes, 'the inner tension created by this discipline . . . gave Brecht's work its own peculiar spell, its tautness, poetic ambiguity, and depth.' Brecht's Galileo—that deeply unheroic, sensual lover of knowledge—obviously contains a great deal of himself, and his own experience of living with a church is reflected in Galileo's. Both Esslin and Hannah Arendt have suggested that the tension between sensibility and ideology led him to a central dramatic *leitmotif* of his work: the man who sets out to improve the world cannot himself be good. 'Where violence rules/ Only violence helps.' 'We/ Who Wished to prepare the ground for friendliness/Could not ourselves be friendly.' But this Marxist-Leninist morality depends on the absolute 'scientific' certainty that the means prescribed by the Party will indeed lead to the desired end. Brecht did not long possess this certainty. At the end of his life, having seen the Measures Taken at first hand, Brecht was compelled by his own fierce poetic intelligence and honesty to acknowledge that the means corrupted those who used them. Embracing the butcher, they became butchers. If, as he says in *Galileo*, the triumph of reason can only be the triumph of reasonable men, how can the triumph of violent men be the triumph of peace, of evil men, the triumph of goodness? You cannot lie your way through to the truth. Brecht died impaled on the horns of this dilemma.

When he succeeded in chaining his natural sensibility, the results were dire. As well as his 'positive' doggerel, much of his writing against fascism is vitiated by his simplistic Marxism. Hitler cannot be understood just as a tool of big business (*Arturo Ui*). Nazi anti-Semitism was not merely a diversion from the class struggle, and it patently did not spare rich Jews (*The Round Heads and the Pointed Heads*). (Hayman rightly mentions what he calls Brecht's 'ambivalent' attitude to the Jews and quotes this extraordinary entry from the twenty-three-year-old poet's diary: 'Why can't the Jews be disposed of? Because for thousands of years they've been quartered, broken on the wheel, tortured, spat at. But the spit runs out before the Jew does.')

Fortunately, Brecht was rarely so successful in chaining himself. In *The Caucasian Chalk Circle*, for instance, ideology is effectively banished to the prologue. If one takes the prologue seriously, then the play tells us that the way agricultural land was redistributed in the Soviet Union under Stalin was a fine example of natural justice, like Azdak's decision to give the child to Grusche. That was Brecht's 'message'. But of course the vast majority of contemporary theatre-goers do not take the prologue seriously. In *The Life of Galileo*, the damage is largely limited to the penultimate scene in the post-war version, where Brecht tries to blame Galileo for Hiroshima. The result is a speech both badly written and out of character.

This dimension, and these connections, are missing in Hayman's Brecht, partly because of his inadequate understanding of the historical and political context, but also because, like most British Brechtians, he is primarily interested in Brecht as a man of the theatre. Like other English-language commentators, he is healthily unbemused by Brecht's theatrical and aesthetic theories. In London in 1936 Brecht read Stanislavsky's *My Life in Art* 'with envy and unease', as he wrote to Erwin Piscator. 'The man has put his system in order and the result is that in Paris and New York they became Stanislavsky-students.' Brecht decided to put his own system in order. Yet the result is most unsystematic. Both the *Messingkauf* dialogues and the *Kleines Organon für das Theater* were written partly as a job application for East Berlin. In paragraph forty-two, for example, Brecht talks grandly about the 'manner of playing (*Spielweise*) tried out between the First and Second World Wars at the Schiffbauerdammtheater' and based on the *Verfremdungseffekt*. In fact he had been involved in only three productions at the Theater am Schiffbauerdamm: The *Dreigroschenoper*, *Happy End*, and Marieluise Fleisser's *Pioniere von Ingolstadt*. None made any notable use of the *Verfremdungseffekt*. But Brecht wanted the Schiffbauerdamm theatre, so he invented a pedigree for it. When he got his company, theorizing gave way to practice. As Hayman writes, 'In Berliner Ensemble rehearsals neither Brecht nor any of the other directors referred to his theoretical works, and probably few of the actors read them.'

His key concept of *Verfremdung*, moreover, is not original. Brecht appears to have taken it directly from the Russian avant-garde theatre, where Meyerhold and Tretyakov had been experimenting with *ostrannenie* for years. And the basic underlying notion is of course much older, as Brecht himself implies with his examples from Goethe. To make the strange familiar and the familiar strange has long been part of the poet's trade.

Furthermore, in his best plays he invariably breaks his own rules: creating memorable individual characters with whom we emotionally identify and sympathize. Again, this was not his conscious intention. For the famous 1949 Berlin production of *Mother Courage* he altered the text in an attempt to alienate sympathy from the central character. At the end of the play we are meant to feel that she has 'learned nothing', but to understand that this is what life will be like until capitalism is destroyed, for, said Brecht, 'war is the continuation of business by other means.' But that is not what we feel. And if you read Kenneth Tynan's early reviews, you will see that is not what he felt, watching the original productions. In the marvellous last scenes—dumb Kattrin's life-saving defiance, the Mother's lament over her dead child—we are not 'alienated' from Mother Courage; we are almost unbearably moved by her. We do not think: Silly old cow, that's what comes of not learning from History; we feel the lump in the throat and the hairs rising on the nape of the neck. Leaving the theatre, we do not reflect: Such is the inevitable cruelty of life under capitalism; we think: Such is the inevitable cruelty of life.

None the less, no one would dispute the brilliance and originality of the theatrical style that Brecht developed in practice with the Berliner Ensemble in the last years of his life. We know this from Tynan, and from the impact on the British stage after 1956. Brecht did not make his compromises for nothing. 'My first impression,' Tynan wrote of the Ensemble in *Caucasian Chalk Circle*, 'was of petrified amazement at the amount of money involved.' According to Hayman, 'the funding made it possible to scrap sets or even whole productions after great quantities of time and money had been spent on them.' He gives us a vivid portrait of Brecht as a director: passionate about every detail, teasing suggestions from his collaborators and disciples, but given to outbursts of calculated tyranny. (He admitted to Eric Bentley that he allowed himself two major tantrums per production.)

Hayman finally seems to regard the Berliner Ensemble as Brecht's crowning achievement. He quotes Brecht's parable of the man who for seven years faithfully serves the agent of a repressive regime who has occupied his house, refusing only to answer the agent's first question: 'Will you serve me?' When the agent dies, the man gets rid of the body, fumigates the house, and then at last answers: 'No.' The seven years, Hayman suggests, were 1949 to 1956: 'Brecht would apparently submit to pressure in East Germany but would succeed in creating the Berliner Ensemble.'

If he means that Brecht's place in the history of theatre was assured by the impact of the Berliner Ensemble in the 1950s, this is of course undeniable. If he means that the Berliner Ensemble said (or says) no to a repressive regime, then I must ask him: When? If he means that we can judge Brecht's achievement by looking at the Berliner Ensemble today, then his verdict is more damning than he may know. For the productions of the Berliner Ensemble today (which I have attended regularly for several years) are a sorry business: stale, slow, and deeply conventional. 'Brechtian' devices are deployed as ornaments, rather as the whole Brecht business is used as an ornament by the regime. (In the 'Brecht House' you are offered 'Weigel's Viennese recipes' on menus called *Versuche*. How Brecht would have squirmed.) Partly, this is because the dead hand of the executors weighs like a nightmare on the theatre of the living—rather as at Bayreuth in the first generation after Wagner's death. Partly, it is because the Brecht epigones have tried to work from what Brecht said rather than from what he did. Hayman gives a fine example from the end of Brecht's life, when Manfred Wekwerth (now head of the Ensemble) tried to evolve a production style for *The Playboy of the Western World* on the basis of Brecht's remark that the Irish people are 'expressionism mixed with Schiller'! Brecht was appalled.

Furthermore, it is, for obvious reasons, difficult to attract first-class directors or actors to East Berlin, or even to keep the ones they have. This was a problem already in Brecht's lifetime. And then, of course, there are the constraints of censorship. Most East Germans do not go to the theatre for a critical view of life under capitalism. They have enough of that in the newspapers. What they demand from theatre, besides entertainment and escape, is a critical, humorous, or at least honest view of some part of their own experience of life—under communism. Theatre in East Germany, as elsewhere in Eastern Europe, *is* more political than in the West, less because the left has a tradition of political theatre than because in these societies the theatre is one of the very few places where a political argument can be presented publicly at all. But owing to the special status of the Berliner Ensemble as East Germany's cultural shop-window, this is the last place where a genuinely critical (Brechtian) examination of their own society will be made. While some 'between-the-lines' criticism has been attempted in the recent work of Volker Braun, much more exciting contemporary political theatre is to be seen at the *Volksbühne* or Max Reinhardt's old *Deutsches Theater*.

My point here is that the professional deformation of the Berliner Ensemble today follows historically from the nature of Brecht's commitment and the position he took in East Berlin in the last years of his life. The political apotheosis of Brecht has brought a kind of nemesis for his Ensemble.

Finally, though, regular attendance at the Berliner Ensemble is a disappointing experience because Brecht just did not write enough good plays to occupy a whole Ensemble. For a Royal Shakespeare Company you do need a Shakespeare. Most of the minor plays and adaptations have not stood the test of time. Turn them how you will, there is too much hedgehog.

Fascinated by the theatrical Brecht, and deaf to the music of his German, Hayman does not seriously consider Auden's judgement (quoted by James K. Lyon in his invaluable *Brecht in America)* that Brecht was 'a great lyric poet, but not as good as a playwright.' Indeed, Auden admired the poetry almost as much as he disliked the man. Now that most of the poetry is accessible and now that we can see the theatrical work (plays, productions, and theories) in some historical perspective, the case for Auden's view is stronger than ever. As the editors of the English edition of *Poems 1913–1956* remark, Brecht's poetry was 'the primary aspect' of his writing 'both in time . . . and in terms of artistic importance.'

The great poems from the period of Scandinavian exile capture, as few others have done, the Central European experience of that time—and that is the *central* European experience of our time. Like Kipling, whom he admired and copied, Brecht had the ability to condense common experience into a single unforgettable phrase—'changing countries more often than shoes'; the 'dark times' when 'a talk about trees is almost a crime/ Because it implies being silent about so many horrors'—so that when we think of these experiences, we find ourselves thinking of them in *his* words. Here we find again that quiet celebration of human endurance in adversity (which is the real rather than the intended 'message' of *Mother Courage*), and here the quite un-Leninist conclusions of Laotse:

> *Dass das weiche Wasser in Bewegung*
> *Mit der Zeit den mächtigen Stein besiegt.*
> *Du verstehst, das Harte unterliegt.*

('That the soft water in motion/ In time conquers the mighty stone/ You understand, the hardness is defeated.')

Moreover, we can see now that Hannah Arendt was wrong to suppose that when he returned to live in East Germany, amidst 'the very horrors he used to play with,' the 'gods of poetry' avenged themselves by drying up his poetic faculty. The gods of *politics* have avenged themselves on Brecht, with results that are visible in East Berlin today. But the gods of poetry move in more mysterious ways.

True, when he wrote to order he wrote badly. He was a hopeless hack. Yet at the moment of his worst political compromises, in the summer of 1953, he produced some of his most beautiful poetry: the Buckow Elegies. Indeed, as in some of his exile poetry, the beauty and the tensions derive largely from his own doubts and sense of guilt:

> Last night in a dream I saw fingers pointing at me
> As at a leper. They were worn with toil and
> They were broken.
>   Unknowing ones! I cried
> Guiltily.

To his poetry one can apply a remark of Tolstoy's to the effect that the writer takes the best out of his life and puts it into his work. 'His work is therefore beautiful and his life—bad.'

The poet Brecht is superbly subversive of every orthodoxy—including his own. As he himself wrote to Alfred Döblin in 1928, half-jestingly but, I think, prophetically: 'My lyric poetry is the most powerful argument against my plays!' (*Meine Lyrik ist nämlich das schlagendste Argument gegen meine Dramen!*). The East German authorities may hang him in censored remnants on the Wall, like the horse's head in the Grimm fairy tale (*O du Bertolt, da du hangest!*). But when my East German friends wanted to protest against the Soviet invasion of Czechoslovakia, they sang his marvellous resistance song from *Schweik in the Second World War:*

> *Am Grunde der Moldau wandern die Steine*
> *Es liegen drei Kaiser begraben in Prag.*
> *Das Grosse bleibt gross nicht und klein nicht das Kleine.*
> *Die Nacht hat zwölf Stunden, dann kommt schon der Tag.*
>
> *Es wechseln die Zeiten. Die riesigen Pläne*
> *Der Mächtigen kommen am Ende zum Halt.*
> *Und gehn sie einher auch wie blutige Hähne*
> *Es wechseln die Zeiten, da hilft kein Gewalt.*

—and the authorities put them in prison.

(DECEMBER 1983)

The Pope in Poland

They have come as pilgrims from all over Poland, marching softly through the night. Now at last they are massed on the meadow before the red-brick fortress walls of Jasna Góra monastery, which is for the Poles at once Westminster Abbey and Windsor Castle. Amid the religious insignia on the banners that flutter above their heads you see everywhere the unmistakable red jumbly lettering of Solidarność—not just the name of the outlawed movement, but a whole anthology of variations on the theme: the papal motto *Totus Tuus* with the Polish flag flying from the *T*; 'You strengthen the students of Gdańsk' (with 'students' in Solidarity lettering); 'We greet the defender of human rights.' This is a gathering of youth—of the Solidarity generation—yet there is none of the relaxed festive joyfulness of four years ago. Straining against the cold wind, their faces are drawn, tense, nervously expectant.

Suddenly he is with them, high up on the huge white-and-gold dais erected before the monastery battlements. For minutes they drown him in wave after wave of emotional applause. Again and again, now from one corner, now from another, you hear the rhythmic chants, 'Long live the Pope, long live the Pope'; 'The Pope with us, the Pope with us.' The rhythms are those of a political demonstration, not a religious chant, the rhythms we heard on the first evening of the visit, when tens of thousands marched from Warsaw Cathedral past the Communist Party headquarters shouting, 'Sol-i-dar-ność, Sol-i-dar-ność,' Lech-Wa-łęs-a, Lech-Wa-łęs-a,' 'Dem-o-kra-cja, Dem-o-kra-cja,' 'In-de-pend-ence, In-de-pend-ence . . .'

Finally, his voice booms through the loudspeakers: 'I want to ask you if a certain person who came today from Rome to Jasna Góra may be allowed to speak.' 'Go-a-head, go-a-head,' they chant; and then, 'Clos-er-to-us, clos-er-to-us' . . . 'Do you hear me?' he replies above the tumult. 'I'm coming closer.' And the red figure marches down the white steps toward them. A monk stumbles after the Pope, carrying the microphone. 'Thank-you, Thank-you,' chants the crowd, and then: 'Chair for the Pope, chair for the Pope.' Another monk stumbles down the steps behind him. When he stops, he is still fifty yards from the nearest pilgrim. But with this single theatrical gesture he has come closer to them. For the first time on this visit, he has established that almost magical, spontaneous contact with a vast crowd that we saw four years ago. He is talking to them. They are talking to him.

And then, as suddenly, the crowd is silent, reverent, half a million people listening with such attention that you could hear a rosary drop. It is a great and simple homily, not a political speech. He preaches a love that is 'greater than all the experiences and disappointments that life can prepare for us.' He shows them that he knows and shares their disappointments, without needing to mention martial law directly. He tells them what they can do: to begin with the reformation of themselves, which must precede any social or political reform; to listen to their consciences; to 'call good and evil by name.' 'It is up to you,' he says, 'to put a firm barrier against demoralization.' Then and only then does he mention, for the first time, the word *solidarity*, letting it drop very quietly into the silent crowd, not Solidarity the outlawed movement, but 'fundamental solidarity between human beings.'

Of course there is an instant rally of applause: But it is not the thunderous chanting of an hour before—already it is something gentler, more mature. 'It would be difficult,' he goes on, 'to enumerate here all the forms of solicitude that surrounded those who were interned, imprisoned, dismissed from work, and their families. You know better than I. I just received sporadic news about it . . .' Finally, speaking as it were directly to the icon of the Black Madonna in the monastery behind him, he appeals, 'Mother of Jasna Góra, you who have been given to us by Providence for the defence of the Polish nation, accept this call of Polish youth together with the Polish Pope, and help us to *persevere in hope*.'

As he walks slowly off the dais, waving to left and to right, they send up a last emotional message, 'Stay with us, stay with us, stay with us . . .'

Later in the evening there is a small Solidarity demonstration in the centre of town, but virtually all that vast crowd disperses peacefully. He has worked the catharsis, turning thunder into hymns, and at the same time he has perhaps shown them the beginning of a 'way out' from circumstances where many of them thought there was no way out.

Kraków

'Stay with us, stay with us,' they chant again, these vast gentle crowds, in an outpouring of love, and the pope's every gesture says: If only I could, if only I could. The aeroplane that rose above the meadows of his beloved Kraków last Thursday afternoon bore a great and very homesick man back to Rome. But it left a society certain that Karol Wojtyła's second fantastic pilgrimage to his native land, which he described to close friends beforehand as the most difficult of all his journeys (including Nicaragua), has been a triumph.

As much Western news coverage has amply demonstrated, it is impossible to translate into foreign newsprint what he had to say. It is impossible because he speaks to the Poles through a tapestry of symbols and allusions—historical, literary, philosophical, Mariological—each of which requires at least a paragraph of explanation. It is impossible because so much depends on a theatrical delivery that John Gielgud once called 'perfect'. It is impossible because poetry is what gets lost in translation.

Yet since the Poles have been doing the impossible ever since the pope's first visit four years ago, we may at least attempt it, beginning with what he did not say. In sharp contrast to his last visit, he said nothing about one leitmotif of his pontificate: the future of the churches elsewhere in Eastern Europe and the special mission of the Slav Pope to reassert the unity of Christian Europe from the Atlantic to the Urals. This was the Vatican's one major concession to Moscow. On the other hand, although he talked a lot about peace, he gave no gifts to the Soviet media. In his only major reference to nuclear disarmament, he recalled a memorandum of the Pontifical Academy of Sciences on the effects of nuclear war, sent to both the Soviet Union and the United States. But this was a cycle of homilies written by a Pole, for the Poles, about Poland.

To the people of Poland he said, first of all, that he shares their disappointment and their suffering since the imposition of martial law. He said this through his bowed head and sombre mien from the moment he stepped onto the tarmac at Warsaw airport. 'He is sad,' said the old woman standing next to me. 'You see, he understands.' He said it in his first homily, in St John's Cathedral in Warsaw: 'Together with all my compatriots—especially with those who are most acutely tasting the bitterness of disappointment, humiliation, suffering, of being deprived of their freedom, of being wronged, of having their dignity trampled on—I stand beneath the cross of Christ...' And again, referring to the late 'primate of the millennium,' Cardinal Stefan Wyszyński, 'Divine Providence spared him the painful events connected with the date 13 December 1981.' A chorus of applause rose from the tens of thousands massed in the streets of the old town around the cathedral. So far the censors have not allowed this sentence to appear anywhere, even in the small-circulation Catholic press. But everyone has heard it.

His theme, however, was victory. Out of this political defeat, he told them, they are called to win a moral victory. In part this must be an internal, spiritual victory: 'Man is called to victory over himself,' the victory of martyrdom, the victory of the cross. 'It is the saints and the beatified,' he declared in Kraków, 'who show us the path to the victory that God achieves in human history.' As the individual, so also the nation is called to the moral victory.

This moral victory, however, is not to be won merely by patient suffering in faith. No, it demands 'living in truth.' 'It means,' as he explained at Jasna Góra, 'that I make an effort to be a person with a conscience ... I call good and evil by name ...' 'It means: love of neighbour; it means: fundamental *solidarity* between human beings.' It means fighting 'demoralization'—both in the sense of declining morale and of decaying morals. Effortlessly recapturing the word *renewal (odnowa)* from the communist dictionary, he preached the imperative of 'moral and social renewal.' The nation must bear witness to the truth as it did in August 1980, 'that witness which amazed the whole world, when the Polish worker stood up for himself with the gospel in his hand and a prayer on his lips.' Today, too, the Poles must not cease to stand up for certain fundamental human and civil rights.

And then he told them, with a clarity that thrilled his listeners and dismayed the government, precisely what those rights are. First, Poland has a right to independence, to national sovereignty, to take 'her proper place among the nations of Europe, between East and West,' as he put it to General Jaruzelski at the Belweder Palace, in a speech that, unlike most of his homilies, was televised nationwide. At the end of the open-air masses, he intoned the stirring hymn that has long been a second, unofficial national anthem. The original version of 'God Who Protects Poland . . .' concludes, '*Restore* to us, O Lord, a free fatherland.' The Communist authorities, however, have tried to encourage the version introduced when Poland regained its independence in 1918, which concludes, '*Bless* for us, O Lord, the free fatherland'—thus implying that People's Poland is in fact a free fatherland. But the Pope's huge congregation did not hesitate for a moment: It was the original version they sang. What is more, the Pope himself quoted it, in the central religious celebration of his pilgrimage: 'Yes. Here at Jasna Góra there also rested the hope of the nation and the persevering effort toward independence . . . "Restore to us, O Lord, a free fatherland . . ."'

In Katowice, the industrial capital of Upper Silesia, addressing an audience subdued by temperament, pouring rain, and strict Church discipline, he went on to spell out the specific rights of workers: 'The right to a just salary,' 'the right to security,' 'the right to a day of rest' (work-free Sundays were only won after a long struggle in the mines here). 'Connected with the area of worker's rights is the question of trade unions,' and the right of all professional groups, including agricultural and white-collar workers, to form unions as 'a mouthpiece for the struggle for social justice.' He quoted a speech by Cardinal Wyszyński (which at the time referred specifically to Rural Solidarity) on 'a people's right to free association.' 'The state does not give us the right, it has only the obligation to protect and guard it. This right is given us by the creator who made man as a social being.' 'It was in this spirit,' the Pope continued, 'that I spoke in January 1981 during an audience granted to the delegation of Solidarity'—and even the dour Silesians raised a cheer at his first (and only) direct mention of the outlawed movement—'accompanied by'—they nudged each other and whispered, 'Lech Wałęsa'—'the representative of the Polish government for permanent working contacts with the Holy See.' This problem, he concluded, can only be resolved through 'a true dialogue between the authorities and society.'

However, in order to revive the dialogue that was severed on 13 December, 1981, the Polish people must learn to forgive. Forgiveness should liberate them from 'the fetters of hatred—for hatred is a destructive force, and we must neither destroy nor allow ourselves to be destroyed by it.' 'Forgiveness is love's might, forgiveness is not weakness. To forgive does not mean to resign from truth and justice.'

This, in crude summary, was the burden of the Pope's message to the Polish people. To the Polish authorities he spoke no less clearly. He told Jaruzelski at the Belweder that the starting point for 'social renewal' must be the 'social accords' that concluded the strikes of the summer of 1980—and gave birth to Solidarity. The authorities and society must find 'means of dialogue that are truly effective.' Addressing more than a million people from the windy heights of a Warsaw football stadium, he demanded 'an order in which man's fundamental rights will be respected.' He went on to say, 'Such an order can be simultaneously a victory of the governed and a victory of those who govern. That point must be reached by way of dialogue and agreement, which is the only viable way for the nation to achieve the *fullness of civil rights* and the social structures that correspond to its just requirements and are capable of fostering the consensus needed by the state if it is to fulfil its role. Through this consensus the nation expresses its sovereignty concretely.'

At Jasna Góra he returned to the theme of sovereignty: 'The state is firmly sovereign when it *governs* society and also *serves* the common good of society and allows the nation to realize its own subjectivity (*podmiotowość*), its own identity.' Later, turning again to the icon of the Black Madonna in the monastery behind him: 'Queen of Poland, I also wish to entrust you with the difficult task of those who wield authority on Polish soil . . . The state gains its strength first of all from the support of the people.' In short, he said to the authorities: You never tire of proclaiming your sovereignty—OK, then behave like a sovereign power.

His third audience was the Polish Church itself. This Church is now stronger than it has been at any time since the war—spiritually, institutionally, and politically. It is the only institution in Poland to have been strengthened both by the rise of Solidarity *and* by the state of war. On the one hand, since 13 December, 1981, a great charge of frustrated hopes, idealism, and energy has run from Solidarity to the Church. According to surveys, in the last year the percentage of regular churchgoers has soared from an already high sixty to sixty-five per cent to an astonishing ninety to ninety-five per cent—especially in working-class parishes. The badges and banners that one saw everywhere with the papal motto *Totus Tuus* and slogans like 'in Solidarity with the Pope' or even *'juventus semper fidelis'*, all in the unmistakable red jumbly lettering of 'Solidarność,' express this transference symbolically. On the other hand, the Jaruzelski government needs Church co-operation more than any of its predecessors, and has made more concessions to win it. Never before has the Church had so much broadcasting time on TV and radio (a right originally won for it by the workers in the summer of 1980), so many newspapers, seminaries, schools, and permits for church building. Two hundred churches are being built in the Kraków diocese alone.

In fact, the Church is frankly alarmed at its own strength—and under the uncertain leadership of Cardinal Józef Glemp, it has been divided about how to use that strength. How far should it co-operate with government at the highest level? How far should it help persecuted workers and Solidarity activists at the parish level? In Warsaw, one church in the working-class quarter of Żoliborz (once a Socialist stronghold) has a famous Solidarity altar. In Kraków, the bishop recently instructed a vicar to dismantle his Solidarity altar and stop the worker education groups that were being held in the vestry. Parish priests have been outspoken in their criticism of the primate.

One of the Pope's main purposes in this pilgrimage was to give the Polish Church its instructions. Politely ignoring the dumpy figure of Primate Glemp, he spoke, in effect, as the pope-primate. His speech to the Episcopate, largely overlooked in media coverage, may in the long term prove to have been as important as any. In it he singled out for special praise the communiqués of the plenary sessions of the Episcopate, which have spelled out the rights of society and the conditions for dialogue most explicitly: 'It seems to me that the communiqués of the Episcopate respond to the need to hear the truth, which is so acute in society. The truth is the first and fundamental condition of social renewal. Without it, one cannot speak of social dialogue, which the Episcopate so justly demands, and which society certainly expects.' It is necessary, he went on, 'to defend every citizen, to protect every life, to prevent injuries, which occur so easily in the case of beatings, especially with young and weak organisms'—a characteristic allusion to the recent case of a Warsaw schoolboy who died after police interrogation. Finally, 'the Christian doctrine of work demands both the solidarity of workers among themselves and the need for honest solidarity with workers.'

Whatever the immediate political effects of the Pope's visit, it is a fact of immense significance that thousands of priests all over Poland will be preaching and ministering along the lines he set for years to come. In the Polish Church, as in economics, there is a 'multiplier effect.'

Meanwhile, the government declares itself broadly satisfied with the visit, which it says both illustrated and facilitated the process of 'normalization'. Spokesmen for the government hint broadly that perhaps on the Communist anniversary of 22 July, it will lift martial law, currently just 'suspended'. In sharp contrast to 1979, it has made this very much a state event, garlanding the Pope with chains of police and security men, which angered and depressed the Poles: 'As if *we* would want to shoot him,' they exclaimed as he was whisked away in his bullet-proof box. The government tried, rather unsuccessfully, to use the presence of some two thousand Western newsmen to put its political point across. Predictably, when the meadow in front of the Jasna Góra monastery turned into a forest of hands raised in the V-for-victory sign and half a million voices cried, 'Restore to us, O Lord, a free fatherland,' the state TV cameras were flashing back to the Belweder meeting with General Jaruzelski.

Like so much else in contemporary Poland, the position of the Jaruzelski government is paradoxical: it is both exceptionally strong and very weak. Its strength derives from the simple fact that it has a monopoly of physical force, which it has shown itself prepared to use and use again. (General Jaruzelski is the first Polish Party leader since 1956 to have had Polish workers shot, breaking the first unwritten commandment of the Polish national tradition—'Pole shall not kill Pole'—and to have survived.) Its weakness is manifested in its inability to find any political way out of the continuing crisis.

Surprisingly, even people who are active in opposition concede that General Jaruzelski's personal intentions are different from—and in some senses, better than—those of his predecessors. In his

Belweder speech he spoke Polish—not translated Sovietese. His obligatory reference to Soviet-Polish friendship was almost papal in its allusiveness, quoting a famous poem, 'To Muscovite Friends', by Adam Mickiewicz, the Polish Byron. He did not once mention the Communist party, but instead spoke emphatically about the necessity of a strong *state*, a state that implements reforms through the laws. Moreover, he said, 'Our law does not punish for views: it only bans anti-state *actions* incompatible with the constitution.' It is possible, even plausible, that this enigmatic man wishes to be an authoritarian rather than a totalitarian ruler of a state in which, as Frederick the Great used to put it, 'the people say what they like and I do what I like.' Even now, articles are published in the official press that could not have been published under Gierek or Gomułka.

But if these are his intentions, can he realize them? At the moment, he still seems to be stymied on all sides. Within his own politburo he faces stiff opposition from a faction led by the wily Stefan Olszowski—a faction that opposed the Pope's visit all along and will now be saying, after the accompanying Solidarity demonstrations and Western news coverage, 'We told you so.' Behind that faction is the stubborn conservatism of the whole bureaucratic apparatus of the Party-state, threatened by reforms and pressure from those 'Muscovite friends.' Against rumours of an imminent deposition of Jaruzelski must be placed the weighty fact that he is backed by the Soviet military, which was, after all, instrumental in the elevation of Mr Andropov. None the less, pressure from the Polish and Soviet Party apparatuses drastically reduces his room for manoeuvre.

Moreover, he is stymied by the economic crisis. Although supplies of basic foodstuffs have improved in recent months, Poland has not begun to sort out its basic problems of long-term neglect of agriculture, catastrophic misinvestment, bureaucratic centralism, and foreign debt. By all accounts, the bloated bureaucracy is already 'rolling back' the vaunted economic reform, as it has rolled back every attempted economic reform since 1956. Industrial production fell last year by a further two per cent. The government hopes that the pope's visit will help break its diplomatic quarantine, bringing Western statesmen and credits in his wake. While the primate and his advisors discreetly let it be known that they do not favour the continuance of sanctions, John Paul II made only one Delphic public utterance on this subject. 'I ardently desire,' he told Jaruzelski at the Belweder, 'the re-creation of conditions of "good co-operation" with all the Western nations on our continent, as well as the Americas, above all the United States of America, where so many millions of citizens are of Polish origin.' Does that mean that Reagan should lift sanctions on Jaruzelski's terms? That Jaruzelski should lift martial law on Reagan's terms? That they should both come half-way, in the spirit of Christian 'forgiveness' and 'dialogue'? What Jaruzelski and the pope said in their subsequent private meeting, and in its even more extraordinary, unscheduled 'continuation' on the Pope's last evening in Kraków, we do not know.

Yet one of their themes must have been the regime's crippling lack of popular support. If Jaruzelski is to begin to regain even a measure of popular acceptance, he must, as the Pope told him publicly, reinstigate a genuine dialogue. But dialogue with whom? The Patriotic Movement for National Salvation (PRON in its Polish acronym), which the government has set up for this purpose, is still an unpopular joke. The new official trade unions do not represent the workers. Independent professional associations like the Polish Journalists' Association and the Polish Writers' Union have been or are being dissolved. The only institution with which there is still something that might be called 'dialogue' is the Church. It seems that this is the dialogue that the regime would most like to pursue today.

In return for the lifting of martial law and perhaps a partial amnesty for political prisoners, the Church should move into closer public co-operation with the authorities. In the medium term, Church sources suggest, the regime might be prepared to enter into a kind of 'corporatist compromise' with the Church, conceding to it large areas of religious and cultural autonomy and perhaps even sharing power with it over some areas of social and economic life. From the Solidarity period there still survive two lay Catholic government ministers—though their current lot is to hold responsibility without power. One Catholic intellectual even talks of a 'Church PRON'. Between them, these two vast authoritarian corporations would guarantee Poland's stability and internal peace to Moscow. It would be as on the streets of Katowice last week, where order was kept by three-man patrols: one soldier, one policeman, and one priest.

Arguably, the Church is so strong that it could afford the loss of popularity that such a 'corporatist compromise' would entail. There are ecclesiastical politicians close to Glemp who are obviously tempted by the prospect. But last week the Pope said an unambiguous public no to this temptation. He spelled out to the people, the authorities, and the Episcopate the conditions for a genuine 'dialogue'—and those conditions included the participation of authentic trade unions. Does this mean the outlawed movement Solidarity? Does this mean Lech Wałęsa? Despite the authorities' glosses on a 'strictly private meeting,' and despite the strange affair of the *Osservatore Romano* article (which sheds light mainly on tensions within the Vatican), what the Pope meant to say with this meeting is unclear. 'There are no private meetings with the Pope,' declares his friend the Kraków theologian Father Józef Tischner. Was he indicating that Wałęsa is still a partner for the dialogue, the true representative of the Polish working class, as many Poles believe? Or was he, as it were, elevating Wałęsa to the peerage of Polish martyrs—a symbol of the great ideals of August 1980, but no longer a political actor?

The authorities' position, by contrast, is already clear. 'Lech Wałęsa ... will never again be a partner of the authorities,' says government spokesman Jerzy Urban. 'There will be no dialogue ... with the former leadership of "Solidarity".' To see the Pope's visit as one great boost for Solidarity, as some Western media have suggested, is at best an oversimplification. The number of active, banner-bearing Solidarity demonstrators was, in fact, relatively small: a hard core of a few thousand, mostly young men, many of whom followed the Pope from place to place, like pilgrims. 'Come with us, today they won't beat you,' they chanted. The surrounding crowds seemed delighted to see them. Children danced along the verges and old women flashed V-signs from rusty balconies. On Wednesday they marched five long miles from the Kraków meadows to the model workers' town of Nowa Huta, where the Pope was to dedicate a church in the afternoon. 'Sol-i-dar-ność,' they chanted. 'End the war'; 'Long live the Pope'; 'Lech Wa-łę-sa'. Their chants were, however, somewhat indiscriminate: when they passed a van hired by NBC, the cry of 'Don't beat for money' (addressed to the police) suddenly changed to 'N-B-C, N-B-C, N-B-C'. I must truthfully report that they also got lost en route to Nowa Huta, but somehow they managed to wind their way back across dusty allotment gardens, making a superb entrance, banners flying, just ten minutes before the Pope. The concourse of workers roared its approval. It was pure Polish theatre.

But when the chanting was over, many of them made a rather sober assessment of their position. 'That was our last day of freedom,' said one standard-bearer, and another: 'Many of us feel it was a kind of glorious funeral for Solidarity—as an organization.' Theirs is the traditional, superb Polish theatre of defiance—and it has a huge and enthusiastic audience—but they do not see any prospects of converting the moral support into effective political action. They cannot force the authorities to talk to them. I understand that Solidarity's underground leadership is uncertain whether to call a demonstration at all for the anniversary of the Gdańsk agreement on 31 August. For on that day the police will not make a U-turn and speed away from the demonstrations, as I saw them do on the road to Nowa Huta. On that day they will charge with batons raised, even though the crowd chants, as it did last week, 'Dem-on-stra-cja pok-oj-ow-a!' 'peace demo, peace demo!'

What does have a future, they argue, is the *samizdat* newspapers, magazines, and factory bulletins that are still being produced on a scale unmatched anywhere else in the Soviet bloc. In large factories, too, Solidarity's clandestine factory commissions continue to collect regular union dues and pay out benefits to the sick and those sacked for political reasons. Some of them discuss attempting to use the limited pluralism of official unions for which the 1982 trades-union act provided. Solidarity survives not only as a symbol and a myth but as a world of diverse local initiatives, of social self-organization, a habit of behaviour, and a set of values that the pope preached and blessed. But Solidarity the nationwide social movement—not even the activists can envisage the conditions in which it could be restored.

As everyone says, we had to wait a year before we saw the effects of the Pope's last visit and we will probably have to wait another year to discern the effects of this one. 'The first visit broke through a barrier of fear,' a senior Catholic intellectual speculated beforehand. 'Perhaps this one can break through the barrier of hopelessness.' This time, however, the effects are unlikely to be seen in any single political breakthrough but rather in countless small ways, in the strengthening of habits of solidarity, dignity and honesty that is already visible. A university lecturer comments that although few of his students are active in the underground, almost all of them are prepared to say exactly what they think, even about the most sensitive political subjects. The students 'call good and evil by name', as the Pope exhorted. Solidarity, says Father Tischner, 'was a forest of awakened consciences.' The forest is growing. It is not for the forest to go to the government. The government must come to the forest. In this sense, for all the depression and repression, Poland may be said to be in a better condition than any of its neighbours—including even Hungary. This transformation of consciousness, this moral revolution, is a lasting achievement of the Pope and Solidarity.

Whatever develops in Poland over the next few years, it will be different from anything we have seen before. Though the police rule the streets, this country cannot be 'normalized'—i.e., returned to Soviet norms. Though the totalitarian communist system remains in outward form, in reality it is still being dismantled from within.

(JUNE 1983)

Czechoslovakia Under Ice

Every day last month young Czechs lit candles and laid wreaths with the simple message 'We Remember' on the grave of Marie Jedličkova, in Prague's main cemetery. Every night the candles and flowers were removed by 'persons unknown'.

Who was Marie Jedličkova? I don't know. None of her mourners could tell me. All they knew was that fifteen years ago, a young man was buried in this same grave. His name was Jan Palach and he set fire to himself to bear witness against the Soviet occupation. To extinguish his memory, the Husák regime subsequently had his remains removed to a country graveyard and put the unknown Marie J. in his place. But Palach's mourners will not be cheated. So every year, on the anniversary of his self-immolation in January 1969, they light candles before the tombstone of the unknown stranger.

Across the road, I made my way through the ivy-covered Jewish cemetery to the tomb of Franz Kafka, whose fiction has become a reality at the grave of Marie J. But the Husák regime tries to forget Kafka, too. The centenary of his birth last year was commemorated only unofficially, by the country's best, and therefore banned, writers. As one of them has observed, Gustav Husák is 'the President of Forgetting'. And how much he has to forget! Prague cinema-goers were recently treated to an official film biography of that broken old communist. After skimming lightly over Husák's wartime collaboration with the Nazis, the film leaped at one bound from 1948 to 1968. The appalling Stalinist trials, in which he was one of the accused; his long imprisonment; his rehabilitation and crawl back up the greasy pole: all this had just disappeared down the memory hole.

Forgetting is the key to the so-called normalization of Czechoslovakia. In effect, the regime has said to the people: 'Forget

1968. Forget your democratic traditions. Forget that you were once citizens with rights and duties. Forget politics. In return we will give you a comfortable, safe life. There'll be plenty of food in the shops and cheap beer in the pubs. You may afford a car and even a little country cottage—and you won't have to work competitively. We don't ask you to believe in us or our fatuous ideology. By all means listen to the Voice of America and watch Austrian television (*sotto voce:* so do we). All we ask is that you will outwardly and publicly conform: join in the ritual "elections", vote the prescribed way in the "trade union" meetings, enroll your children in the "socialist" youth organization. Keep your mind to yourself.'

One can describe this unwritten deal in different ways. A Western observer might describe it as a retreat from totalitarianism. An angry young Czech describes it as the perfection of totalitarianism. Czech ex-communists describe it as Husák's social contract. But all agree that in the last decade, the deal has more or less worked for the regime. By comparison with Warsaw, Bucharest, and even East Berlin, the streets of Prague look prosperous. Butchers' windows display a rich variety of sausage and meat. Of course there are shortages, but several housewives told me that supplies slightly improved last year. They had even seen fresh *lettuce* in the greengrocer's. They have been hit by price increases—for example, on petrol, oil, and electricity—without compensatory wage rises. Workers have been officially threatened with wage cuts. Consumer durables are scarce and expensive. But they still have much to lose.

In return for this relative prosperity, most Czechs have watched passively while the regime has systematically purged the Party and state, the economy, the arts, the universities, and the media of anyone who dares to speak critically, independently, or even intelligently about what the regime defines as politics—an infinitely elastic category. The scale of the purges is breathtaking. Roughly half a million people resigned or were expelled from the Party after 1968: one in every three Party members. If one assumes they each have two dependents, then they make up ten per cent of the whole population. Philosophers, lawyers, journalists became bricklayers, waiters, clerks. They joined an existing circle of the damned: Christians and non-communists whose degradation began with the communist coup in 1948. And they are still being joined by others. That window cleaner over there: his thesis was on Wittgenstein. Ask your waiter about Kafka: before his trial, he lectured on *The Trial.* Yes, the nightwatchman is reading Aristotle. Your coal will be delivered by an ordained priest of the Czech brethren. Kiss the milkman's ring: he is your bishop.

The Czech nation has been stood on its head. (In Slovakia, conditions are rather different and easier; I confine myself to the Czech lands.) The most independent, intelligent, and best are at the bottom; the worst, stupidest, and most servile, at the top. The Party is little more than a union for self-advancement. A director will tell an ambitious young man, 'Well, of course you must join the Party,' and many do so quite cynically. The country's politics are frozen into immobility—a fifteen-year winter after one Prague Spring. Husák and his politburo fear that even their timid, tinkering, economic reforms could have untoward political consequences. No impulses for reform come from the purged, cowed, and corrupt *apparat.* Younger Party members are devastatingly critical—but cynically and in private; while most Czechs do not look to the Party for anything at all. I have never been in a country where politics, and indeed the whole of public life, is a matter of such supreme indifference.

Czechoslovakia today can be compared to a lake permanently covered by a thick layer of ice. On the surface nothing moves. But under the ice, among the philosopher-labourers, the window-cleaning journalists, and nightwatchman-monks—here, things are on the move.

In the West this subglacial movement is known, if at all, by the label Charter 77. Charter 77 is often thought of as a dissident political organization. This it is not, and cannot be. The original Charter declaration on 1 January, 1977, proclaimed a 'free, informal, open community of people of different convictions, different faiths, and different professions' united to work for the respect of human and civil rights. It emphasized that 'Charter 77 is not an organization' and 'does not form the basis of any oppositional political activity.' Of course these disclaimers were partly tactical, since to form *any* independent organization ('political' or not) is a crime in Czechoslovakia's totalitarian law book. But there are more than sufficient reasons why Charter 77 has not in practice built the kind of organization that its Polish cousin, KOR, developed before August 1980. 'KOR began where the Charter leaves off,' one Chartist told me. From the start, the Chartists were fiercely and systematically persecuted. Détente did not help protect them as it helped protect leading KOR members until 1980. Czechoslovakia's hard-currency debt had never been so large as to provide a significant 'lever' for the West. In autumn 1979 the playwright Václav Havel and four other members of the Committee for the Defence of the Unjustly Prosecuted (VONS) were themselves unjustly prosecuted and summarily convicted, despite worldwide protests. Havel was released from prison only last year, seriously ill. He described to me the oppressive police surveillance under which he now lives: the threat of a house search hanging over him whenever he sits down at the typewriter; the knowledge that every visitor is photographed and every conversation bugged; police narks following him wherever he goes—even into the sauna.

In the most recent example of Husák's justice, a thirty-one-year-old worker, Jiří Wolf, was condemned to six years' imprisonment for 'subversion'. His offence: writing a letter to the Austrian embassy about prison conditions. This is the longest sentence yet given to a Chartist, and follows a previous sentence of three and a half years. As the Good Soldier Schweik once commented: 'I never imagined they'd sentence an innocent man to ten years ... sentencing an innocent man to five years, that's something I've heard of, but *ten*, that's a bit too much.'

Wolf's fellow workers react in a similar vein. 'Why bother to make trouble for yourself by saying these things out loud?' the philosopher and former Charter spokesman Ladislav Hejdánek was asked by his factory workmates. 'We all know them anyway.' This lack of active support from the industrial working class—not to mention the prosperous agricultural workers—is the second main reason why Charter cannot follow the path of KOR.

A third, grave, disability is the lack of support or protection from the Church. The majority Catholic Church has, since the Stalinist period, been persecuted, broken, and corrupted to an appalling degree. Historically identified with Habsburg domination over the Czech lands, it lacked that massive popularity that alone enabled the Polish Church to resist communist *Gleichschaltung*. In the early fifties, all its monastic orders were simply dissolved: some 8,000 of the country's 12,000 monks disappeared into labour camps. Bishops, priests, and theologians were imprisoned for up to fifteen years. The minority Protestant churches were co-opted or coerced.

Since then, all the clergy in Czechoslovakia have been, in effect, employees of the communist state. Their salaries are paid by the government, which has a veto on all church appointments. If a priest displeases the state by preaching 'political' sermons, or simply by attracting too many young people to church, he is forbidden to practise his vocation. That is why the man the Vatican appointed as bishop of Hradec Králové had to work as a milkman. So whereas in Poland the Catholic Church plays a great, independent role, whereas in East Germany the Protestant hierarchy can do something to shield peace activists, in Czechoslovakia, the official churches are crippled and corrupted and the most courageous priests banned from the pulpit.

In these conditions it is a miracle that Charter has survived at all—like a candle burning under water. It has done so thanks to the extraordinary fortitude of people like Václav Benda, a Catholic intellectual who, emerging from four years' imprisonment, has once again taken up the job of Charter spokesperson (one of three), despite illness and reprisals against himself and his children. (The punishment of children for the conduct of their parents—the Nazis' *Sippenhaft*—is one of the most revolting regular practices of the communist state.) Benda, a stout, bearded man in his mid-thirties, admits that the ranks of the thousand-odd signatories of the Charter have been depleted by emigration, imprisonment and, sometimes, resignation. None the less, the eight-year-old Charter can claim to be the longest-lived human rights movement in Eastern Europe, and he quotes its first spokesman, Jan Patočka: 'This is not a battle but a war.' The Chartists, he says, have served as the 'front line', behind which hundreds of newcomers have quietly joined the ranks of nonconformity.

Who knows how many hundred people are seated at their typewriters every evening typing out a manuscript with ten carbon copies for *samizdat* distribution? Judging by the quantity of *samizdat* I saw in a short visit, it must be hundreds if not thousands. Besides the *samizdat*, there are unofficial seminars and discussion groups. For obvious reasons of secrecy, no one person can know all about this miniature counterculture; but its main concerns are visible. After 1968 the Czech lands became what Louis Aragon called a 'literary Biafra'. Virtually all the best contemporary Czech writers are published only in *samizdat*.

Secondly, they try to salvage Czech history from the regime of forgetting. In the study of a former professor of literature I noticed a fine bust of Tomáš Garrigue Masaryk, president of the pre-war Czechoslovakian Republic. He explained that the bust was commissioned for his university in 1947. After the communist takeover in 1948, it could not be exhibited. 'So I am keeping it in trust until it can be returned to its proper place.' Only recently, he told me, the citizens of Nové Mesto (in Moravia) woke up one morning to find their statue of Masaryk gone from the main square—'the spot was already half paved over.' Another blow for the President of Forgetting. But wherever I went, in private flats I found busts of Tomáš Masaryk. For the Czechs, as Kundera has written: 'The struggle of man against power is the struggle of memory against forgetting.'

The Czechs are intensely proud of their interwar democracy, which they justly claim was unique in Central and Eastern Europe. Yet the counter-culture is distinguished by a fiercely self-critical approach to that history. 'We regard the expulsion of the Sudetan Germans in 1945 as the first act of totalitarianism in our country,' one passionate Czech patriot told me. To most British observers, the three national tragedies of Czechoslovakia—1938 (Munich), 1948 (communist coup), and 1968 (Warsaw Pact invasion)—would seem to have been events beyond the Czechs' control: *our* fault in 1938, the Russians' (and ours) in 1948, the Russians' in 1968. But they ask: What could Masaryk, Beneš, or Dubček have done to prevent it?

Predictably, the closer the event the fiercer the controversy, so 1968 is the subject of fierce polemics among Chartists. Ex-Party members are still the tightest single group within the Charter, and many of them still cherish the hope of 1968: that change will come through the Party. Consequently, these self-styled 'Euro-communists' insist on the necessity of 'dialogue' with the communists in power—their former comrades. I was told that a group of them even addressed a letter to Andropov on his accession, virtually offering their services as an alternative politburo. However, as one ex-communist wryly remarked, 'The only "dialogue" I have is with my interrogator.' 'Please don't imagine I have any illusions about the "dialogue",' Dr Jiří Hájek, Dubček's foreign minister in 1968, hastened to assure me. He no longer expects any major political results from talking to the Party; but this 'dialogue' would be a stimulus and example to society at large.

Non- and anti-communist Chartists call these residual hopes residual illusions. But they do not yet have any alternative political strategy. Where the Eurocommunists think in terms of power and diplomacy, they think in terms of metaphysics and theology. The difference is nicely illustrated by the underground (or subglacial) debate about peace. On this issue the range of opinion among Chartists is as wide as in the West. I met passionate Reaganauts and supporters of Western 'peace movements'. But whereas the Euro-communists, like Western peaceniks, pose direct political questions—What is to be done? Which argument will persuade whom?—the non-communists argue at a deeper level. Western peace activists who come to Prague seeking allies (or alibis?) are confronted with philosophers like Ladislav Hejdánek, asking, 'But what *is* "peace"?'—and reaching back to Spinoza and St Luke for the answer. Václav Havel describes the arms race as merely part of a 'worldwide crisis of human responsibility.' 'Western governments overestimate the power of missiles.' However, all the Chartists I spoke to stressed one point: What they have in Eastern Europe is not the peace that we enjoy in Western Europe. Peace is not just the absence of war. A lasting, full peace can only be achieved with and within countries whose governments respect human rights and are democratically controlled.

Do they envisage their philosophical ideas ever being translated into political realities in Czechoslovakia? For Havel there are 'two crucial questions: Does the Charter speak the truth? And if it does speak the truth, has this truth reached wider circles of society?'

Of course in a communist state there cannot be public opinion. But there is something that we might call private opinion. There are issues on which large numbers of people think and speak alike in private, although they dare not in public. The Charter, and its surrounding counter-culture, has had a considerable impact on this private opinion, Havel argues. After four years in prison, he finds that the gulf between public life and private opinion has grown. People are complaining more openly—in pubs and trams as well as in the privacy of their homes. Compared with what happened in Poland, the change is imperceptible; compared with Czechoslovakia when he went to prison, it is substantial.

Private opinion has been particularly incensed by the deployment of new Soviet missiles, announced last November. What infuriated the Czechs was the absurd *volte-face* of official propaganda. For three years they were inundated with diatribes against Pershing and Cruise. *Any* new missiles will increase the danger to the country in which they are stationed, said the propagandists. In the town of Pardubice, a mass meeting was held under a banner exhorting 'No New Missiles in Europe.' Next day, the government announced that new Soviet missiles would be stationed in Czechoslovakia. People returned to photograph the banner, which was hastily removed. The authorities displayed their anxiety by threatening leading Chartists with prosecution for 'undermining the national defence capability' if they criticized the deployment. In spite of this, a petition against the missiles has collected some thousand signatures in Prague. In the Moravian capital, Brno, a similar petition was apparently started spontaneously by apprentices and Christian students: it is said to have collected more than a thousand signatures, and baffled the police. An 'unofficial peace movement' like that in neighbouring East Germany (with Church protection) is not possible here. But the anger of private opinion is unmistakable.

The same is true of one other issue: pollution. 'Golden Prague' is a dirty rust-colour these days, with accumulated grime from low-grade brown coal, petrol fumes, and industrial smog. A friend drove me through devastated parts of north-western Bohemia—what was once the Sudetenland. Near the town of Most, we stopped before the huge, belching Chemical Works of Czech-Soviet Friendship. Through choking acid fog we could just read the banner on the façade: 'Together with the Soviet Union for Peace and Future Happiness for Our People.' In the mountains I saw whole forests destroyed by acid rain—a landscape by a war artist. On our way home we passed another building with a banner proclaiming 'The Leninist Way for the Development of Our Country.' 'Yes, that building is the Leninist way,' snorted my companion. It was the prison where the Husák regime incarcerated Václav Benda. The Leninist way . . .

Unlike the Chartists' philosophical, literary and historical concerns, the issues of peace and pollution have an immediate popular appeal. You do not need to be an intellectual to feel threatened by missiles and acid rain. Nor can one assume that Czech workers have been wholly pacified by Husák's 'social contract'. On the wall of one Prague factory there recently appeared a large graffito: 'We envy the people of Grenada!' When a Party official tried to collect signatures in support of the new Soviet missiles at an official trade-union meeting, the workers sent him packing. Now and then they like to frighten the managers by muttering: 'Solidarność.'

Of course the Chartists see that a Czech Solidarity is as likely as fire under ice. But they also see that the development of the *samizdat* counter-culture, and the growing alienation of private opinion, combined with economic and political stagnation, have begun at least to make the ice mushy on the underside. If ever a real thaw comes—from above? after change in Moscow?—they will be ready with their busts of Tomáš Masaryk, their editions of Franz Kafka, and their memorials to Jan Palach. They know from their own experience in 1968, and from the Polish experience in 1980–81, how suddenly a society that seems atomized, apathetic, and broken can be transformed into an articulate, united civil society. How private opinion can become public opinion. How a nation can stand on its feet again. And for this they are working and waiting, under the ice.

(FEBRUARY 1984)

The German Question

1

The 'German question' as it has been posed with renewed intensity in Western capitals over the last five years is really two questions. First, is the Federal Republic still a fully committed and reliable member of the Western alliance? Do not its distinctive foreign policy towards East Germany, Eastern Europe, and Soviet Union (*Deutschlandpolitik* and *Ostpolitik*), its harking back to détente, and its disagreements with the Reagan administration reflect a revived yearning for reunification and Germany's historic, geopolitical propensity for manoeuvring between East and West? Second, is West Germany still a stable pillar of Western liberal democracy? Do not the so-called peace movement, the spread of anti-Americanism, and the rise of the Greens presage a slide away from the Anglo-Saxon style of parliamentary democracy imposed after 1945, towards a more 'national' and 'socialist' policy that would altogether reject 'bourgeois democratic' institutions, capitalism, and NATO as the lock, stock, and barrel of an alien 'system?' Rapallo is a catchword for the first fear; neutralist nationalism, for the second.

West Germans have always been extremely sensitive to comment from abroad. Every Sunday morning, instead of going to church, millions of West Germans tune in to Werner Hofer's *Frühschoppen* TV discussion programme to hear what '*das kritische Ausland*'—that is, a group of foreign journalists—has to say about their country's performance the previous week. But with the new self-confidence that the Federal Republic acquired under Helmut Schmidt, politicians from all parties do not conceal their irritation at the revival of suspicious questioning from Washington, London, Paris, or Rome. In otherwise diplomatic memoirs of his time as head of West Germany's *Ständige Vertretung* (i.e., quasi embassy) in East Berlin,

Klaus Bölling, one of Schmidt's closest advisers, suddenly explodes:

> We could not discount leading articles about the dangers of German nationalism in *Le Monde* and *The Times* as mere journalistic opinions. Leadership circles (*Führungszirkel*) in Western capitals found that it paid to revive fears of an over-mighty, reunified Germany in order the better to discipline us. Who would be surprised that a man like Carter's Security Advisor Brzezinski, being of Polish origin, helped to spread rumours—for which he then found a grateful audience in certain floors of Foreign Offices.[1]

A neurosis speaks through this extraordinary outburst.

It may be, as the former *Die Zeit* editor Josef Joffe has written, that post-war Germany is 'doomed to suffer the fate of Caesar's wife: it has to be above suspicion.' What is certain is that West Germany has a Caesar's-wife syndrome. Even if no accusations came from other Western capitals (and I must say I cannot recall a single *Times* leader about the dangers of German nationalism in the period to which Klaus Bölling refers), the ghosts of the past would constantly be raised in Bonn.

No one is more suspicious of the Germans than the Germans themselves. You cannot pass a week in the Federal Republic without seeing at least one article asking, 'How Stable is Our Democracy?' or, 'Is Bonn Weimar?' or, 'How Open is the German Question?' West Germany is like one of its own model businessmen: a hearty, sun-tanned forty-year-old, hair neatly parted, smartly dressed (Harris tweed jacket, grey flannels), with nice manners and a stock of sensible conversation—but forever dashing into the *Apotheke* to check his blood pressure, or glancing at his reflection in shop windows, to make sure he hasn't developed a nervous tic. To nations with happier pasts, this relentless self-examination may seem excessive or even faintly comical; but we would really start worrying if the Germans stopped worrying.

Out of this historical moment, poised between self-doubt and self-assertion, come German answers to our German questions.

---

[1] *Die Fernen Nachbarn: Erfahrungen in der DDR*, by Klaus Bölling, (Hamburg: Stern Buch, 1983)

'*Deutschlandpolitik* is not reunification policy,' insist the diplomats and politicians who make it. 'The only kind of reunification we are talking about is the reunification of families.' Much of the misunderstanding in Western capitals, they say, comes from confusing the long-term perspective of reunification with the short- to medium-term perspectives of their current policy towards East Germany. The current policy begins by acknowledging the fact of Germany's division into two states, with opposed systems and alliances. (Indeed, the process of rethinking that led to the new *Deutschlandpolitik* and *Ostpolitik* may be dated from the building of the Berlin Wall in 1961.)

The modest announced aims are to make the consequences of division as humanly bearable as possible, particularly for the Germans in the East ('*menschliche Erleichterungen*'); to promote contacts between Germans in East and West; to keep alive the consciousness of common nationhood on both sides of the Wall (quite as necessary in the Federal Republic as in the GDR); and thus to keep open the possibility that in the unforeseeable future, the Germans might yet 'achieve in free self-determination the unity and freedom of Germany'—as they are 'called upon' to do by the preamble to the Federal Republic's 'Basic Law'. But for the foreseeable future, this means recognizing and dealing with the German Democratic Republic (GDR).

Such was the policy that the Christian Democrats (CDU) and Franz Josef Strauss's CSU furiously opposed when the Brandt-Scheel (SPD-FDP) government introduced the 'Basic Treaty' (*Grundlagenvertrag*) with the GDR in 1972. It is the same policy that the Christian Democrats are themselves pursuing today. Despite a change in rhetoric, there has been a truly remarkable continuity in *Deutschlandpolitik* from the social-liberal to the conservative-liberal coalition governments. The Christian Democrats came into office swearing they would be tougher about linking new credits to concessions from the Honecker regime in East Germany (*Gegenleistungen*), but in practice they have carried on much as their predecessors did. When I asked Herr Heinrich Windelen, the minister for intra-German affairs (not *inter*-German affairs—a fine distinction), what concessions his government had won in return for guaranteeing 2 billion Deutschmarks in loans to the GDR, he said the GDR had speeded up border-crossing procedures for transit traffic between West Berlin and West Germany and reduced the amount that West German pensioners have to exchange into East German Marks for every day they spend in the East.

Two billion Deutschmarks' worth of concessions? As under Schmidt, the hotline continues to run from the federal chancellery (*Bundeskanzleramt*) in Bonn to the quasi embassy (*Ständige Vertretung*) in East Berlin—or directly to Honecker's office. The present head of the *Ständige Vertretung*, Dr Hans-Otto Bräutigam, is a highly respected professional diplomat who was instrumental in shaping the practice of *Deutschlandpolitik* under the previous government. Most remarkable is the *volte-face* of that most intemperate right-wing critic of the social-liberal *Ostpolitik*, Franz Josef Strauss; for today it is Strauss who arranges new credits for Erich Honecker.

Of course the change of rhetoric has been a problem. It is characteristic of Chancellor Kohl's monumentally relaxed style of leadership (less *laissez-faire* than *laissez-parler*) that he lets his ministers make quite different noises in public—and blithely maintains they are all right. It is also a fact that the associations of Germans from the former Eastern territories (Silesia, Pomerania, etc.) are a significant lobby inside the CDU and CSU. As a result, people like Friedrich Zimmermann, the CSU interior minister, have been getting up at Sunday meetings and talking about the old *Vaterland* within the frontiers of 1937. They have, in other words, done precisely what the government charges its Western critics with doing—confusing the long-term perspectives of reunification with the short- to medium-term *Deutschlandpolitik*. So the Kohl government has appeared to say one thing on Sunday and do another on Monday.

This may have raised eyebrows in Washington or Paris; it has been a heaven-sent gift to Moscow. Whether or not the old men in the Kremlin still (irrationally) believe in a 'German threat', they have every political reason to wheel out the propaganda bogey of West German 'revanchism' today. Inside the Soviet Union, patriotic mobilization in the preparations for the fortieth anniversary of the glorious victory over Nazi Germany, in May, is an irresistible alternative to risky measures of economic reform, upon which the Politburo can probably not agree. In Eastern Europe, the tired old German bogey must serve once again to legitimize Soviet domination and to justify the continued existence of the Warsaw Pact. Kohl's colleagues have offered chapter and verse, as if to a Soviet propagandist's order.

It is tempting to suggest that the Kohl government paid the price of preaching what it does not practice when Honecker postponed his planned visit to West Germany last autumn. But the rhetoric of the CDU/CSU right was probably more a pretext for Honecker's change of plans than a cause of it. The basic reasons for the 'postponement' are to be sought in Moscow and in what Erich Honecker calls the *Grosswetterlage*—the climate of East-West relations. In late August or early September, Soviet leaders seem finally to have agreed among themselves that if someone *must* talk seriously with the West, it had better be Russians talking to Americans. So Gromyko met Reagan instead of Honecker meeting Kohl. What is permitted to Jove is not permitted to an ally.

Yet the quiet practice of *Deutschlandpolitik* goes on. Last October the secretary of state in the federal chancellery responsible for *Deutschlandpolitik*, Herr Philipp Jenninger (now president of the Bundestag), told me that the East German government was, if anything, more friendly than before the cancellation. Despite the embarrassment of East German citizens squatting in West German embassies across Eastern Europe, the GDR continued to release a steady trickle of its citizens to the West—either political prisoners 'bought free' by the Bonn government (for 15,000 to 25,000 dollars a head) or those allowed out in the course of 'family reunification'. During a trip to Finland, Honecker said his West German visit had been called off because 'preparations were not sufficiently advanced.' Both German governments are obviously keen to preserve their good working relationship, without advertising it to the East or West; both privately hope that a German-German summit may yet prove possible—when the Soviet victory celebrations are over, the Warsaw Pact renewed, and the superpowers have returned to the negotiating table.

Who could have imagined a decade ago that a conservative government in Bonn would attach such importance to good relations with the communist government in East Berlin? Why has Strauss changed his tune? Because he and most of his colleagues see the benefits that the *Deutschlandpolitik*, initiated by the opposition, has brought to the Federal Republic and, they would say, to 'Germany'.

Western observers ignore at their peril the evidence that the development of German-German relations since the basic treaty has been a success story for *both* German states and for the German people. Anyone who has lived in West Berlin will appreciate the relative ease of communication (by telephone or in person) with East Berlin and West Germany—by contrast with the island fastness of fifteen years ago. Anyone who has lived in East Germany will know that the millions of West Germans who come visiting each year (5 million in 1983) are generally welcome guests—though there are mixed feelings. The number of East Germans below pensionable age who are allowed to visit the West is still pitifully small (some 112,000 in 1983)—but it, too, is larger than a decade ago. Even the normal non-privileged GDR citizen can now hope that in ten or fifteen years' time he might be allowed out for a few days in West Germany, if only to attend his grandmother's funeral.

The Honecker regime feared, and no doubt still fears, that these mass contacts with the West might be destabilizing. On balance, they have had the reverse effect. Honecker's *Westpolitik*, his 'opening up' to West Germany, has been popular, especially when—as during the rumpus over his planned West German visit—he is perceived by his own citizens to be 'standing up to Moscow.' (A perception fuelled by West German television, which the great majority of East Germans watch in preference to their own!) Those whose discontent *has* been stimulated by Western contacts are mostly led, sooner or later, to try to escape or to apply to leave legally. Honecker can then export his dissidents for hard currency—a trick that General Jaruzelski can only dream of. During the last two years, this has been a highly cost effective way of bleeding the independent 'peace groups' in the GDR. There are now more Jena 'peace activists' in West Berlin than there are in Jena.

Direct payments of more than 1 billion Deutschmarks a year from the Federal Republic, favourable credits, and the GDR's 'secret membership' in the EEC have helped it maintain its place among the world's top ten industrial nations, and a better level of consumer supplies than its Eastern neighbours. The contrast with impoverished Poland is a source of national pride among ordinary East Germans. Finally, the GDR has, thanks to West Germany's *Deutschlandpolitik*, achieved wide international recognition—the *Anerkennung* for which it so long fought. In his keynote speech at last

October's thirty-fifth anniversary celebrations, Erich Honecker proudly declared that the GDR maintains diplomatic relations with 132 countries 'the world over'. The printed version of his speech actually said 131, but at the last minute the GDR scored yet another diplomatic triumph by securing recognition from the Ivory Coast.

The former GDR dissident Rudolf Bahro comments interestingly in one of his interviews with the *New Left Review* (collected in *From Red to Green*):

> You find that workers will grouse and swear about conditions when they are in their factory, but when some well-heeled uncle arrives on a visit from West Germany, they stand up for the GDR and point out all the good things about it, all the disadvantages they had to overcome after 1945, and so on. Although the state's demands for loyalty are widely resented, I would say that in normal, crisis-free times there is sufficiently high degree of loyalty to assure the country's stability... The increase in international recognition has certainly boosted the sense of loyalty to the state.[2]

In my experience, many GDR citizens truly appreciate the modest security of life in an efficient police welfare state. The East German state's increasingly explicit acknowledgement of its own undoubted Germanness—with the equestrian statue of Frederick the Great back on Unter den Linden, and even Bismarck partially rehabilitated—has also contributed to this qualified loyalty.

West Germany, for its part, has abandoned the SPD's original notion of '*Wandel durch Annäherung*'—'change through coming closer.' Politicians from all established parties now claim that their policies are not aimed at changing the political system in East Germany—or in the rest of Eastern Europe. Thus Richard von Weizsäcker (CDU), president of the Federal Republic, in a revealing introduction to his collection of essays and speeches describes the idea of *Wandel durch Annäherung* as an unrealistic 'burden' on West Germany's policy towards the Soviet Union. Minister Windelen writes, in *Aussenpolitik* (a German counterpart to *Foreign Affairs*): 'We have no intention of harming or destabilizing the GDR.'

[2] *From Red to Green: Interviews with New Left Review*, by Rudolf Bahro, translated by Gus Fagan and Richard Hurst, (London: Verso, 1984)

In return for helping stabilize the communist regime in East Germany, the Federal Republic has been able to 'buy free' some thing in the order of 150,000 of its citizens; to make life for the remaining 16.7 million more bearable; and to bring the Germans in East and West closer together. Intra-German trade, a major factor for the GDR, has been no more than a fringe benefit for West Germany—just 1.8 per cent of its total foreign trade in 1983. But West German commentators point out that the Federal Republic has reaped one major benefit for itself: a new freedom in foreign policy. The Hallstein doctrine of the 1950s—that West Germany would not recognize any state that recognized East Germany—had been a manacle on both German states. The 'normalization' of Berlin's position following the Four-Power Agreement means that Bonn does not feel such a pressing day-to-day dependence on the Western allies for the defence of Germany's once and future capital. Opening up to the East is an essential part of West Germany's emergence, under Brandt and Schmidt, from its anomalous position in the 1960s as 'an economic giant but a political dwarf.'

If West Germany's political leaders and opinion makers have a rational, political investment in their distinctive foreign policy toward the East, many also have a deep emotional investment in it. And the emotions are far from ignoble—patriotism, a sense of Germany's special historical responsibility, pride in the Federal Republic's appearance on the world stage. Travelling through East Germany—in the lush forests of Goethe's Thuringia, or at the Wittenberg church where Luther nailed up his Ninety-Five Theses— even a foreigner can become emotional about this 'old Germany', which has disappeared in the West. (The Americanization of the Federal Republic goes far deeper than the Sovietization of the GDR.) Few would be unmoved by the courageous witness of the Protestant churches in the GDR—the heirs of Bonhoeffer. And if you have seen at first hand what the division of Germany means in human suffering and what relief the quiet practice of *Deutschlandpolitik* brings, then you too may rail against a superpower conflict—a *'Grosswetterlage'*— that seems to put all this in question.

The memoirs of West Germany's first two quasi-ambassadors to East Berlin, Gaus and Bölling, are shot through with this emotional involvement, this sense of shared Germany. Bölling also gives a riveting account of the December 1981 summit meeting between

Schmidt and Honecker—on the shores of the Werbellinsee, in the Mark Brandenburg. There was, he writes, a 'very German' atmosphere about the occasion (*'so etwas wie eine sehr deutsche Grundstimmung'*). In his presentation, Schmidt told Honecker: 'We must remain predictable [*berechenbar*] for each other,' and later, 'The world powers have an obligation toward us. We must pressurize the great powers.' The formula repeated publicly by both leaders—'a war may never again start from German soil'—has acquired an almost shamanistic significance for many people in both Germanies, people who want to believe that both German governments have learned the same lesson from the same disastrous history.

Finally, there is a strong sense that the Federal Republic's own self-respect, its role as a leading European power, is inseparably bound up with its *Ostpolitik*. This was, after all, the Federal Republic's major contribution to world politics during the last decade, and one inspired by a noble vision of a new peacemaking Germany that might begin to undo the damage Hitler did.

Now, it may be that Honecker too has such an emotional investment in the intra-German détente. Certainly, he is identified with it politically; and he would seem to have adequate support for it in his own politburo and central committee. Polemical exchanges in the Soviet-bloc press last summer seemed to suggest that East Germany's Communist leaders, like Hungary's and Poland's, have an understanding of their 'national' interests that is far from identical with Moscow's understanding of their 'internationalist' obligation. Yet the upshot of that controversy has shown just how little room for manoeuvre they have, if indeed they seriously seek more. Whatever East Berlin's executive independence from Moscow, it is certainly far less than Bonn's independence from Washington. However important the GDR is to the Warsaw Pact, it cannot be more important than the Federal Republic is to NATO.

We can therefore be led—not by outdated, irrational fears of the 'German menace', but by a sympathetic, rational reading of what authoritative West Germans say and do—to wonder how Bonn's policy towards the East might affect its policy towards the West.

2

The Kohl government has not one but two answers to this question. The first is that there is simply no conflict between the Federal Republic's integration into the West (*Westintegration*) and its policy toward the East (*Ostpolitik*), between its security policy (*Sicherheitspolitik*) and its intra-German policy (*Deutschlandpolitik*). On the contrary. The latter would not be possible without the former. *Westintegration* is the premise of *Ostpolitik*. 'The more firmly bedded we are in the Western alliance, the easier it is to work with the GDR,' a senior emissary to East Berlin told me. Good fences make good neighbours. The second answer is, in a characteristic Kohl phrase: 'Freedom has the right of way before unity' ('*Die Freiheit hat Vorfahrt vor der Einheit*'). 'Faced with a choice between intra-German relations and the security of the Federal Republic within the Western alliance,' as the minister for intra-German affairs reassured an American audience in February last year, his government 'would decide in favour of the latter.' But both these statements imply that there *might* be a choice, a decision; in short, a conflict of interest.

And of course there *is* a potential conflict. As Chancellor Kohl himself acknowledged in a discussion after his Adenauer Memorial Lecture in Oxford last year, the key to what the East German government does lies in Moscow. Now, since all the established parties in Bonn perceive good relations with the German Democratic Republic to be in Germany's national interest, and since good relations with the GDR are rightly seen to depend on relations with the Soviet Union, it must follow that West Germany (like all previous Germanies) has a special interest in good relations with Russia. Insofar as their purpose is to keep the nation together—at least in spirit, human contacts, and so forth—Moscow is more important than Washington. The Federal Republic's 1970 treaty with the Soviet Union *necessarily* preceded its 1972 treaty with the GDR. Eastern approaches, not Western alliances, allow German to meet German in Weimar or East Berlin.

It is refreshing to find the president of the Federal Republic, Richard von Weizsäcker[3], frankly acknowledging this potential

---

[3] *Die Deutsche Geschichte Geht Weiter*, by Richard von Weizsäcker (Berlin: Siedler, 1983)

conflict. Germany's division, he writes, has created for West Germany a lasting tension between two basic facts: its connection to the West *(Westbindung)*, based on a commitment to liberal democracy, and its geopolitical position 'in the centre' *(die Mittellage)*. 'This is not simple or comfortable for anybody, not for our allies and certainly not for ourselves. But everyone would do well not to shut their eyes to it.' Von Weizsäcker continues:

> The priorities of the western German state in foreign policy and *Deutschlandpolitik* follow from this position. On the basis of our freedom, protected by the alliance, we must concentrate our efforts on a good relationship with the eastern leading power *[Führungsmacht]. This is our most important task.* [my italics]

So, according to its head of state, West Germany's most important task is to establish a good relationship with the Soviet Union.

During the last five years, moreover, we have seen the Kremlin trying to exploit this special interest by setting it against the Federal Republic's commitment to NATO. If you deploy Cruise and Pershing II, you cannot expect your relationship with the East to be unharmed, was the unmistakable message from Moscow. One major party, the SPD, has accepted this linkage. 'I have to represent German interests,' says Karsten Voigt, the SPD's parliamentary spokesman on defence, explaining that if the SPD came to power tomorrow, it would 'call on the United States to stop the deployment of new missiles.' *Sicherheitspolitik*—security policy—explains Voigt, is not just defence policy. The whole web of political, economic, and cultural ties with the East is as important for 'European security' as new NATO missiles. Therefore, the SPD would defend intra-German relations against American pressure. But what would be the basis of those relations under the SPD? 'If we are serious about our national belonging together [*die nationale Zusammengehörigkeit*],' writes Bölling, 'we will always have to give more than the other side is prepared to. One can call this our vulnerability to blackmail. It is not dishonourable.' Western fears could hardly be better expressed.

The Kohl government, in contrast, has responded to Moscow's attempted blackmail by ignoring it. Nelson-like, it has placed the telescope to its blind eye and said, 'We see no linkage,' sailing ahead with both deployment of Pershings and *Ostpolitik*. Naturally, its relations with the East have been damaged, and its own nationalist rhetoric has added unnecessary insult to necessary injury. But Kohl, 'Adenauer's grandson', has followed Adenauer's example, with a demonstrative commitment to the Western alliance. He has also pressed for more political integration in the Western European community.

Yet the conflict identified by von Weizsäcker remains a basic fact of West German life, for nationally minded Christian Democrats as much as for nationally minded Social Democrats. As the distinguished historian Hans-Peter Schwarz shows in his Adenauer Memorial Lecture,[4] there was nothing inevitable about Adenauer's grand commitment to the West. During the 1950s there were compelling reasons for the western half-nation-state to return to Germany's traditional *Schaukelpolitik* of manoeuvring between Russia and the West; for 'the conviction was general that Moscow held the key to reunification.' And Professor Schwarz concludes that if, in the future, Bonn 'opted again for a middle path, Adenauer's decision in favour of an anti-Russian policy and a lasting alliance with the Western democracies would only be a temporary affair in the long course of German policy toward Russia.'

In the 1980s, Moscow still holds the key to relations between the two Germanies (*vide* the cancellation of Honecker's visit); but West Germany has a greater freedom of manoeuvre in the West. If the Western commitment was a painful choice, it remains both: a choice and painful. Considerations of Realpolitik and national sentiment tug eastward. The crucial westward anchors are ideological and economic rather than diplomatic or 'national'. It is a voluntary commitment to the shared values of liberal democracy, the mixed economy, the rule of law, and so forth that keeps West Germany firmly in the West. That is a sufficient reason for alarm at any widespread questioning of those values in West Germany. That is why our first German question, about the Federal Republic's foreign policy, necessarily leads to our second German question, about its internal affairs.

---

[4]Reprinted in *The Konrad Adenauer Memorial Lectures 1978–1982* (St Antony's College, Oxford; Konrad-Adenauer-Stiftung).

3

Poor Caesar's wife. After all, as a senior German diplomat wearily observed, Britain's main opposition party has a policy of unilateral nuclear disarmament—which the SPD does not—while opinion polls show more general anti-Americanism in Britain than in Germany. So why aren't the Americans getting wild about 'the British question'? The answer is two words: German history.

What is truly remarkable in the light of that history is the *lack* of serious challenges to the Anglo-Saxon type of parliamentary democracy in the Federal Republic over the last thirty-five years. The Soviet-model socialism of the GDR sits far more easily on the foundations of Germany's pre-1945 'political culture', on the *Untertanmentalität*, on the undemocratic, illiberal, and militaristic part of the Prussian-German heritage. In West Germany, one can almost agree with the doyenne of German liberal journalists, Countess Dönhoff, who said in an interview to mark her seventy-fifth birthday that 'the Germans have become another nation. One may regret it, but the old faith in authority [*Autoritätsgläubigkeit*] is no longer there.' The questioning of authority by the younger generation is in itself a positive sign.

Moreover, the economic foundations are solid. According to a recent analysis in the *Financial Times:*

> The Germans can reasonably expect faster economic growth in 1985 (perhaps around three per cent in real terms), largely stable prices, a visible trade surplus which stands to be bigger than this year's figure of a likely DM 50 bn, and a current account still firmly in the black.

Despite metalworkers' and printworkers' strikes and eight per cent unemployment, industrial relations are still smooth and co-operative. Despite cuts by the present government, the social-security network is still one of the most generous and comprehensive in the world. The Federal Republic remains a model of welfare capitalism. Again, a comparison with Britain is salutary.

This background is essential when considering the impact of the Flick affair or the rise of the Greens. The 'German Watergate', which revealed that leading politicians were receiving money from the huge Flick conglomerate, has certainly cast a garish light on the intimate connections between big business and politics in the Federal Republic. It is not merely that three former ministers stand in the dock on charges of corruption. It is not just that all the established parties and many of West Germany's leading companies conspired to break the law (or 'not to observe legal stipulations,' as Chancellor Kohl more delicately put it to a parliamentary hearing), evading tax on contributions to party funds by 'laundering' them through a shadowy network of charitable foundations, through bogus Institutes of This or That, through the Bonn seminary of a monastic order and, oh dear, yes, through cash in plain envelopes, personally handed to leading politicians like Helmut Kohl by leading industrialists like Eberhard von Brauchitsch, the former managing director of the Flick concern.

Von Brauchitsch's own extraordinary notes of his lobbying campaign, with which the news magazine *Der Spiegel* has been regaling us week by week, give the impression that half the political establishment was 'bought' by Flick ('outfitting the gentlemen in Bonn,' was von Brauchitsch's delightful euphemism); that, indeed, it was he who decided who should be leader of the CDU. Last November, Rainer Barzel was forced to resign as Bundestag president when it emerged that he had received more than 450,000 dollars from Flick & Co. (via a lawyer's office) after he stepped down as CDU leader in 1973 to make way for Helmut Kohl. Von Brauchitsch had noted: 'Decided on Aktion Kohl.' But he wondered: 'Where is K's leadership potential?' and gave his own answer: 'a) hasn't had a chance; b) no one else around. *So* don't go down one-way street K. *Therefore* no adulation status [*Adlatusstatus*].' Not very flattering for Kohl.

Finally, there was the attempted cover-up. Leading members of all the established parties made at least one concerted attempt to vote themselves a free pardon—in the form of an amnesty for all tax evasion on donations to party funds. But they failed. Like Watergate, the Flick affair has shown both the weakness and the strength of a democracy. The weakness, that it happened; the strength, that it was exposed. Now German commentators are talking about a 'crisis of confidence' in the system. Of course they are—just as they did at the height of the peace movement and during the terrorist crisis in the late 1970s and in 1968, and . . . and . . . West Germany would not be

West Germany if her commentators did not start talking, very solemnly and responsibly, about pneumonia every time she sneezed. It is the Caesar's-wife syndrome again. This is no good reason for foreign observers to follow suit.

What public opinion polls and local government elections do show is that the Flick affair has been damaging to Chancellor Kohl and a gift to the Greens—the one party with clean hands. The Greens! Another cause for hypochondriac hysterics, with the awful prospect of 'red-Green chaos' (i.e., an SPD-Green government) brandished before us. Again, the reality is less dramatic. On present evidence, there is but a tiny chance that the Greens will come into the federal government after the 1987 election. Perhaps the CDU/CSU's candidate for chancellor in that election will be Gerhard Stoltenberg, the popular finance minister, or Lothar Späth, premier of Baden-Württemberg, rather than Helmut Kohl; but whoever he is, he is most likely to be elected.

If, however, the Kohl government does continue to trip over its own big feet for another two years and if the economy does not perform as predicted and if the Free Democrats get below five per cent of the vote in the 1987 elections[5]—three big ifs—then it is possible that the SPD would emerge strong enough to demand a share in government. But even then, the SPD's likely first choice would be a 'grand coalition' with the CDU/CSU (as in 1966–1969) rather than an accommodation with the Greens. The experiment of 'red-Green' government in the state of Hesse has already foundered on the issue of nuclear power. For every 'pragmatist' Green member of the Bundestag who wants alliance with the SPD there are a hundred 'fundamentalists' outside who want nothing of the sort.

Moreover, a mid-term protest vote for the Greens, mainly on the domestic issues of Flick and ecology—which they have single-handedly moved to the centre of political debate—rather than on 'peace' or foreign policy, is no sure indicator of their prospects in a national election two years hence. The government, in the unlikely person of Mr Zimmerman (he of the 1937 frontiers), is making strenuous efforts to steal the Greens' clothes on environmental issues; and who will remember Flick in 1987?

[5] Under West Germany's proportional representation system, a party that gets less than five per cent of the national vote has no seats in the Bundestag.

So American policy- and opinion-makers should not exaggerate the medium-term impact of the German Watergate or the danger of red-Green chaos. None the less, the Greens are symptomatic of a certain climate of opinion in West Germany today, and this climate may be important in the longer term. I deliberately do not say public opinion because the phenomenon is not so general. Intellectual opinion might be a better label: more specifically, the ideas, attitudes, and loyalties of university-educated West Germans born after 1945. A significant minority. Unlike the practice of *Deutschlandpolitik*, this climate of opinion does not lend itself to logical, rational exposition. Any account of it must be fragmentary and impressionistic: a patchwork coloured by personal experience. Moreover, it is as difficult as it is important to say which parts of the patchwork are peculiarly German and which parts are common to intellectual opinion in other countries. For example, I hear quite as much criticism of an American president who talks about the possibility of a limited nuclear war from my neighbours in Oxford as I used to from my neighbours in West Berlin. There is a perfectly serious case to be made against the transatlantic chain of decisions that led to the deployment of new land-based INF missiles in Western Europe. It is hard to maintain, after reading Strobe Talbott's *Deadly Gambits*, that all the blame for last year's breakdown of arms-control talks lies with the Russians.

Yet I think it is undeniable that the fear of nuclear war is more urgently, radically, and even hysterically articulated in West Germany than in any other Western country. 'I have hope for the world,' Petra Kelly reassures us in her personal manifesto[6], 'although it is ten minutes before Doomsday.' The apocalyptic timekeeping is almost matter-of-fact. Even sober-minded politicians like Helmut Schmidt have contributed to this hysteria, by comparing the situation today with that in 1914. The exiled Soviet international relations expert Mikhail Voslensky, who now lives in Munich, told me that in his experience, expressions of fear are obligatory among *bien pensant* German intellectuals: 'If I say, "I'm not afraid," they regard me as almost a fascist!' Voslensky said. 'But I'm *not* afraid, so long as both superpowers have an adequate second-strike capability . . .'

[6] *Fighting for Hope*, by Petra Kelly, introduction by Heinrich Böll, translated by Marianne Howarth, (London: South End Press, 1984)

One reason given for this special fearfulness is geography. As Günter Gaus writes, in a book heavy with foreboding[7], 'Germany lies . . . in the middle of the first battlefield, in the event of a new war in Europe.' But this popular fear—'Germany is the battlefield'—is only rational if Reagan is right and a limited war in Europe is possible. If, as these same German commentators argue, Reagan is wrong and escalation to a full-scale nuclear conflict would be inevitable (as the Soviets have always maintained), then the fact that Germany is on the front line is really irrelevant: I'm no better off in Oxford (or San Francisco) than I am in West Berlin. Yet one can appreciate the emotional force of the Germany-as-battlefield motif.

A second reason advanced is history. Having started the last two world wars, the Germans are determined not to start another one. This admirable sense of historical responsibility is displayed by writers on both sides of the Wall. There is, to take a phrase from the minister for intra-German affairs, 'an all-German intellectual opinion.' But what opinions! We find Günter Grass calling on West German youth to practice *Wehrkraftzersetzung*—a word used by the Nazis to describe sedition (literally, 'the subversion of military power'). We find the fine East German novelist Christa Wolf retelling the Cassandra legend as a warning against intermediate nuclear missiles[8]. And here is Rolf Hochhuth, a writer who has done much to remind German readers of the realities of life under Nazi rule (*A German Love Story, Tell 38*), with his new play *Judith*[9]. In the prologue we are shown how a Russian girl assassinates Hitler's commissar-general (a mass murderer) in Minsk in 1943. The main action is set forty years later, in Washington. The journalist heroine, Judith (Hochhuth suggests she may be played by the same actress), with a brother crippled by Agent Orange in Vietnam, decides she has a moral duty to assassinate an American president who is prepared to spend 150 million dollars over five years on armaments—including nerve gas. So she kills him with a canister of that same nerve gas. '"They that live by the sword shall die by the sword,"' quotes Hochhuth.

[7] *Wo Deutschland Liegt: Eine Ortsbestimmung*, by Günter Gaus (Hamburg: Hoffmann und Campe, 1983)

[8] *Cassandra*, by Christa Wolf, translated by Jan van Heurck (New York: Farrar, Strauss, 1984)

[9] *Judith*, by Rolf Hochhuth (Hamburg: Rowohlt Taschenbuch, 1983)

Underpinning this 'peace' discussion is what may conveniently be called equilateralism: a feeling that the United States is as dangerous as the Soviet Union, if not more so, and the best thing for humankind in general, and Germankind in particular, is to get as far away as possible from both of them. 'A plague on both your armouries.' Of course the Reagan administration has helped fuel this feeling with its 'evil empire' rhetoric and military planning leaks that many in the peace movement confuse with policy. Of course the feeling is present elsewhere in Europe: the British historian E.P. Thompson is its most eloquent voice. But there is a question why it should be strongest in the most thoroughly Americanized country in Europe, and the one closest to people living under a system of the Soviet type.

One may just understand it in insular Oxford, but how on earth can a West Berliner fail to see the difference between the two sides of the Wall? Richard Löwenthal, a grand old man of the SPD, offers one partial explanation in a 'Letter' to the *Partisan Review:* 'a failure of political education.'[10] In its efforts to promote détente, the social-liberal establishment has bent over backward to stress what unites East and West rather than what still divides them. The result: 'in a large part of the young generation, a loss of the understanding that the conflict with the Soviet Union is *not only* a conflict between two great powers and their associates, but also a conflict between freedom and tyranny.' The Gaus and Bölling memoirs illustrate his point. In one passage, Bölling describes the two systems as *Geschäftsbedingungen*—'terms of business'—while Gaus compares them to two religious denominations. *Deutschlandpolitik*, he writes, should be 'the attempt to achieve a Peace of Augsburg without the religious war which preceded it.' So, by implication, the difference between communism and liberal democracy is no more than the difference between Protestantism and Catholicism or between the 'terms of business' of public as opposed to private companies.

I would add a personal observation. In my experience, most West German intellectuals seldom visit East Germany. However, if they do, they often find a warmth of welcome and an intensity of human relations that contrast favourably with the 'atomization' and 'alienation' of life in the capitalist West. It is easy for the intellectual

[10] No.2,1984

tourist to take this for a positive product of the communist system. But if you actually live in East Germany, you realize that this community spirit is a product of the system only in the sense that the community spirit of Londoners during the blitz was a product of the war. (German has the fine but I think untranslatable portmanteau word—*Schicksalsgemeinschaft*—for such a community). The casual visitor, who may not notice that people are particularly cordial just because he comes from the West, enjoys the camaraderie without the hardship. In West-East encounters there is the added element of discovering an 'old Germany', by contrast with the Americanized West. The 'old Germany' is especially enjoyable if you can pop back to West Berlin to do your shopping, use the telephone, have your car serviced, and generally suffer all the hardships of the consumer society. To be fair, the Western visitor will also encounter in East Germany that genuine qualified loyalty to the state described by Rudolf Bahro.

Obviously, I don't give too much weight to a personal impression. But the West Berlin writer Peter Schneider, in his 'novel' *The Wall Jumper*, demonstrates that you can cross the Wall and come back with 'equilateral' conclusions[11]. Schneider portrays his East Berlin friend Pommerer and himself as victims of different but equally insidious forms of indoctrination:

> The first English sentence Pommerer learned: Ami, go home.
> My first English sentence: Have you chewing gum?
> Thirty-five years later, these differences are the cornerstone of defence budgets.

Switching to and fro between Western and Eastern television news (as you can in Berlin), he comments: 'Network executives on both sides are laughably alike: in their own camp, they let only the rulers speak; in the enemy camp, only the oppressed.'

The Americanization of the Federal Republic is undeniable. West German democracy is the stepchild of American democracy. West German consumerism is the closest European copy of American consumerism. *Der Spiegel* was modelled on *Time*. And so on. Consequently, when younger West Germans rebel against their

[11] *The Wall Jumper*, by Peter Schneider, translated by Leigh Hafrey, (New York: Pantheon, 1983)

parents' values, against the 'industrial system', or the Flick-like mores of what Baader-Meinhof used to call the Raspberry Reich, they find themselves, inevitably, rebelling against things American. It is not despite the Americanization but *because* of it that German anti-Americanism has a particular emotional edge—a kind of adolescent extremism—that you don't find in more traditionally anti-American (and less Americanized) countries like France. Petra Kelly, with her US Army stepfather, her Virginia high school education, and her volunteer work for Robert Kennedy, personifies the paradox. Learning that the Greens' model for their campaign of civil disobedience against American missiles is Martin Luther King, one is tempted to comment that even their anti-Americanism is American.

Yet Petra Kelly's personal manifesto reads very oddly indeed in its American version.[12] 'The system is bankrupt,' proclaims her first section. 'The system is bankrupt when $2.3 million a minute are spent on perfecting the machinery of destruction' while millions starve in the Third World; 'when micro-electronics undermines the deterrent model'; 'when doctors have to issue warnings against nuclear war'; 'when more than 3,000 accidents are reported in American power stations in one year.' 'To people who advise us to "Go East if you don't like it here", we say East German principles apply in our country too. There is minimal provision for the poor and less and less of an opportunity to speak out. *The system is the same; the differences are only of degree'* (my italics).

So what is 'the system?' In Part Two of Kelly's book, it would appear to be parliamentary democracy ('we have stepped into the system in order to change it'). By Part Four, 'the system' seems to be men. 'Masculine science and masculine thinking were applied in the concentration camps of Auschwitz, in Dresden, in Nagasaki, in Vietnam, in Grenada, in Afghanistan and in Prague in 1968.' In Part Five, the cancer wards in which her younger sister died and the X-rays that she believes caused her to lose a child in the sixth week of pregnancy are added to the list. 'These experiences brought it home

---

[12] The US edition carries a note warning of 'grave translation errors' and 'excerpts that shorten and/or take out of context many relevant sections of the book.' Unfortunately, I have not been able to compare it with the original German text.

to me that we are all victims of ecological atrocity.' All this is 'the system.' The system is bankrupt. The system must go.

And what shall we put in its place? 'Ecofeminism.' 'Women must lose all fear of speaking up and demanding what is theirs and their children's. Only if we begin to rediscover our own nature can we discover new ways of wholeness, balance, and decentralization—can we forge a bond with the Earth and the Moon, living with co-operation, gentleness, nonpossessiveness and soft energies.' In a concluding section entitled 'For an Erotic Society', Petra Kelly tells us, after 'leafing through books on Tantra temples, art and Tantra yoga,' that 'love and life are indissolubly linked with one another.' She 'agree[s] with David Cooper (*On the Need for Freedom*) that "the simplistic view that the man is there to penetrate the woman is a culturally conditioned belief that is easily refuted by experience." For example, Tantric yoga is based on *mutual* penetration . . .' But *how?* is the urgent question this leaves me with. But *how?* is the question that every part of this sloganizing, dilettantish, muddle-headed, hysterical tract persistently begs—whether the subject is decentralization, disarmament, or mutual penetration.

Stefan Heym conjures up a more sober utopia in his *Schwarzenberg* (published in West Germany)[13]. Heym imagines that in 1945, through an oversight, a small corner of Germany on the Czech border is left unoccupied by both the Western allies and the Russians. His 'novel' recounts how independent, upright, democratic German anti-fascists strive to build their dream of a 'free German republic'. In the end they fail—Schwarzenberg falls into the Soviet zone—but to most of his readers, Heym's 'realistic' ending will be less important than the 'dream' he paints with such manifest sympathy: a 'political utopia' that, as the blurb quite unhistorically asserts, 'might almost have become reality.' *Schwarzenberg* speaks powerfully to a notion abroad in Germany today—not a popular notion, but a quietly influential one—that somehow Germany's national and democratic development was frustrated by Allied occupation; that left to themselves, the survivors of the German anti-fascist resistance in 1945 could have found their own way forward to an authentic socialist democracy in a demilitarized, united Germany.

[13] *Schwarzenberg*, by Stefan Heym, (Munich: Bertelsmann, 1984)

But if the 'opportunity' was 'missed' in 1945 (though in historical fact there was no opportunity), couldn't we start feeling our way back to it now? Schwarzenberg—'a model for later times?' as the blurb rhetorically asks. If only Germany could free itself from the imprisoning military 'blocs' . . . This is a perspective on the German question that is popular (though by no means undisputed) among the Greens, in the peace movement, and (insofar as the label is meaningful) 'leftward' from the left wing of the SPD. Some Greens talk about getting back to the pre-unification Germany of principates—but ecoprincipates, naturally. Rudolph Bahro, too, plays with the idea of 'many smaller German states.' But, he says, 'in practice, if we want to build an ecological, decentralized Germany, we have first to free German territory. The Federal Republic is now under NATO and is the NATO country with the least sovereignty. For our perspective to work, we must first acquire sovereignty over our own territory.'

The Social Democrat Gaus argues passionately for disassociating the idea of German *nationhood* from that of *statehood*. The Germans must give up the idea of returning to the Bismarckian unified nation-state. They can rediscover their national identity, and their patriotism, in the present, divided post-Yalta Europe. The fact that they have two different *states* is not so important, Yet he is dismissive of Chancellor Kohl's enthusiasm for the Western European Community. The road to German unity, he writes, does not go through Brussels. He, too, is not content with a status quo *Deutschlandpolitik*. For under present conditions, he says, 'a war in Europe is probably unavoidable' (that apocalyptic vision again). The US will not commit nuclear suicide for Europe. Therefore, 'is it entirely unthinkable to establish in the West European part of NATO, with France, a nuclear deterrent power that would be directed in those European interests? And if that's not possible, wouldn't we still be better off under the French national nuclear umbrella than under the American?' (One wonders what the French think about that.)

Now, he continues, if we try to imagine such a reform of the alliance—*reform*, not dissolution, he stresses—'accompanied by Western renunciation of further nuclear armament,' then 'wouldn't the West have some promising suggestion to make to the Soviet Union for . . . all-European arrangements?' 'In a nuclear-free zone, secured by a European balance of power and guaranteed by Washington and Moscow, could there develop in Central Europe, where Germany too lies, the beginnings of Confederations in Part-territories?' The prose is convoluted, the last concept obscure, but the direction of his thinking is plain enough.

'Almost everything stands in the way of such an all-European future,' Gaus concludes soberly. And so it is with all the other fragments of utopia we have passed in review. They are books, not policies. No party that is likely to find itself in the West German government in the foreseeable future has adopted any such policy. Moreover, as Karsten Voigt of the SPD sadly observes in connection with disarmament: 'The Soviet Union has not given us what we need. It has given us words; we need deeds.' This is even more true of the path back to national unity (if not nation-statehood) via the mutual neutralization of both German states. According to Richard Löwenthal, 'there has literally not been a single hint to Bonn of such a deal, official or unofficial, since 1955.' (Really? Not a single, unofficial hint? One Soviet diplomat certainly made such a hint to me only a few months ago.) So unless Moscow suddenly changes its position or the Greens pull off an electoral miracle in 1987, none of this talk of neutral Central Europe is part of any real political agenda.

But it is, as I have argued, symptomatic of a certain climate of intellectual opinion in West Germany today. There is no single 'ideology' here, no unified, internally consistent set of ideas. It would be wrong to impose coherence where there is none. But two ingredients are common to this *Urbrei* (to borrow a term from Freud)—this primeval porridge of myths and notions.

First, there is a general undervaluation, if not outright dismissal, of the existing West German state and system (parliamentary democracy, welfare capitalism, nuclear power, the rule of law and all) as corrupt and inadequate and inauthentic and, as Petra Kelly says, 'bankrupt'. If the generations before 1945 were inclined to be uncritically loyal to the state (the *Untertanmentalität*, the *Autoritätsgläubigkeit* to which Countess Dönhoff refers), this generation has lurched to the opposite extreme. Partly in conscious reaction—witness the Hochhuth play. Partly out of political romanticism and utopian idealism. But the best may be the enemy of the good. Perhaps it needs a foreigner to point out that the Federal Republic has the worst possible system, apart from all the other systems that Germany has tried from time to time.

If you seriously compare it with utopia, then the best state Germany has ever had can, of course, be written off. If you seriously compare it with any real alternative, for example East Germany ... But you don't. For the second common ingredient in the *Urbrei* is a consistent undervaluation—if not outright dismissal—of the qualitative differences between the systems of Eastern and Western Europe. *'The system is the same ...'* Petra Kelly proclaims.

I wonder how many people in Eastern Europe would agree? Travelling to and fro between West Germany and Poland over the last five years, I have been struck again and again by the contrast between the two countries. The Poles enjoy a deep and confident national identity but are struggling for freedom. The Germans enjoy freedom but are struggling for a national identity. Each, in a sense, is reaching out for what the other enjoys: West Germans, for an authentic national community; Poles, for authentic democratic participation. In both countries, large popular movements arose at the same time—Solidarity and the peace movement. Both brought together Christians and socialists on the same platform, both driven by the energy and idealism of the younger generation—but what a world between them!

'There is nothing more important than peace,' my friends in the West German peace movement would tell me. Not freedom? No, 'better red than dead.' Meanwhile, their Polish contemporaries risked another invasion by the Red Army in order to win for themselves a portion—just a portion—of the freedoms enjoyed by every West German.

In Göttingen, university students who had lived all their lives in a stable liberal democracy questioned and doubted the primacy of its traditional values—representative government, the rule of law, individual freedom—when faced with economic recession, the north-south divide, and the threat of nuclear war. In Gdańsk, young workers who had lived all their lives under communism were daubing on a crane in the Lenin Shipyard the words 'Man is born and lives free.' Polish *schoolchildren* chose as the motto of their *samizdat* journal 'Dangerous freedom is dearer to me than safe bondage.' In West Germany, Reagan was compared with a Nazi mass murderer. For most Poles, he was a hero. Between the two mass movements there was a gulf of mutual incomprehension. (The Poles could misunderstand almost as much as they were misunderstood—but that is the subject of another essay.) When someone like Petra Kelly did (exceptionally) try to draw conclusions from the crushing of Solidarity, it came out like this: 'Precisely because the peace movement is independent, it cannot turn a blind eye to Poland. Nor should we ignore the current erosion of trade-union rights in Britain, where new legislation is being drafted...' etc., etc., etc. So everything is mixed up together: martial law in Poland and an act of the British Parliament; Thatcher and Jaruzelski; deterrence and genocide; Auschwitz and Grenada. All this is 'the system'. The system is bankrupt. The system must go.

4

If Poland since August 1980 has been a foil to the movement of intellectual opinion in West Germany, it has been a touchstone for the *Ostpolitik*. German reactions to the Polish crisis illuminate the premises and direction of that policy. In Gaus's and Bölling's memoirs, the Polish crisis is seen entirely through the East German prism. Solidarity appears as a nuisance and a danger. Both authors carefully distance themselves from the crude anti-Polish sentiments that, as they observe, were audible in East Germany—and discreetly encouraged by the Party. But Bölling approvingly quotes East German judgements that

> the Poles, particularly some intellectual advisers of the shipyard worker Walesa, overestimated their strength, desired willfully to push the conflict further, inclined— encouraged by the Western response—to a policy of all-or- nothing, and had a very Polish remoteness from reality (*eine sehr polnische Realitätsferne*).

East Germans, he writes, appreciated the fact that in his statements on Poland, Helmut Schmidt 'abjured the pathos favoured by Washington, London, and Paris.' They were thankful that Schmidt 'joined the minority in the West who thought ahead.'

Here is the thinking ahead: 'After a bloodbath in Poland ... we, we Germans in both states, might have to wait a whole decade before we could talk to each other again.' Already, in summer 1980, the strikes that gave birth to Solidarity had compelled Schmidt to postpone his planned summit meeting with Honecker. The Polish events were seen to be the main cause of the GDR's dramatic increase in the compulsory minimum exchange (of hard currency) for West German visitors in autumn 1980—a major setback for intra-German relations. And then, when Schmidt and Honecker did at last get together, at the Werbellinsee, Jaruzelski declared his 'state of war' on the last day of their meeting! Naturally, Western journalists at once asked Schmidt for his reaction to martial law. 'Herr Honecker is as dismayed as I am,' said Schmidt, *'that this was necessary . . .'* (my italics). According to Bölling, Schmidt subsequently felt 'that it had been a mistake to portray the Poles as an interference factor in German-German relations.'

For, of course, the Polish revolution of 1980–81 did get in the way of the intra-German détente. And since December 1981, General Jaruzelski's 'restoration of order' in Poland, like the restoration of good working relations between the United States and the Soviet Union, *has* been a desideratum—if not a prerequisite—for further progress in German-German relations. So Kohl's foreign minister, Hans-Dietrich Genscher, has been vigorously encouraging the one and the other: the 'normalization' of East-West relations and, yes, General Jaruzelski's 'normalization' in Poland. And not only Genscher. On visits to Poland, the SPD leader, Hans-Jochen Vogel, and the CSU leader, Franz Josef Strauss, both expressed their support for General Jaruzelski's 'stabilization'. The harmony of Strauss and Vogel is startling, until one recalls how the *Deutschlandpolitik* was disrupted by the challenge to Communist rule in Poland. Whatever their political differences, both see the continuation of the *Deutschlandpolitik* as being in Germany's national interest.

West German policy makers are not happy with the analysis I have made—although it is based on what they themselves write and say at home. They insist that their policy is actually in the best interests of the Polish people. Only gradual, evolutionary change, carefully controlled from above, is possible in Eastern Europe. The first priority must be to rebuild the shattered Polish economy. The Poles should be 'realistic' rather than 'romantic'. (I am quoting from a number of conversations with German policy makers over the last three years.) If the West builds up a relationship with Jaruzelski, particularly through new credits and trade, it can influence him to pursue more 'liberal' policies, as it did with Gierek.[14] The Polish people, instead of unreasonably demanding more freedom and self-determination, should settle for a more comfortable life under the more economically efficient and possibly more tolerant dictatorship that they, the West Germans, will help Jaruzelski construct. In short, Poland should be more like East Germany.

The only problem with this approach is that most Poles don't share it. They have other priorities. For example, they tend ('romantically' and 'unrealistically') to put freedom before efficiency or security. The *Ostpolitik* approach to Poland is thus profoundly *anti-democratic* in the same way that the Reagan approach to Nicaragua is anti-democratic: because it acts in contempt of the clearly expressed aspirations of the majority in the country affected. (This is not to equate the aspirations of the Sandinistas with those of Solidarity—that is quite a different argument.)

Günter Gaus suggests a possible answer to this change. Stability in Eastern Europe, he insists, is essential for the peace of Europe— and he praises Franz Josef Strauss for saying as much in Warsaw. 'Polish conditions such as prevailed in the last three years, such a "Polish economy" (*polnische Wirtschaft*) in central Germany—"Polish economy" understood in the sense of the old, evil, arrogant German metaphor—such conditions would be the eve of war in Europe.' By implication, the Poles must sacrifice their democratic aspirations to the higher cause of peace. Or, as Bölling puts it, 'according to a general consensus in East and West, peace just is a higher good than paragraphs devoted to the idea of freedom, which are also to be found in the constitution of the GDR.'

The Polish case is important, because in the last three years West German commentators and politicians have held up East-West German relations as a model for East-West European relations and indeed for East-West relations altogether. The automatic equation of German with European interests is a staple ingredient of West German political rhetoric from Strauss to Bahro, through Kohl and Vogel. You find it in all the books I have discussed here. In a note

[14] Schmidt was extraordinarily impressed by Gierek. 'I'd take him straight into my cabinet,' he said, according to Bölling. And hours before the 'state of war' was declared in Poland, he was (by Bölling's account) asking Honecker to intervene with his Polish comrades—for 'fair treatment' of Edward Gierek!

entitled 'German Model,' in the influential weekly *Die Zeit*, Countess Dönhoff takes things a stage further:

> The whole world, East and West, is anxiously asking: What's up with the two Germanies? The puzzle is easily solved. It infuriates the Germans to the right and left of the Elbe to have to stand idly by while the two superpowers arm like crazy, or play 'pass the buck' like children. After all, this policy—if one can call it such—affects not only the two great powers, but several hundred million Europeans.
>
> Erich Honecker declared in an interview some time ago: 'Whatever controversial international problems appear, however complicated they are—we must regulate them not by the law of the jungle, but by negotiation.'
>
> And Foreign Minister Genscher has just convincingly explained what policy should look like today: 'The significance of Europe requires that no single power aims to achieve a dominant position [*Vormachtstellung*] on the old continent'—and: 'It gets us nowhere if both sides attribute responsibility for the worsening of the situation to the other, and demand a change in the other's behaviour as the precondition for a contribution.'
>
> If only the superpowers would show so much insight!

The self-righteous tone is worth noting.

Yet, as I have tried to show, the equations are far from proven. Let us suppose, for the sake of argument, that all Eastern Europe becomes more like East Germany and all Western Europe behaves toward Eastern Europe as West Germany behaves toward East Germany. Will Europe then be a safer place: more peaceful or more free? I doubt it. East Germany is the sturdiest pillar of the Soviet empire. It is the nearest Eastern Europe comes to a properly functioning Leninist Party-state. Its powerful and relatively modern economy is of immense value to the Soviet Union. Its large and highly professional army is vital to the Warsaw Pact.

Poland, by contrast, is the Spanish ulcer of the Soviet empire. Its economy is a burden on Comecon and the Soviet Union. Soviet military commanders must fear that they cannot rely on Poland in the event of war. (Any such fears about the East German army?) Arguably, with the Polish problem in its 'backyard', the Kremlin is less, rather than more, likely to take risks abroad. Moreover, the Polish people have won for themselves (at great cost), and are struggling to defend against Jaruzelski's 'normalization,' far greater areas of *de facto* freedom and pluralism than the East Germans can dream of.

West Germany, meanwhile, has virtually abandoned the original hope of changing the way East Germany is governed (*Wandel durch Annäherung*). Instead, it makes a huge contribution to the stability and prosperity of Honecker's police welfare state. Both Gaus and Bölling say frankly that Bonn gives more than it gets. 'Anyone in the Federal Republic who cannot put up with the partial bitter powerlessness connected with this,' writes Gaus, 'had better not pursue *Deutschlandpolitik*.' And we recall Bölling's striking phrase about West Germany's 'honourable vulnerability to blackmail.' Is that what we want for all of Western Europe in our dealings with the East?

This is not to suggest the opposite: that East Germany needs 'Polish conditions'. No. I have little doubt that the majority of East Germans prefer the gradual material and human improvements achieved by the patient practice of *Deutschlandpolitik* to any 'romantic' Polish bid for more political freedom. They have a perfect right to these priorities. Let every nation pursue its own idea of happiness in its own way. In Europe's house are many mansions. But because *Deutschlandpolitik*, and the *Ostpolitik* that goes with it, is in the Germans' interest, it is not necessarily in everyone else's. For as long as there have been nations in Europe, their interests have been in conflict as often as they have coincided. There is no reason to believe this is no longer the case. What we saw in the last years of the Schmidt government was, tendentially, in a mild and muted form, what we have seen so many times before in the history of Central Europe: the clash of Poland's national aspirations and interests with those of Russia and Germany. Which of those interests and aspirations best serve the peace of Europe remains very much an open question.

5

If this essay has only hinted at the complexity of the 'German question' as it appears in contemporary Europe, it has served its purpose. Over the last fifteen years, the position of the Federal Republic in international relations has changed fundamentally. A new *Deutschlandpolitik* based on good working relations with the communist regime in East Berlin has been the epicentre of this change. Such a policy now enjoys a broad consensus in Bonn, and probably in East Berlin. We ignore at our peril the great benefits that it has brought to both German states and to the German people— especially the Berliners.

This successful, pragmatic *Deutschlandpolitik* is inextricably intertwined with Bonn's distinctive foreign policy toward Eastern Europe. It has definitely strengthened what is inevitably—because of the geopolitical position—West Germany's special interest in relations with Moscow. So far these special, national interests have been accommodated in the Western alliance and the West European community without too much strain. There is no reason to believe they cannot be so accommodated in the foreseeable future. But as President von Weizsäcker observes, we do well not to shut our eyes to them. With the new self-confidence that the Federal Republic has acquired in this period, with the political, economic, and emotional investment it has made in its *Ostpolitik*, Bonn will forcefully assert what it regards as German national interests. A federal government including the SPD might partially accept Moscow's reverse linkage between defence policy and *Deutschlandpolitik*—a linkage that Helmut Kohl, Nelson-like, contrives to ignore.

These considerations, and a knowledge of Germany history, make us, and still more the Germans themselves, hypochondriacal about the health of the best state Germany has ever had. On a sober diagnosis, however, the Federal Republic is still one of the most stable, prosperous, and liberal democracies in the world. Even the hypochondria, and the restless questioning of authority, are symptoms rather of health than of sickness. Only a minority, but a significant minority, has taken this questioning to extremes— undervaluing, or rejecting outright, the state, the 'system', and the values that distinguish it from other systems, including the Soviet-type systems of the East. Utopian idealism, political romanticism, an over-reaction to the Nazi past, a kind of adolescent rebellion against stepfather America: all this comes through in the voices of German intellectuals—voices that sound a strange, high note of apocalyptic alarm. But these are not the deciding voices of German politics—nor will they be, for as far ahead as we can see. Moreover, if Christian Democrats can say one thing on Sunday and do another on Monday, so can the Greens. To hear Petra Kelly preaching is one thing; to watch her at work in a parliamentary committee is quite another.

Finally, if this essay has highlighted some rich confusion in German answers to the German question, the confusion is not theirs alone. Günter Gaus writes bitterly that 'our allies have happily got used to the reduction of our national *engagement* to lip-service on certain anniversaries.' The reality is a little more complicated. We may sometimes feel, like François Mauriac, that 'we love Germany so much that we're happy there are two of them.' On the other hand, anyone can see that the road to an eventual European reunification must lead via Germany. So if we are at all serious about a long-term, peaceful 'evolutionary liberation' of Central and Eastern Europe from Soviet domination, about overcoming Yalta, then we too must be serious about overcoming the division of Germany. But how?

(JANUARY 1985)

The Uses of Adversity

'I think it very encouraging that it's here that Marx's dream is being fulfilled,' Kurt Vonnegut told the leading underground weekly *Tygodnik Mazowsze* on his recent visit to Poland. He meant Marx's 'dream of the withering, or rather ignored, state.' Vonnegut's nice conceit captures the extraordinary quality of Polish intellectual life today. For here is a communist state in which the best writers are published by underground publishers, the best journalists write for underground papers, the best teachers work out of school; in which banned theatre companies just carry on performing, in monasteries, while sacked professors carry on lecturing as 'private guests' at their own seminars; in which churches are also schools, concert halls, and art galleries. An entire world of learning and culture exists quite independent of the state that claims to control it—a real world of consciousness floating high and free, like Mohammed's coffin, above the false world of being.

Of course, every Polish schoolboy knows that since the time of the partitions, the *inteligencja* has had a mission to uphold the spirit and culture of the nation against the political powers that be. This romantic version of noblesse oblige is at the heart of the traditional Polish definition of what it is to be an intellectual or, more broadly, a member of the educated class—an *inteligent*. It is a subjective, idealistic self-definition in which the idea takes absolute precedence over reality and consciousness determines being. In the condition of unfreedom, it proclaims the principle of As If. Try to live *as if* you live in a free country, it says, though today your study is a prison cell. Or, as the contemporary Polish poet Ryszard Krynicki puts it, in a poem dedicated to Adam Michnik:

> living here and now
> you must pretend

95

that you live elsewhere and in other
    times
and, at best, fight with the dead
through the iron curtain of clouds.

But when Krynicki wrote these lines, in the mid-seventies, the number of intellectuals who actually tried to live by the principle of As If was still tiny. Indeed, the typical student or academic of the Gierek years was cynical about all ideas and ideals, almost unthinkingly paying lip service to the ruling ideology, inasmuch as this served life's real purpose: the serious pursuit of material betterment and private happiness.

What transformed the 'dissident' minority into a 'dissident' majority was the Solidarity revolution of 1980 and 1981. The Solidarity revolution was a revolution of consciousness. What it changed, lastingly, was not institutions or property relations or material circumstances, but people's minds and attitudes. 'Solidarity,' said the Kraków theologian Józef Tischner, 'is a huge forest planted by awakened consciences.' Behind the front line of confrontation between Solidarity's national leadership and the communist authorities, millions of people across the country—in factories, offices, universities, schools—suddenly found that they no longer needed to live the double life, that they could say in public what they thought in private. They began to discover the true facts about their country, its history, its economy, the privileges of its governing class, its relations with the Soviet Union; and they experienced, for the first time, free speech, free assembly, democratic elections, and the taste of self-government. For a few months it really was *as if* they lived in a free country. As a rule the younger you were, the more intense was the experience—students and schoolchildren were among the most active and radical of all. At the same time, in a collapsing economy, the state had fewer and fewer material goods with which to lure the young generation back to outward conformity.

After General Jaruzelski's declaration of the 'state of war' in December 1981, this transformed and galvanized young intelligentsia threw itself, passionately, into the business of resistance—conspiratorial and open, passive and active. Many saw themselves as the (non-violent) heirs of the wartime Home Army

(AK), in which the young intelligentsia also predominated. Some went into hiding, 'underground', reading books about the AK for practical advice on the organization of conspiracy. Others began to live in 'semi-conspiracy', slipping away of an evening (check behind you for the tell-tale white Fiat used by the secret police) to service a carefully hidden offset machine and run off a few hundred copies of the latest unofficial journal, or book about the AK. More still, thousands more, helped distribute and avidly consumed this unofficial literature. Nobody knows how much of it has been produced: In Warsaw I was given an estimate of 1,600 periodical titles, with the important caveat that many titles only lasted for an issue or two.

Today this world of independent culture—culture understood in the broadest sense—is probably the most extensive field of opposition in Poland. For the workers' Solidarity, which originally created the space for this cultural revolution, has itself been ground down and fragmented. Of course the national leadership still exists, underground and above-ground; its statements still have great symbolic importance; but it no longer has the capacity to organize effective nationwide industrial action. For one thing, the government has again been jailing Solidarity leaders. After the amnesty last July, there were probably fewer than forty political prisoners left in Poland's jails; now there are at least 160, and the regime is pushing ahead with the trial of Adam Michnik, Bogdan Lis, and Władysław Frasyniuk in Gdańsk. Solidarity's basic units, the factory committees, where they exist, cannot operate on a day-to-day basis as trade unions, representing the real interests of the work force—which is, after all, their *raison d'être*. (This is not to suggest that the workers are satisfied or that another round of meat-price rises this summer will not provoke strikes and protests. Far from it. But the strikes are likely to be sporadic, spontaneous, and uncontrolled — more like pre-Solidarity forms of industrial action—and one thing this state certainly can do is break strikes.)

It would obviously be wrong to draw too clear a line between workers and intelligentsia. One of the hallmarks of Solidarity in 1980–1981 was the close links it established between intellectuals and workers, and many of these links have been preserved. They are symbolized at the highest level by the relationship between Wałęsa and his advisors. Moreover, most people involved in producing this independent culture are at pains to make it available to workers as well.

In the steel town of Nowa Huta near Kraków, for example, there is a 'Christian University of the Workers' based at the huge new church in Mistrzejowice, which the Pope dedicated on his last visit. Here Father Jancarz, who is to the Nowa Huta steelworkers what Father Popiełuszko was to the steelworkers of Huta Warszawa, has organized regular lecture courses, films, concerts, a permanent exhibition of photographs, and what he grandly calls an 'independent television service'—meaning video-cassette recordings, mostly of interviews with famous Poles. At the regular weekly 'mass for the fatherland' (a tradition begun in Warsaw by Father Popiełuszko), on the evening I attended, the Kraków philharmonic orchestra and choir sang the Hallelujah chorus from Handel's *Messiah*, and a buxom *prima donna* sang arias from the organ loft. But Mistrzejowice is exceptional. As a rule, the people who benefit most from the world of independent culture are, inevitably, those whose trade is thinking and whose tools are words.

Take a first-year university student from Warsaw, Kraków, Wrocław, Poznań, or Gdańsk. (Things may be somewhat different in the smaller towns.) If he is lucky, his schoolteacher will have taught him using syllabuses largely agreed on during the Solidarity period. In addition, he may already have used one or another of the National Education Booklets (known by their Polish acronym as ZEN), giving, for example, a true account of Poland's part in the Second World War. The ZENs are produced by the Committee for Independent Education—one of three linked unofficial committees (the other two are called the Social Committee for Scholarship and the Committee for Independent Culture) whose anonymous members are, besides the Church, responsible for co-ordinating much of Poland's independent cultural life.

Arriving at the university, he will find almost complete freedom of speech in the classroom. One of his first-term seminars may be on 'critics of totalitarianism'—Arendt, Orwell, Hayek. The basic texts— *1984, The Origins of Totalitarianism, The Constitution of Liberty*, and so forth—are published underground, naturally, and can be purchased from vendors among his fellow students. Indeed, I was told by one lecturer that her students can more easily obtain books produced unofficially than those from state publishers. In addition, he will have on his shelves at home a random selection of underground papers: for hard news, the two closely printed sheets of *Tygodnik Mazowsze* (the *Newsweek* of the underground); for opinions, one of the many 'irregular monthlies' (a distinct category)—perhaps the Orwell number of the Kraków-based *Arka*, including Norman Podhoretz's piece in *Harper's*, or *Bez Dekretu*, with a contentious essay about Central America reprinted from the *New York Review*, or the organ of the Catholic nationalist Young Poland movement, *Polityka Polska*, with articles about Poland's need for a new right wing. In the Catholic chaplaincy attached to the university, and in the city's Club of the Catholic Intelligentsia, he will be able to hear leading independent intellectuals—former Solidarity advisors like Tadeusz Mazowiecki, for example, or the historian of Solidarity, Jerzy Holzer—giving talks on a very catholic range of topics. If he is lucky, he may get tickets for a play about Osip Mandelstam performed (beautifully) by the Poznań-based Theatre of the Eighth Day. The Theatre of the Eighth Day has been officially banned—so this performance will take place in a Dominican monastery.

Back on the campus, our first-year student will also find a very active students' self-government committee (its identity proclaimed in the unmistakable jumbly Solidarność lettering, red on white), which represents the students' interests and distributes all the funds for social activities—student clubs, sports, excursions, and so forth. Indeed, one of the most remarkable features of contemporary Polish university life is a degree of internal democracy that at moments recalls the more moderate demands of 1968 in the Sorbonne or even Berkeley. Student representatives are elected (by secret ballot, supervised by the students' self-government committee) on to the university governing bodies. In some faculties at Warsaw University the students not only have a say in their plan of studies but also mark their professor's performance. 'I got 4.7,' the newly elected rector, Professor Białkowski, told me with a satisfied smile. (In Poland, marks go from 2.0—disgraceful—to 5.0—excellent.) 'One of my colleagues got 3.1 last year,' Rector Białkowski added. This year his colleague had prepared his lectures better—and jumped to 4.5.

Both the elected rector and the elected students' representatives are warm in praise of each other—'I have learned a lot from them,' Białkowski says—and there seems to be excellent co-operation between them. 'You see, many of us were interned together in 1982,' one student activist explained. 'Sharing a prison cell does help bridge the gap between student and professor.' And both sides underline what is perhaps the most remarkable fact of all: that the autonomy and internal democracy of the universities is based on the letter of the Higher Education Act, which was passed *during the 'state of war'*—in May 1982—a law which, although it did not go quite as far as the draft worked out when Solidarity was still a legal organization, is none the less the most liberal that communist Poland has seen.

At this point the Western visitor, if he has any knowledge of the Soviet bloc, and even more the Eastern visitor, will be able to restrain himself no longer. 'How on earth is all this possible in the fourth year of so-called normalization?' he will ask. 'If Husák could silence his intellectuals, why can't Jaruzelski?' (That from the Soviet visitor.) Where is the state? Where, indeed, is the Party? Just recently, the state and the Party seem to have been asking themselves these questions as well. One obvious answer is that the Polish regime has had much more to 'normalize'. Its first aim was to crush the *workers'* Solidarity, and this has absorbed most of its political skills and police energies. So the pessimist could say: 'It's just the old familiar salami tactics—when they've finished slicing off the workers, they'll move on to the intellectuals. You wait and see.'

A second speculative answer is that in this initial phase of re-establishing a minimum of political control, with on the whole (it must be said) a minimum of physical terror, the co-operation of the Catholic Church was (and is?) a tactical necessity for the Jaruzelski government. And if this greatly expanded world of spiritual, educational, and cultural activity, in which the values of solidarity, with a small *s* (as preached by the pope), are preserved and carried forward—if this is part of the price that Church leaders exact for their co-operation, well, the regime must pay the price, for as long as the tactical necessity exists.

Yet these two reasons together still do not quite suffice to explain why the Jaruzelski government passed such a charter of academic liberties in the first year of martial law and why, while dissolving the writers', artists', actors', and journalists' unions in sound Husák style, it has yet been quirkily tolerant in allowing quite outspoken criticism in the official and (censored) Catholic press and permitting the official publication of books by authors who are otherwise published in *samizdat* or in the West.

Some have plausibly suggested that in the first year of martial law, they hoped—and may still hope—to win over parts of the intelligentsia to their side by demonstrative tolerance, following the motto of János Kádár in Hungary: 'He who is not against us is with us.' It is wryly noted that if they did *not* publish some writers who publish unofficially, they would have no writers of repute to publish at all. There is also what I might call the prosopographical theory. Several of General Jaruzelski's closest political advisors—Deputy Prime Minister Mieczysław Rakowski, for example, and government spokesman Jerzy Urban—themselves come from the Warsaw intellectual milieu. (The general himself, incidentally, must have a fairly good idea of the atmosphere at Warsaw University: his wife lectures and his daughter is a student there.) These advisors are still, at least notionally, on first-name terms with leaders of the intellectual opposition who are their former comrades from the bygone golden days of the 'Polish October' of 1956. They cannot (one perhaps sentimentally hopes) altogether enjoy the contempt of former friends. They cannot (one perhaps naïvely feels) entirely have abandoned that commitment to free debate that was so much a part of the Polish October. Somewhere inside them still lurks, perhaps, the shadow of an *inteligent*.[1]

Yet the political auguries are bad. Since the autumn of 1984, the pressure on the academic community and the world of Church-protected and underground culture has increased, with threatening articles in the official press and speeches at Party meetings, police action, the sacking of two well-known academics, and proposals for new repressive changes in the law. The emergence of this campaign roughly coincided with the Popiełuszko affair, and many observers at first suggested that the propaganda offensive against the Church was a tactical quid pro quo for holding the unprecedented trial of Father Popiełuszko's secret-police murderers—a quid pro quo 'for Moscow'. Probably, there is an element of truth in this supposition; and Mr Gorbachev would surely be as delighted as any of his predecessors if the Polish Party were to revive itself with a good vicious campaign against the Church.

[1] But I remember the precise judgement of a distinguished Polish philosopher on, so to speak, the socio-intellectual status of Deputy Prime Minister Rakowski. 'Mietek,' he said, for they were former comrades, 'is certainly intelligent; but he is no *inteligent*.'

But the quid has gone on so long now as to become its own quo. The 'reformist' weekly *Polityka* has published a direct attack on the pope that could have come from the pages of the Russian or Slovak *Pravda*. A 'reader's letter' in the Warsaw evening paper suggests that, as in Polish law the instrument of a crime is confiscated, so the pulpit of Lech Wałęsa's parish church in Gdańsk should be confiscated too. The ministry for culture and arts has collected detailed reports on church-protected cultural activity from all the provinces. Characteristically, these confidential reports have been 'leaked' to the Church, probably by Church sympathizers inside the ministry. Another 'leaked' document (the frequency of 'leaks' is one small way in which Warsaw has become more like a Western capital since 1980) suggests very strongly that the sustained attack on the entire world of independent spiritual and cultural life springs quite as much from the government's own domestic fears as from the putative concerns of its 'Muscovite friends'.

This twenty-five page document, marked 'Confidential—material for pt. 2.b. of the meeting of the Council of Ministers, 1985-03-22,' is entitled 'Threats in the Sociopolitical Sphere in 1985.' One's doubts about its authenticity are diminished by the inimitable Newspeak in which it warns, for example, against a 'lack of feeling for Poland's *raison d'état* among some creative artists' (translation: some artists are rude about the Russians). What is most striking about this document (if it is genuine) is the sheer range of human activities that it categorizes as 'threats in the sociopolitical sphere', and the inclusion in this category, point by point, of virtually all the independent cultural activities I have sketched above. Any political scientist who wishes to maintain that the Jaruzelski regime is *by design* authoritarian rather than totalitarian will have a hard task explaining the character of this report.

But of course the performance falls far short of the desire. In practice, intellectual and cultural life is emancipated from the would-be-totalitarian ideological control of the Party to a degree unthinkable anywhere else in the Soviet bloc. Moreover, so decayed is the Polish Party that the Jaruzelski government attempts only, so to speak, *in form* to use the Party as the main instrument for the restoration of order. In practice, the key instruments of control are now the police and the law. While moving energetically to curb some independent actions by the secret police (like the murder of Father

Popiełuszko or the recent attack on a priest connected with Father Jancarz's church in Nowa Huta), it has steadily changed the laws so that, in respect of most forms of Solidarity activity, the legal process has become the continuation of policing by other means.

It is therefore typical of the Jaruzelski regime that the sharpest threat to the academic community should come in the form of proposed 'amendments' to the 1982 Higher Education Act. The first project for these amendments became known last autumn, in a (deliberate?) leak from the ministry of higher education. A few quotations give the taste of this 'project':

- · In art. 35 sect. 1, delete 'elected'
- · In art. 54 sect. 1, in place of 'by election' read 'by nomination'
- · In art. 97, delete 'self-governing'
- · In art. 100, delete 'students' self-government'

You get the general idea. If implemented in full, this 'project' would clearly demolish the legal foundations of the universities' autonomy and internal democracy: their senior officers would all be appointed by the education minister, not elected; academic staff would have yearly contracts rather than tenure; students could be dismissed by the minister if they 'offended against the principles of social coexistence and public order'; and so on and so forth.

The response of the academic community was immediate and immense. At the main universities, the governing bodies not only protested but also organized internal staff referenda on the main points of the proposed changes. At Warsaw University the responses ranged from seventy-four per cent against a reduction in the representation of students and younger academic staff on the governing body (not all older professors are as tolerant as the rector) to ninety per cent against giving the minister the right to sack professors for 'activities contrary to the interests of the Polish People's Republic.'

The students' self-government organized its own referendum, with the results scrupulously tabulated and presented—an average of ninety-eight per cent opposed on most points—and copies were sent to the minister, the Sejm (parliament), and the Polish Press Agency. The main council on higher education (consisting of one delegate each from most higher education institutions) more cautiously told the government that it should wait another year or two, until the law had been thoroughly tried out in practice. And most surprisingly, even the government's own favoured front organization—the Patriotic Movement for National Salvation (PRON)—took up a similar position.

Faced with this united front, the government seemed for a time to recoil. But the recent plenary session of the Party central committee devoted to the intelligentsia called quite clearly for changes to the law, and it now seems almost certain that repressive amendments will after all be pushed through the Sejm before it is dissolved in July. Perhaps the government will soften its original proposals somewhat, to demonstrate its 'liberalism' and attentiveness to public opinion. (Probably, that is one reason why the original proposals were so tough.) No doubt it will accompany them with the sweetener of pay raises—academic salaries are now pitifully low. But there is no mistaking the attempted reassertion of Party-state control.

As I have suggested, the response of the intellectual community to this assault has been to follow the great principle of As If, in what might be called its qualified and its absolute forms. The qualified form consists in saying, in effect, to General Jaruzelski: 'You, sir, claim to head a strong but civilized state that is governed under the rule of law. A Polish *Rechtsstaat*. To us and to the West (although not to your own Party and to the East), you claim to derive your legitimacy not from the transvaluated values of Marxism-Leninism but from certain recognizable old European standards of law and order and sovereignty and statehood. All right, we believe you— though millions wouldn't. Here are your proclaimed standards. Here are your own laws. *Now stick to them.*' This may be a pretence, but in Poland over the last few years it has been a curiously effective pretence. At times it has almost seemed as if some of those in power wanted to pretend too.

The absolute form consists simply in teaching, writing, researching, painting, acting, publishing as far as possible and for as long as possible *as if* the state (to recall Vonnegut's conceit) has withered away; *as if* you live in a free country. Both forms of the As If principle are finely illustrated by the case of Professor Leszek Nowak of Poznań University. Professor Nowak, a philosopher, was suspended from teaching last September and summarily dismissed by the minister in February. This was clearly a political act '*pour encourager les autres'*. The response has been twofold. First, the governing body of Poznań University has protested to the minister about the way the dismissal was carried out: the present law required a disciplinary tribunal (of academic colleagues) as a precondition for dismissal. That is qualified As If. Secondly, Professor Nowak has just carried on teaching, as a 'private guest' at his own seminar, even though the minister paid a personal visit to Poznań to demand that he should be banned from the campus. When I went to see him, he had to hurry off to teach a seminar on (if I understood him aright) the significance of factions in one-party systems. Instead of his professional salary, he is being paid a roughly equivalent monthly sum by sympathetic colleagues, while he writes a book on captivity and revolution. That is absolute As If.

But how far and how long can Polish intellectuals carry on living As If? The political answer to this question depends on so many unknowns—on the unpredictable response of a barely subordinated working class to a further deterioration in living standards, for example—that speculation is rather fruitless. The only safe prediction is that, since this is Poland, all government measures— whether of repression or reform—are likely to be half-measures, honoured mainly in the breach. It is more interesting to ask a less obvious question. Even if they can carry on living As If for years, how will this affect the content and quality of the country's intellectual life?

The Western intellectual who visits his colleagues in Poland feels admiration, excitement and, yes, envy. Here is a place where people care, passionately, about ideas. Here is a place where intellectuals matter. Here, in a figure like Adam Michnik, is the Intellectual as Hero. Here historians make history. The Western intellectual tourist enjoys the thrill of being in the front line—in the safe certainty that he will not be shot at.[2] War without tears. And often he returns to view

---

[2] The distinguished medievalist Bronisław Geremek was recently fired from the Polish Academy of Sciences, where he has worked for thirty years. This was almost certainly punishment for his work as an advisor to Lech Wałęsa, and in particular for taking part in a private meeting— alongside other Solidarity advisors—with the British foreign secretary. When I talked to him shortly after that meeting, he told me he had just finished a paper on 'Suffering and Laughter in the Work of François Villon.'

with weary disdain our workaday world of Western culture, with its hypermarket profusion of ideas, for none of which anyone risks anything; a world in which intellectuals don't matter.

But if you stay a little longer and look a little deeper, doubts and questions multiply. In Poznań, I spent an hour talking to an extraordinarily impressive and mature student self-government leader—also a historian. How long would one have to search to find such a student in Oxford, I wondered. Then, just before we parted, I asked what he was going to do with his degree. 'I think I'll become a carpenter,' he said. With his university record, he explained, the security services would stop him getting a good job in a state enterprise. Working privately as a carpenter, the police couldn't get him; and he'd earn more than he ever would as a historian. He would go on reading and writing in his spare time. In Warsaw I heard many similar stories—the most able and independent-minded students going to work as taxi drivers, postmen, or market vendors. Now, of course, it is possible that these students will sustain their intellectual and cultural engagement. One thinks of the extraordinary catacomb intellectual life of Prague, with its philosophers working as window cleaners, priests as milkmen, historians as gardeners. But how many and for how long?

Beyond this question about the future of individuals there is the larger question about the collective future. How can a country prosper when the best part of its educated class refuses, or feels unable, to collaborate in running it? (Unable, that is, on the terms offered by this state.) The fact that this question is constantly posed by the regime's intellectual apologists does not make it a non-question. Indeed, the question is also posed, increasingly, by deeply anti-communist, Catholic, and nationalist intellectuals; and this line of questioning is clearly encouraged by the primate. When Poland is finally free, so the argument goes, it will need a solid 'infrastructure' of good roads and factories and technical schools; it will need experienced managers, lawyers, civil servants—and this must mean working, here and now, to some extent with the state. Historians will immediately recognize the argument for 'organic work' from the great debate after the crushing of the January Rising of 1863-1864.

There is also a real question about the effect on the country's political culture of this divorce from the state. There is, for instance, something faintly adolescent about the current proliferation of political grouplets with grand titles—the Liberal Democratic party (three students and a dog)—and grander programmes ('Our Policy Toward the Ukranians'), a phenomenon that surely grows in direct proportion to the reduction in possibilities of real political action. (This is not, of course, an argument for collaboration with a state that does not afford such real possibilities.)

Finally, there is what I might call the question of Poland's European future. In the offices of Poland's best weekly paper, the independent Catholic *Tygodnik Powszechny*, someone has pinned up a cartoon that shows an elderly intellectual (he seemed to me to bear a faint resemblance to the paper's venerable editor, Jerzy Turowicz) toiling across a desolate, half-ruined landscape—an unfinished Soviet-style housing development, smashed windows, broken water mains, fallen telegraph wires—with the water soaking through his shoes. He is repeating, through gritted teeth, 'We belong to Europe, we belong to Europe, we belong to Europe.' The sense of hanging on at the edge of Europe is as acute as the European patriotism is fierce. For the uses of adversity are also sour. Scientists desperately bemoan the lack of modern equipment, which puts their research years behind that of their Western colleagues. Scholars feel acutely the shortage of foreign books and periodicals—partly the result of the state's shortage of foreign currency. Many are the doctoral students quite demoralized by the lack of the basic literature in their fields. Private funding and Church support can hardly begin to fill the well of needs.

We may sometimes grow tired in the West of the ways of the literary free market—the ceaseless hype, the sheer superabundance of publications and reviews—but if there is one thing worse than a literary market it is the lack of a literary market. The political division of culture can also distort judgement: second-rate work may be lauded just because it is officially criticized, first-rate work ignored because it is officially lauded. Yes, it is wonderful to find three thousand young people turning up at a poetry reading. But what questions do they ask the poet? Should we demonstrate on 1 May? How should we treat someone who joins the Party? What should we think about the local elections? How should we live? The poet wants to be a poet, not a confessor, political leader, economist, or citizens' advice bureau. He has, so to speak, an abnormal importance. And it is no surprise to find that so many of Poland's best intellectuals, faced with these pressures, limitations, handicaps, and demands, have come West, away from the front line, for a breath (long or short) of, so to speak, European normality (a notion that certainly includes New York and Chicago). Yes, intellectuals in Poland matter—perhaps more than intellectuals ever should.

'Unhappy the land that has no heroes,' cries Galileo's angry pupil. But Brecht's Galileo replies: 'Unhappy the land that has need of heroes.'

(JUNE 1985)

The Life of Death

Here are two enormous films about subjects central to the history of our time: Claude Lanzmanns's nine-and-a-half-hour-long film about the Holocaust, *Shoah*, and Edgar Reitz's even longer rendering of German experience in the twentieth century, *Heimat*. Both have won great critical acclaim, and both have provoked bitter controversy. They speak to us about Germans, Poles and Jews in the worst and final period of their common history.

1

Heimat is a film about memory. Memory plays tricks. So does *Heimat*. One of its most persistent tricks is a seemingly arbitrary chopping and changing between black-and-white, full colour, one-colour filter, and sepia, a device sustained throughout the fifteen and a half hours of the film. In the first hour or two—covering the Weimar Republic—I found this device both a cliché (sepia photographs from an old family album—what could be more obvious?) and increasingly irritating. But when we reached 1945, I saw the point of it. For when you are shown the 1930s as a golden age of prosperity and excitement in the German countryside, when you are shown the Germans as victims of the war, then you inevitably find yourself asking: But what about the other side? What about Auschwitz? Where is the director's moral judgement? To which the colour filters insistently reply: Remember, remember, this is a film about what Germans remember. Some things they remember in colour. Some in sepia. Others they prefer to forget. Memory is selective. Memory is partial. Memory is amoral.

With this simple trick, Reitz manages to escape from the chains that have weighed down most German artistic treatments of twentieth-century history. 'We try to avoid making judgements,' he writes. Not for him the agonizing directorial evenhandedness, the earnest formulations of guilt, responsibility, or shame. Not for him the efforts to 'come to terms with' or 'overcome' the past. Not *Vergangenheitsbewältigung*. Not Bitburg. Just memory and forgetting.

This is the main key to *Heimat's* artistic success. The other reasons are more obvious and more familiar. A small cast of well-defined characters enables the viewer to identify with their suffering where statistics and documentation would leave him cold. Reitz has said that he conceived *Heimat* partly in reaction against the American soap opera *Holocaust*, which had such a huge and cathartic impact in West Germany six years ago. Yet much of the success of *Heimat* as a West German television series (which is how the film was first shown in 1984) was owing to the very same soap-opera qualities that made for the success of *Holocaust*. This is, however, very superior soap opera.

It is beautifully acted. Marita Breuer brings off the extraordinary feat of portraying the central character, Maria, Reitz's Mother Courage, from the age of nineteen (in 1919, when the film starts) to the age of eighty-two (in 1982, when the film ends with her death). In re-creating the physical detail of pre-war village life in the Hunsrück hills of the southern Rhineland, Reitz displays a remarkable capacity for taking pains. When that village life was slower, he has the courage to let his film go slowly. It was lived in dialect, so most of his characters speak the heavy Hunsrück dialect (and he has used local people, not professional actors, for some important parts). Much of the film's charm and humour is carried in this dialect, and sadly lost in the English subtitles. (Perhaps the loss was inevitable, given the subject: *Heimat*, like poetry, is what gets lost in translation. The word itself has no adequate English equivalent. 'Homeland'? 'Motherland'? 'Native soil'?) And *Heimat* is funny.

'In Munich the Spartacists have plundered the trams,' someone announces to a small gathering in the remote village of Schabbach in 1919. 'Thank God there are no trams here.' No trams or cars or electricity or telephones . . . but the blacksmith's son, Paul Simon, back from the war, builds the first radio in Schabbach (actually, a fictional compound of several villages in the Hunsrück) and wins the hand of Maria, the mayor's daughter. They have two sons, Anton and Ernst. They seem happy. Then one day, in 1928, Paul just puts on his cap and walks away. Nobody knows where he has gone. Nobody knows why. Maria carries on bringing up the children—Mother

Courage alone. A few harvests later, we suddenly see a torch-lit march through the streets of the local town. Hitler has come to power. Nobody in the Hunsrück seems to know quite how or why. Another act of God? Hitler comes to power—and the telephone and the motor car come to the village. Nazism, which presents itself in the city as the guardian of old German rural life, of everything called *Heimat*, appears in the countryside as a revolution of technological modernity. It's a great time. Eduard, Paul's weakling elder brother, becomes the Nazi mayor, and his loud ambitious wife, Lucie, the former madam of a Berlin brothel, builds a large villa.

In 1938, thousands of men from the Organization Todt (the state engineering and construction empire named after its chief, Fritz Todt) arrive in the neighbourhood to build one of Hitler's new autobahns. A supervising engineer, Otto Wohlleben, is quartered in Maria's house. They fall in love. Meanwhile, business is booming for the farmers and shopkeepers. Maria's brother-in-law, a jeweller, does a roaring trade in death's-head rings for the men from the Organization Todt (*Tod*–death). In the Hunsrück, they've never had it so good. Only the one-eyed village ragamuffin thinks to follow the telegraph wires back to their point of origin. They lead him to a concentration camp: But we are shown only a glimpse of it, from outside.

A year later, the happiness of Maria and the *Heimat* is shattered. Maria receives a letter from Paul, who now owns a factory in Detroit, and ends her affair with Otto in emotional turmoil. The *Heimat* goes to war. Maria's younger brother, Wilfried, an SS officer, rules over a village of women, children, and foreign labourers. Ernst is a fighter pilot; Anton, a soldier on the Eastern front. Maria's lover, Otto, has volunteered to work as a bomb disposal expert. In 1944, finally learning that he has a son by Maria—little Hermann—he arranges to pass back through Schabbach. Maria and he are reconciled, but the next day he is killed by a bomb. The *Heimat* and Maria are stricken. The Americans arrive.

This long first half of the film, up to 1945, is superb: funny, sad, haunting. It displays a real historical intelligence in its evocation of the complex connections between modernization and nazism. It shows us, most movingly, German experience of the war, and German suffering—surely a legitimate undertaking. I can see no justification at all for the charge made by the French Jewish writer

Marek Halter in an article in *Le Monde* that Reitz idealizes the war and trivializes nazism. On the contrary, he skilfully exposes the Nazis' cinematic idealization of war: Anton is attached to a war photography unit, and we are shown all Goebbels's favourite tricks for aestheticizing violence. Anton later recalls that in all Nazi newsreels Germans are only shown marching *from left to right* across the screen: advancing even when they are retreating.

Moreover, Reitz is far from suggesting that his 'ordinary Germans' knew nothing about Nazi crimes. Anton's unit has to film the mass execution of partisans on the eastern front. At a party in Lucie's villa, Wilfried, the SS officer, proudly tells a group of army officers about the final solution. Earlier, we are shown Wilfried cold-bloodedly finishing off a wounded English pilot who has come down in the woods near Schabbach. In historical truth, did the Hunsrück villagers see more than these glimpses of Nazi barbarism? I think not. Of course they *could* have seen more—but like most Germans, they preferred not to look (as President von Weizsäcker observed in his magnificent speech to the Bundestag on the fortieth anniversary of the end of the Second World War). Indeed, Reitz almost breaks his own artistic convention. For he shows us more of what his villagers actually saw than they would probably ever remember having seen. In this respect, he is more just than memory is.

The charge of excessive justness cannot, however, be levelled against his first post-war episode, which is entitled 'The Americans'. Lucie, the former brothel madam and Nazi, now prostitutes herself again—before the American conquerors. Her son Horst (presumably named after the Nazi hero Horst Wessel) is the first to take chewing gum from the black GIs. A few months later, a large well-dressed man walks into Schabbach, followed by a large black limousine driven by a large black chauffeur. It is Paul Simon, Maria's husband, returned as a rich American who hardly remembers his native tongue. He is fat, brash, and insensitive beyond belief. He lays on an American military band to welcome himself home in the village hall (where earlier—in the thirties—Maria had danced so happily with Otto); he provides a groaning table of free groceries from American military stores for the villagers and, in case they have not yet noticed how well he has done, delivers an endless speech about his own success and the glories of America. Little Horst is pushed forward by a delirious

Lucie to recite the names of the fifty states. Later that night, Paul enters Maria's bedroom, on the pretext that he is cold, but obviously expecting to reconquer his long-lost bride. Maria gives him a blanket. 'I don't want you to freeze,' she says, 'but I don't want you to have any illusions.' American is repulsed. Germania remains intacta.

In this crucial episode, the partial and unjust memory is surely Reitz's own. And what is most striking about the entire film is not anything it reveals about a contemporary German attitude to the Nazi past but what it reveals about an attitude to America. From the first mention of America that I noticed—a reference in a twenties radio broadcast to 'the land of the electric chair'—the image of the United States is consistently appalling. America is the antithesis of *Heimat*. Paul is the Germany that has sold itself to America; Maria, the Germany that remains true to itself. Moreover, though the director would probably deny this, I think it is not entirely fanciful to detect a kind of implicit alignment that goes: nazism—modernity—Americanism. Certainly, these are the three elements most vividly opposed to the authentic community of village life. When Paul re-enters the village, he walks slowly down the road under the telegraph wires—the wires that led to the concentration camp. A chance image only?

In the next episode, set in 1955 and 1956, the enemy is less America than parental jealousy and the restrictive mores of Adenauer's Germany. As Maria's own great romance with Otto was destroyed by Paul and the war, so now it is she who destroys her son Hermann's romance with the beautiful Klärchen. When the family finds out that Klärchen has had an abortion (which was of course still illegal in 1956), they threaten to denounce her to the police unless she breaks off all contact with Hermann. But in destroying the romance, Maria also destroys her relationship with him. Soon she is left, once again *mutterseelenallein*.

By 1967, the villain seems to be international capitalism. A multinational concern wishes to buy up Anton's small, high-quality optics factory. Anton decides to consult his father. He finds Paul, now a truly revolting caricature of the loud, fat American abroad—and learns that he has sold out, to IBM. This apparently persuades Anton not to sell. So the values of *Heimat vs* America return, in the guise of a paternalistic employer. But already the film is losing conviction, and with the death of Maria, which opens the last episode, it completely falls to pieces, in a tedious, half-surreal village-fair sequence, ending quite feebly with all the dead assembled in the village hall to greet the ghost of Mother Courage.

Less would have been more. Reitz should have seen that he could not handle the last two decades within his chosen artistic convention and his chosen historical pattern (or myth). Memory fails him, not because the events are too remote to be remembered, but because they are too close. With his profoundly romantic view of the pre-1945 *Heimat*, and his deep anti-Americanism, he is incapable of treating contemporary West Germany with the same sympathetic naturalism that he applies to the 1920s and 1930s, for if he did so, he would be bound to show at least some of the ways in which this new, rootless, machine-age, Americanized Germany is actually better than the old *Germania intacta*. For example, in having democracy—a small point not, so far as I can recall, noticed in the whole second half, except in the American Paul's revolting speech. Reitz cannot be fair to Paul's children—because he is one of them himself.

2

Shoah is also a film about memory. Memory plays tricks. So does *Shoah*. But the tricks of *Shoah* are quite different from those of *Heimat*. Reitz allows the Germans their forgetting. Claude Lanzmann compels everyone to remember. *Shoah* has been described by a French critic as 'a monument against forgetting', beside it, *Heimat* looks like a monument *to* forgetting. Reitz's position is deliberately amoral ('We try to avoid making judgements'). Lanzmann is fiercely moral. 'I am deeply convinced,' he has explained in an interview with *L'Express*, 'that there is identity between art and morality.' The tricks of *Shoah* are those of art: but art in the service of morality.

Lanzmann's unique artistic achievement is to have re-created the life of the death camps. The life of death. Re-created out of nothing—no, out of less than nothing, out of nothingness, *le néant*, as Lanzmann himself says. There were not even the ashes. Re-*created*, not merely reconstructed. *Shoah* is not a documentary. It has none of those familiar black-and-white sequences: hysterical crowd chanting *'Sieg Heil'* CUT to pile of corpses at Bergen-Belsen. No Hitler, no corpses. Instead, we have nine and a half hours of interviews with surviving Jewish victims, German executioners, and

Polish witnesses (spectators? bystanders?—every word anticipates a judgement), long, harrowing, astonishing interviews intercut with one another and with slow, lingering camera shots of the extermination camps as they are today, and the railway lines leading to them, of the surrounding countryside, and the railway lines again, of the cities where the survivors now live, and again the railway lines. Germans, Jews, Poles: Lanzmann requires, cajoles and, if need be, bullies them all to recall in minute physical detail their experience of the death camps. 'You have to do it,' he insists when a Jewish survivor breaks down. 'Please. We must go on.' 'Can you describe this "funnel" precisely?' he presses the SS officer from Treblinka. 'What was it like? How wide? How was it for the people in this "funnel?"' [1] And by the end of Lanzmann's film I felt that I began to know what it seems by definition impossible to know: 'how it was' for the people in the 'funnel' that led to the gas chamber at Treblinka.

[1] Direct quotations in this essay are from the text of *Shoah* published by Pantheon (New York, 1985). Some small caveats must be entered about this edition and the publisher's bold description of it as 'the complete text' and 'an oral history of the Holocaust.' In fact, as Lanzmann points out in his short introduction, many of the English words we have here are in fact English translation of the French *subtitles* based on the (often hurried) simultaneous interpretation into French from the Polish, Hebrew, or Yiddish, languages Lanzmann 'did not understand.' As Lanzmann observes, 'the subtitling . . . has determined the way in which this book reads: the subtitles reflect very closely the spoken words, but they never express the entirety of what is said.' What is 'unessential' in the film becomes 'essential' in the book.

Unfortunately, at least in the Polish passages, small mistakes that the interpreter understandably made in her haste, or which crept into the subtitles, have also been reproduced in the book. For example, on page thirty-three the train driver apparently gives the distance from Treblinka station to the ramp as four miles, but I am fairly certain he actually said 'eight' in Polish, and surely he would anyway reckon in kilometres. On page ninety-nine, 'Myndjewyce' is an orthographical impossibility as a Polish place-name. On page 174 Karski's pseudonym must be 'Witold', not 'Vitold', as printed, and it should be 'Plac', not 'Platz', Muranowski.

These points might seem too trivial to mention were it not for Lanzmann's own magnificent obsession with accuracy in detail. It does seem a pity that after Lanzmann has spent more than a decade in scrupulous research, it has not been thought worth getting competent language readers to spend a few days checking the English text against the Polish, Yiddish, and Hebrew actually spoken on film. Moreover, the final published text does not contain a rider that I found in the uncorrected

No other film that I have seen about the subject has haunted me as *Shoah* does: images and voices returning unasked and, so to speak, unwanted when I wake in the night or as I play in the park with my baby son. Some written witness, some literature, has come close to it—I think of André Schwarz-Bart's *The Last of the Just* or the stories of Tadeusz Borowski.[2] But there is a particular compulsion that results precisely from *Shoah's* being not a book but a film. 'I couldn't put it down,' says the book reviewer's cliché. Well, you literally can't 'put *Shoah* down.' You can't stop on page forty-three, after reading the description of a mother disowning her own child before the gas chamber, and walk out into the garden to regain your composure. Unless you walk right out of the cinema and, as it were, miss the next fifty pages, you just have to go on sitting through it. You lose your composure. You get thirsty. You get exhausted. Perhaps you even get angry when the camera takes you once again, for what seems like the hundredth time, slowly, oh so slowly, down the railway line to the ramp. But this deadly repetition, this exhaustion, this *having* to sit through it, is an essential part of Lanzmann's re-creation. He deliberately uses the dictatorial powers of the director to lock you in a cattle wagon and send you for nine and a half hours down the line to Auschwitz.

Lanzmann is a supremely self-conscious artist. At a discussion organized by the new Institute for Polish-Jewish Studies in Oxford, after the first showing of the film in England, he analysed, explained, and commended his own achievement with an obsessional artistic self-interest that recalled accounts of Wagner or Joyce. ('He is a monster,' a friend commented afterward, 'a *golden* monster.')

proof, to the effect that 'a small number' of Lanzmann's questions 'have been eliminated in the English-language editions to allow for a clearer flow of the narrative.' Yet in at least one place—on page eighty-eight—it seems to me that this has in fact been done, and a tiny but not unimportant nuance lost.

Finally, one should note that much of the film's power comes precisely from the *clash* of languages—the appalling bureaucratic euphemisms of the executioners' German, for example, put against the survivors' plain English or Polish peasant crudities—and this is inevitably lost in translation. Still, it is probably better to have an incomplete and one-dimensional text than to have none at all.

[2] *This Way for the Gas, Ladies and Gentlemen* (New York: Viking, 1967; Penguin, 1976).

Lanzmann talked about his film as of a symphony, a great work of architecture, a Shakespearean play. Asked why he had not used interviews with this or that famous survivor, he said they were 'weak' as characters, they were incapable of truly *reliving* the experience before the camera, they did not fit into his play. In this film, he went on, every protagonist becomes an actor; it 'is a fiction of reality.' Asked about his criteria of selection, he replied: 'The film is made around my own obsessions; it wouldn't have been possible otherwise.'

'The film can be something else than a documentary,' he said. 'It can be a work of art—and it can be accurate too.' Accuracy is the second extraordinary feature of his work. Behind the nine and a half hours are some 350 hours of recorded film and eleven years of research across the globe. In Oxford, faced with some of the world's leading experts on Jewish and Polish affairs, he answered every criticism on points of factual detail with what seemed to me overwhelming knowledge, conviction, and something more: the justified sense that he had done what none of these historians had done. Why had he not included anyone from the *Einsatzgruppen*—the specially constituted Nazi mass-execution squads? There are very few survivors of the *Einsatzgruppen*, he replied. He tried to interview them. It was very difficult. In one case the camera concealed in his shoulder bag (which he used for secretly filming most of his Nazi interviewees) was discovered. 'I spent one month in the hospital. I was severely . . . extremely beaten. All my material was stolen.'

Yet as he talked, it became clear that his criteria of selection were not only those of the artist's truth ('my obsession') but also those of the historian's truth. He argued for his interpretation of the long-term causes of the Holocaust, and the nature of the extermination process, as a historian debating with historians. In large part, Lanzmann's interpretation follows that of Professor Raul Hilberg, who appears in *Shoah* as the key professional witness. There was a 'logical progression,' says Hilberg, 'because from the earliest days . . . the missionaries of Christianity had said in effect to the Jews: "You may not live amongst us as Jews." The secular rulers who followed them from the late Middle Ages then decided: "You may not live among us," and the Nazis decreed: "You may not live."' However, there was no one clear order that stated 'now the Jews will be killed.' The Final Solution was rather 'a series of minute steps taken in logical order,' at the end of which the 'bureaucrats became inventors'—a 'bureaucratic destruction process' that Hilberg has done more than anyone to reconstruct in scrupulous detail.[3] One may question parts of this interpretation, as Professor Israel Gutman did most powerfully in the Oxford discussion, but there is no doubt that on this central theme, *Shoah* makes a clear and cogent historical argument.

Challenged more closely on his interpretation of Polish responses, Lanzmann said, 'I think I have shown the real Poland . . . the deep Poland,' and, crucially, *'nothing essential'* about the Poles is left out. In that last comment he again explicitly offered up his work as a historian inviting a historian's judgement. For this criterion of fairness, representativeness, completeness, this claim that 'nothing essential' is left out, is always central to the judgement of what historians do but generally peripheral to the judgement of art. To say that a novelist, dramatist, or painter has 'left something essential out' is not usually to say anything meaningful or important. (Why did Leonardo leave out the Mona Lisa's feet?) To say that a historian has 'left something essential out' is always important. We expect historians at least to declare their principles of exclusion.

Lanzmann thus applies to his own work two standards of judgement; not to say a double standard. If I now proceed to question the historical comprehensiveness of the Polish part of *Shoah*, to suggest that here something essential *is* left out, then I shall at once be open to two criticisms: first, that the *artistic* completeness of the film is far more important than its historical completeness, or incompleteness; second, that the Polish part is anyway, historically speaking, the less important part of a film whose subject is the extermination process. I agree. Its artistic completeness *is* more important. The unique and unquestionable achievement of *Shoah* is that it brings home to us what no other documentary film has brought home: it makes us imagine the unimaginable, it re-creates the life of death.

Using the exact opposite of Brecht's 'alienation effect,' Lanzmann succeeds in eliminating the distance between past and present. In so doing, 'he wanted to aid the human conscience to never forget, to

[3] Raul Hilberg, *The Destruction of the European Jews*, revised and definitive edition (New York: Holmes and Meier, 1985; originally published 1961).

never accustom itself to the perversity of racism and its monstrous capacities for destruction.' This moral drawn from Lanzmann's art is the more striking because of the person who drew it. I am quoting Pope John Paul II, who thus singled out *Shoah* in an audience given to veterans of the French and Belgian resistance. Whether Lanzmann himself would agree that it was precisely this, or this above all, that he wanted to do, I do not know. But I have no doubt that this is one of the things he succeeds in doing. His work of art has a great moral effect.

Second, I agree that the Polish part is historically secondary. The Poles were neither the executioners nor the main victims in the extermination camps—Lanzmann's subject. They were only (only?) the train drivers and switchmen, the farmers who worked the fields around the camps, the local population who sheltered, ignored, or denounced the Jews. One Israeli participant in the Oxford discussion privately compared Polish criticism of the depiction of the Poles in *Shoah* to Jewish criticism of the depiction of the Jews in Andrzej Wajda's *The Promised Land:* Both criticisms, he said, miss the main point of what the director is trying to show, to which the depiction of the Poles and Jews, respectively, is largely irrelevant, a backdrop, not the play.

Yet Lanzmann himself is obviously fascinated by the Polish backdrop—indeed, he gives it more prominence in the film than its strict historical relevance to his main theme might dictate. (It is also striking that the image the American publisher of the subtitle texts has chosen for his dust-jacket is that of the Polish train driver who drove the transports into Treblinka.) Moreover, Lanzmann asks that his treatment of the Polish backdrop be judged with the same historical rigour as the main play. The political controversy surrounding *Shoah* has largely concerned the Polish part. The history of Polish-Jewish relations may not be so important to the Jewish nation today (*may* not be), but I have no doubt that it is still of vital importance to the Polish nation: to the Poles' proper understanding of themselves. For all these reasons, I think it is worth devoting the rest of this essay to what is—I repeat—*not the most important* part of the film.

3

Contemporary Polish reactions to the Polish-Jewish question are a mess. This is not an issue where there are clear dividing lines between regime, opposition, and Church. After *Shoah* opened in Paris, the Polish government's first reaction was to fire off an official protest at the Quai d'Orsay. But the government subsequently bought the film for showing (in part) on Polish television and (in full) at a few cinemas. There were stupid and ugly articles about it in the official press, mostly by journalist-propagandists who had never seen it. But there were subsequently intelligent assessments by critics who had.[4] Moreover, both categories of article could also be found in the Catholic and in the underground press.

The debate is hopelessly distorted by the extraordinary degree to which anti-Semitism has remained an issue, and an instrument of political manipulation, in post-war Poland. This was notoriously so in the 1968 'anti-Zionist' pogrom, led by factions in the Party and the security services, which resulted in the expulsion of most remaining Polish Jews from their jobs, but also in the crisis period between 1980 and 1982, when a few anti-Semitic voices could once again be heard in all camps—Party, Church, Solidarity—although this time they were truly marginal. Every politically conscious Pole writing about this subject therefore has a voice in his ear asking: What political use will be made of what I write? How will *Żolnierz Wolności* (the army newspaper that played a leading role in the 1968 campaign) misquote me? Whom will this serve? Indeed, I can almost hear this voice myself, since the last essay I wrote about Poland for the *New York Review* has been made the subject of a charming little attack in *Żolnierz Wolności*, signed by one Colonel (!) W. Zieliński. But this voice is a voice of self-censorship.

Such fears are everywhere and always the bane of free discussion. In Poland they are reinforced by another complex. Every Pole is brought up to believe that his country is one of history's victims: the generally innocent and righteous victim of the predatory nationalism of more powerful neighbours. Then he is confronted with a bitter and sweeping indictment of his nation by an American or British or

[4] An example of the latter is Artur Sandauer, ' "*Shoah*" a sprawa polska,' in *Polityka*, 3 August, 1985.

French or, indeed, Polish Jew—an indictment (and who has not heard it spoken?) that places the Poles right there in the dock between Barbie and Mengele. Brought up to see himself as a victim, he is suddenly told: You were the executioner.

We recognize the nationalism of the conqueror. But there is also a nationalism of the victim. The nationalism of the victim is one of the many things that Poles and Jews have (or, at least, have had) in common. Characteristic for the nationalism of the victim is a reluctance to acknowledge in just measure the sufferings of other peoples and an inability to admit that the victim can also victimize. In his famous 'Notes on Nationalism', Orwell writes that 'if one harbours anywhere in one's mind a nationalistic loyalty or hatred, certain facts, although in a sense known to be true, are inadmissible,' and he goes on to give examples of 'intolerable facts' for different kinds of 'nationalists': British Tory, communist, pacifist, etc. I cite below one 'intolerable fact' for the Polish and one for the Jewish nationalist—using the word *nationalist*, I stress, in Orwell's peculiar, broad, and pejorative sense.

> *For the Polish nationalist:* There was virulent and widespread anti-semitism in Poland during the Second World War.
>
> *For the Jewish nationalist:* The conditions of German occupation were worse for the Poles than for any other nation except the Jews.

To any reasonably detached observer who knows even a little of the evidence, these are both statements of obvious fact. 'Please accept it as a fact,' the commander of the Polish underground Home Army (AK) wrote to the Polish government in London in September 1941,

> that the overwhelming majority of the country is anti-Semitic . . . Anti-Semitism is widespread now. Even secret organizations remaining under the influence of the pre-war activists in the Democratic Club or the Socialist Party adopt the postulate of emigration as a solution of the Jewish problem. This became as much of a truism as, for instance, the necessity to eliminate Germans.[5]

[5] Quoted from Jan Gross's excellent book *Polish Society Under German Occupation*, (Princeton, N.J.: Princeton University Press, 1979), pp. 184–185.

But equally, as Gross and Martin Broszat and many others have amply documented, the Nazi occupation of Poland was special and extreme. Churchill was not using mere hyperbole when he declared, 'Monday [Hitler] shoots Dutchmen; Tuesday—Norwegians; Wednesday—French or Belgians stand against the wall; Thursday it is the Czechs who must suffer . . . But always, all the days . . . there are the Poles.' And consequently, as Nechama Tec soberly observes in her remarkable book about Christians who sheltered Polish Jews, 'obstacles and barriers to Jewish rescue were the most formidable in Poland.'

To present these two 'intolerable facts' is not to imply any symmetry or moral equivalence. It is only to suggest that unless you are able to acknowledge such basic facts—and most of the people who have spoken or written about this subject over the forty years do seem to have been unable to acknowledge either one or the other—then you cannot begin seriously to answer the real historical questions, such as: What is the connection, if any, between the fact of Polish wartime anti-Semitism and the fact that the German extermination camps were located in Poland?

Lanzmann's own answer to this central question, in newspaper interviews and in the Oxford discussion, has been confused. 'The film, you are aware, is an act of accusation against Poland?' he was asked by *L'Express* (in an interview published in May). 'Yes,' he replied, 'but it's the Poles who accuse themselves. They mastered the routine of extermination. No one was troubled by it.' But in the Oxford discussion, he said: 'It's not an accusation . . . against the Poles, because I don't think they could do much.' Yet a minute later, speaking of the Polish village of Grabów, which features prominently in the film, he exclaimed: 'A small village like this just let go of half its population . . . knowing absolutely that they were going to be gassed, because everybody knew.' To say they 'just let go of' the Jews surely implies they could have done something about it. Subsequently, Lanzmann revealed that his whole family was saved by French peasants during the war, and declared categorically, 'There could not have been extermination camps in France.'

But never trust the artist; trust the tale. What does the film actually show us? Most memorably, it shows us long extracts from some of the extraordinary conversations that Lanzmann had in the Polish villages and farms near the death camps. In these conversations, old

Polish peasants describe what they saw of the extermination process, how they reacted then, and what they think now. A farmer laughingly tells how as a young man he used to walk down the line of carriages, drawing a finger across his throat to indicate to the Jews that they were going to be killed. The foreign Jews came in passenger cars, he says. They were beautifully dressed, in white shirts . . . they played cards. The foreign Jews, oh yes, 'they were this fat,' repeat his friends, and, 'we'd gesture that they'd be killed.' And they laugh into the camera. But the same farmer also says, 'When people began to understand what was happening, they were appalled, and they commented privately that since the world began, no one had ever murdered so many people that way.' The Poles feared for their own safety. Weren't they afraid for the Jews too? Lanzmann asks. Well, replies the farmer, it's like this: if I cut my finger, it doesn't hurt you, does it?

Later, we meet the villagers of Grabów, living in houses that once belonged to the Jews. (Notice the beautiful wood carvings on the doors.) They describe how the Jews were herded into the church— the Polish Catholic church—and then transported to Chełmno, just twelve miles away. 'The Germans threw children as small as these into the trucks by the legs. Old folks too.' 'The Poles knew the Jews would be gassed in Chełmno?' Lanzmann asks. 'Did this gentleman know?' 'Yes.'

Then a group of old women. 'The Jewish women were beautiful,' they say. 'The Poles liked to make love to them.' 'It's crazy how the Poles liked the little Jewesses!' What made them so beautiful? 'It was because they did nothing. Polish women worked. Jewish women only thought of their beauty and their clothes.' 'The capital was in the hands of the Jews.' 'All Poland was in the Jews' hands.' And a group of men. Are they glad there are no more Jews here? 'It doesn't bother [us]. As you know, Jews and Germans ran all Polish industry before the war.'

Then the most eerie scene of all. A group of villagers in front of the church in Chełmno. Sounds of prayer and hymns. What's being celebrated? 'The birth of the Virgin Mary. It's her birthday.' And as the old Marian hymns ring out behind them, the villagers describe how the Jews were herded into this very church, how the Jews moaned and cried in the night, before the gas vans came to take them away, to kill them. Why did it happen to the Jews? 'Because they were the richest! Many Poles were also exterminated. Even priests.'

Then a self-important-looking man steps forward. He obviously considers himself a cut above the rest, and the rest seem to agree. 'Mr Kantarowski will tell us what a friend told him. It happened in Myndjewyce [sic], near Warsaw.' 'Go on,' says Lanzmann.

> The Jews were gathered in a square. The rabbi asked an SS man: 'Can I talk to them?' The SS man said yes. So the rabbi said that around 2,000 years ago the Jews condemned the innocent Christ to death. And when they did that, they cried out: 'Let his blood fall on our heads and on our sons' heads.' Then the rabbi told them, 'Perhaps the time has come for that, so let us do nothing, let us go, let us do as we're asked.'

And when Lanzmann questions this fantastic tale, an old woman shouts: 'So Pilate washed his hands and said: "Christ is innocent," and sent Barabbas. But the Jews cried out: "Let his blood fall on our heads!" That's all: now you know!'

The reaction of one of Poland's most respected Catholic intellectuals to all of this was both symptomatic and rather shocking. (Speaks the self-censor in my ear: 'Here comes a passage *Żolnierz Wolności* might want to quote out of context.') Jerzy Turowicz is editor of the leading Catholic weekly *Tygodnik Powszechny*. Turowicz got up early in the Oxford discussion and said approximately this: The film is one-sided. These peasants are simple, primitive people such as you could find in any country. Lots of Poles helped the Jews. There are 1,500 Polish trees in Yad Vashem. Polish Catholicism has precious little to do with Polish anti-Semitism—and anyway, Polish anti-Semitism has nothing to do with the Holocaust.

Now, with the greatest respect to Mr Turowicz, this really will not do; it will not do at all. This reaction is pure *nationalism*, in the special sense in which, after Orwell, I am using that term here. Lanzmann's presentation of Polish peasant Catholic anti-Semitism is a challenge and an implicit rebuke to Polish Catholic intellectuals. It says, in effect: For God's sake, here is a *problem*, a raw, bleeding, horrid problem, and why has it taken forty years and my provocation for you to address it? And all Mr Turowicz could reply was: We see no problem.[6]

Is Lanzmann's presentation of this problem in the film unfair? Yes and no. No, in the sense that everything he shows is obviously true. These people exist. They said these things. To be sure, his questioning is aggressive, even angry. 'They've gotten rich,' he says of one Grabów couple who have moved into a Jewish house: that is to say, a wooden cottage in a poor farming village in one of the most backward corners of Europe. Rich! Lanzmann is clearly shocked and amazed to find himself talking to real, live Christian anti-Semites who could almost have stepped out of the pages of a textbook on anti-Semitism (a textbook that should exist in Polish). But he does not attempt to flatten out the human, all too human, complexities, the bizarre mixture of superstition and earthy common sense in the peasants' mental world. The Jews stank, says one peasant. Why? asks Lanzmann, and we expect an ideological answer. 'Because they were tanners and the hides stank.' An old woman says she is now better off than she was then. 'Because the Jews are gone, or because of socialism?' asks Lanzmann. No, because before the war she picked potatoes and now she sells eggs.

He shows us their callousness but also their compassion. A leathery old railway worker bursts into tears as he recalls a Jewish mother and child being shot. 'Shot her through the heart. Shot the mother. This gentleman [explains the interpreter] has lived a long time; he can't forget it.' A mother and child, the central image of Polish Catholicism: Mary and Jesus. (A *Jewish* mother and child.) These 'primitive' Poles are so much more human than the 'civilized' Germans who would not dream of laughing on camera about the death camps—'*man weiss, das tut man ja nicht.*'

In the end, Lanzmann himself obviously developed, almost despite himself, a kind of affection for 'simple' Poles like the little train driver Pan Gawkowski, who actually drove the transports into Treblinka; an affection no one could conceivably develop for

[6] In fairness it must be said that Mr Turowicz has very significantly developed and refined his position in the years since the first publication of this essay. He has also opened the pages of *Tygodnik Powszechny* to a most wide-ranging, frank, and sensitive discussion of the issue, especially in a remarkable article by the distinguished Polish literary critic Jan Błoński.

'civilized' Germans like the unspeakable Herr Stier, former head of Reich Railways Department 33, who merely organized these 'special trains' from afar and still insists he 'knew nothing' about the nature of destinations 'like that camp—what was its name? It was in the Oppeln district . . . I've got it: Auschwitz!'

In these ways, the Polish part of *Shoah* is not only profound and moving but also fair and true. However, its truth is not the complete historian's truth that Lanzmann claims for it when he says 'nothing essential in what regards the Poles is left out.' Essential aspects of the Polish-Jewish relationship *are* left out, as can be seen by comparing it with the scrupulously fair account in Nechama Tec's book,[7] in which she examines all the published evidence and case histories of more than five hundred Poles who helped Jews. *Shoah* gives no examples of a Pole who sheltered Jews, although it does include a powerful interview with a courier from the Polish government-in-exile, Jan Karski, who vainly tried to alert world leaders to what was happening to the Jews in Poland.

Tec concludes that the only sociological generalization that can safely be made about people who helped Jews is that *peasants* were the class least likely to do so. In *Shoah* one sees almost exclusively peasants. On the few occasions where Poles mention the penalties they had to fear if they helped Jews in any way, Lanzmann seems to cast doubt on this by his own questioning and cross-cutting. In Tec's book, for comparison, we find a reproduction of a German poster announcing the sentencing to death of fifty-five Poles in one region (Galicia) in one day in December 1943, eight of them for the crime of '*Judenbeherbergung*'—sheltering Jews.

At the very end of the film, a survivor of the Warsaw ghetto rising describes how he escaped from the ghetto by a tunnel into 'Aryan Warsaw,' where, to his stupefaction, he found that 'life went on as naturally and normally as before. The cafés operated normally, the restaurants, buses, streetcars, and movies were open.' 'The ghetto,' he concluded, 'was an isolated island amid normal life.' Lanzmann accompanies this with a long film sequence showing Warsaw *today*. Now, as Leszek Kołakowski pointed out in the Oxford discussion, Warsaw in 1943 may well have looked normal to someone who had just emerged from the indescribable hell of the ghetto, but the Polish

[7]Nechama Tec, *When Light Pierced the Darkness: Righteous Christians and the Polish Jews* (Oxford University Press, 1988).

capital under Nazi occupation was certainly not normal in the way that Warsaw *today* is normal. It was a city living in terror.

This, Lanzmann does not mention. But he also does not mention the merry-go-round just outside the ghetto wall, in 'Aryan Warsaw,' the merry-go-round that went on playing even as the ghetto burned, the sound of gunfire from the last desperate fight inside the ghetto mingling with the fairground music, while 'wind from the burning houses/lifted the girls' frocks'—as Czesław Miłosz describes it in his great poem 'Campo di Fiori'. He also does not mention what some people in 'Aryan Warsaw' were saying—as Kazimierz Brandys memorably recalls in his *Warsaw Diary:* 'The nice woman who weighed my meat in the grocery store said that Hitler had disinfected Poland of Jews (the Warsaw ghetto was still in flames at that time).' He also does not mention the criminal Poles who blackmailed Jews (the *szmalcownicy*) or the role of the pre-war Polish police (the so-called *Granatowa Policja*) in helping round up Jews. Are these not also 'essentials'?

The real point is that (*pace* Lanzmann) *Shoah* does not make a historical argument about the Poles and the Holocaust in the way that it clearly does make a historical argument about the extermination process. As we have seen, Lanzmann's own statements outside the film about the connection between Polish wartime anti-Semitism and the working of the death camps on Polish soil are quite confused. Inside the film, there is no coherent statement—no historian's argument—about this connection. On this point, too, there is no key professional witness, such as Hilberg is for the main subject. (Partly, perhaps, because there *is* no Hilberg for Polish-Jewish relations during the Second World War.) This is not at all to put in question Lanzmann's achievement, only to define it. Just as it stands—vivid, personal, raw, and partial—the film within the film about the Polish role should be compulsory viewing in Poland. One would like to think that its very rawness and partiality could provoke Polish intellectuals, and above all Polish historians, into beginning a serious scholarly examination of the entire subject—so that, for the next film, there might be a Polish Hilberg to argue with.

With the Jaruzelski government permitting and apparently even encouraging Polish-Jewish studies in Poland (a political fact to be welcomed, whatever the mixture of motives behind it), and—equally important—with the support of the pope, the external conditions for such an intellectual and moral effort would seem to be more favourable (or, at least, less unfavourable) than at any other time since 1945. But alas, one can equally well imagine its producing an opposite effect: yet another sterile, bitter clash of intellectual nationalism—the (Polish) nationalism of the victim against . . . the (Jewish) nationalism of the victim.

4

Shoah is so obviously a larger film than *Heimat*—more complex, difficult, profound, and important—that one wonders if, after all, there is much point in reviewing them side by side. But on reflection, I think a real point emerges precisely from the very difference in quality between them. Why is Reitz's film about German memory so much 'easier', lighter, more superficial than Lanzmann's film about Jewish and Polish memory? Not because Reitz is a lesser director but because *the German memory of this period is itself 'easier'*. I do not, of course, mean the memory of those historically sensitive and morally anguished Germans who have shaped the Federal Republic's *public* attitude to the Nazi past and who currently have a fine spokesman in the federal president, Richard von Weizsäcker. I mean the popular and private memory of most ordinary West Germans, which is Reitz's subject—the memory, as it were, of Herr Kohl at home. And in comparing the two films, we discover the last monstrous injustice: it is the victims, not the executioners, who suffer most in remembering. It is the victims who break down, while the executioners bask in the happy memories of *Heimat*.

Both films together remind us: Memory is treacherous. Memory is amoral. Memory is also forgetting. There are things that memory cannot look in the face. If German, Jewish, and Polish survivors try to remember exactly the same event, they simply cannot remember it the same. And both films together say: Beware the tyranny of the director. For both *Shoah* and *Heimat* are ultimately shaped, and bent, by the partiality of the directors' own attitudes and biographies. Reitz's America, Lanzmann's Poland—these, too, are the products, the inevitably distorted products, of one man's memory.

The one conclusion to which they both lead me is: Thank God for historians! Only the professional historians, with their tested methods of research, their explicit principles of selection and use of evidence, only they can give us the weapons with which we may begin to look the thing in the face. Only the historians give us the standards by which we can judge and 'place' *Heimat* or *Shoah*. Not that any one historian is necessarily more impartial than any one film director. But (at least in a free society) the terms of the historians' trade make them responsible and open to mutual attack, like politicians in a democracy, whereas the film director is always, by the very nature of his medium, a great dictator. So the historians are our protectors. They protect us against forgetting—that is a truism. But they also protect us against memory.

(DECEMBER 1985)

A Hungarian Lesson

Background Reading

Imagine a garden maze, a maze in which mirrors conceal the hedges, giving the illusion of open space and free movement but also distorting wildly, as in a fairground hall of mirrors. At one corner you look impossibly tall, thin, and pale, like the poet Petőfi; at the next, absurdly squat. First you confidently step forward—and hit a mirror. Then you nervously edge around an open space. But sometimes you can walk straight through a mirror (or hedge), only to find yourself in another alley. Here you meet the administrator of the maze, himself lost in it.

This is Hungary.

At a recent meeting of the writers' union, one of Hungary's most respected writers, István Eörsi, delivered a powerful appeal for censorship. Yes, *for* censorship. Give us censorship! he said. Give us one office that is clearly, officially denoted as the Censors'. Specify its powers. Give us legal definitions of the boundaries. Prosecute us in the courts if we trespass beyond them. At least we would then know where the hedges are. Eörsi's idea was not new. Solidarity in Poland attacked the censorship in precisely this way, by demanding its self-definition, and partly achieved that goal in the 1981 law 'On the Control of Publications and Public Performances.' Even today, the censorship is more explicit and visible in Poland than in any other East European state, which is a kind of progress.

In Hungary, the position is worse and better. Better, because in practice so much can be published officially, including works of Polish writers such as Witold Gombrowicz, that cannot be published officially in Poland. Worse, because since there is no Censor, everyone has become a censor: not just the officials in those departments of the central committee and the culture ministry that are, in fact, politically responsible for censorship, but every

130

newspaper editor, publisher's reader, television producer, and worst of all, the writer himself. Because there is not one censorship there are many censorships; collective and individual, political and social, pre- and post-publication, before, after, and during the very act of writing. In this respect, Hungary is more like the Soviet Union— where, as is well known, there is no Censorship.

The Hungarian difference consists not in the machinery of censorship but in the way it is used. Pierre Kende[1] has identified three main surviving categories of 'outright taboo'. You may not question or criticize the Soviet presence in Eastern Europe, Soviet foreign policy in general, and neighbouring socialist states insofar as they follow Soviet precepts. (This last is the only major constraint on what *economists* can publish officially.) The basic legitimacy of Communist party rule is also sacrosanct. Finally, you cannot directly attack Marxist-Leninist 'socialism' by name.[2] Yet as Kende points out, there are startling exceptions even in these categories: a historical journal has published an astonishingly frank account of how the Communist party rigged the 1947 election, which formally legitimated its seizure of power, and even the great trauma of 1956 has been treated—with the barest of allegorical disguises—in fiction and drama.

Many Western observers apply the word *liberalism* to this state of affairs. Hungarian writers talk rather of *chaos* or *anarchy* in the cultural dictatorship. Nowadays, they say, you simply can't tell what will get through. There's almost nothing that *might not* be allowed; but what was permitted at eight o'clock may be denounced at noon. The instruments of control are out of sync. A new textbook on Hungarian language and literature (which includes a chapter on the Bible) is officially passed for use in schools; then it is fiercely attacked in the official press. Books that have passed through all the hoops of pre-censorship are suddenly withdrawn after being on sale for several days. This happened most recently to a biography of Béla Kun

---

[1] *Censorship in Hungary*, pp. 43-54 in Study No. 9 of the Research Project 'Crisis in Soviet-Type Systems', based in Vienna and directed by Zdeněk Mlynář.

[2] 'Of course socialism remains a name,' a high-placed official intellectual told me after describing his government's further moves toward capitalism. 'I mean "an aim" not "a name",' he corrected himself, tittering. But how often had he made this 'slip' before, in private conversation with Western visitors?

by a scholar at the Institute for Party History—following a protest from the Soviet embassy. And so on. Here is the moving maze.

Two main reasons are given for this 'anarchy': one contingent, one systemic. The contingent reason is that György Aczél, the inventor of the maze, the Kádár of culture for a quarter of a century, is no longer in command. Aczél it was who in the late fifties and early sixties made the essential 'Kádárite' bargain with writers. Its terms were, very roughly, that if they desisted from engaging in politics, as they had done with such spectacular results in 1956, if they observed the political limits, then the state, imposing virtually no stylistic limits, would publish and provide for them, generously, even lavishly. The maze has a deep-pile carpet. The limits were never clearly defined, but on any one borderline book, essay, or film, there was this one overlord who could say: 'That is the wrong side of the hedge.' But at the last Party congress, Aczél surrendered his overlordship of culture.

The systemic cause—which already began to take effect in the latter years of Aczél's reign—is quite simply that the people who administer the system do not believe in it any more than the people they are censoring. Marxist-Leninist ideology in Hungary today is as obviously wax as the face of Lenin in the mausoleum on Red Square. 'If you write a rabidly anti-Russian article,' a friend explains, 'the editor or publisher's reader will not try to argue with you. He'll say: "Marvellous piece. You're so right about 'fifty-six. I couldn't agree more. Have a drink on me."' As a result, the censors have no objective criteria for deciding where the limits are: They too are lost in the maze. 'Accepting the realities' is the slogan. But what are the realities for most editors or publishers? The realities are a judgement of what is acceptable to your superiors. But *their* realities too are mainly a judgement of what is acceptable to *their* superiors, and so on, up to the very top.

And what are the top people's realities? They are, we may surmise, twofold. First, there is the one living piece of Leninist ideology: the question of power. Here is a real criterion: Does this or that strengthen or weaken our power? But the answers to even this question in contemporary Hungary are often far from clear. Is it more strengthening or weakening ('stabilizing' or 'destabilizing,' in the jargon of Western political science) to allow relatively free debate about economic reform, to publish or to prohibit this book, that play?

The second reality for Hungary's top people is the same as everyone else's: a judgement of what will be acceptable to their superiors. As most Hungarian writers are expert at judging what their editors will tolerate, so the top political leadership must be adept at judging just how much the Russians will tolerate. Rulers and ruled are united in self-censorship. The usual effect of these successive levels of self-censorship is to stop the writer or artist well short of the actual limits. But because even Party officials seem to find it increasingly difficult, with the best will in the world, to see things the way the Russians do, they sometimes walk through a hedge (or mirror) themselves. Then the Soviet embassy protests.

The maze has its own language. I call it the Hungarian Periphrastic. It is a language of diabolical circumlocution, of convoluted allegory and serpentine metaphor, all guarded by a crack regiment of sub-Germanic abstract compound-nouns. Nothing is said directly. Everyone is taken from behind. A spade is never a spade. A crime is never a crime. Here is central committee secretary Mátyás Szürös describing how foreign policy was made in the 1950s under the Comintern: 'Essentially it was done by a collective and pluralistic decision.' Pluralistic! 'In certain specific cases this may have been harmful and as a whole perhaps objectionable in principle.' This is Newspeak turned against its makers.

Yet the great majority of Hungarian writers, intellectuals, and academics also live and work in the maze. They, too, write dialects of the Periphrastic. Their criticisms of the authorities are oblique, implicit, elliptical, or metaphorical. To the initiated and sophisticated reader, their meaning is no doubt entirely clear. The non-maze dweller and non-Hungarian speaker must hesitate to gloss what he does not understand. I am told that the finest contemporary Hungarian poetry and fiction are written and published in the maze. Their artistic quality I cannot judge, because so pitifully little is available in translation. Yet anyone can see that the Periphrastic is not a language to bring you to the barricades. It is the intellectual version of an attitude that prevails in the whole society: that of getting around the system rather than confronting it, of finding loopholes and niches rather than making demands of the state; and the premise of this attitude is, again by contrast with Poland, the essential permanence and immutability of the system.

Not everyone works inside the maze. Since the mid-seventies,

Hungary, like Poland and Czechoslovakia, has seen the growth of an intellectual opposition with its own independent *samizdat* publications and a pronounced allergy to the Periphrastic. Today there are two leading *samizdat* reviews, *Beszélő* and *Hirmondó*, and three *samizdat* publishers, AB, ABC, and Hungarian October. The publishers have produced some twenty books in the last year. The reviews probably reach some ten thousand readers. So far, their main strength has been their treatment of social and political problems inside Hungary—poverty, inequality, alcoholism—and of developments in other Soviet-bloc countries. As the publisher's name suggests, the Hungarian October of 1956, that central *negative* reference point of officialdom, is the central *positive* reference point for the opposition. While officials, and all too many Western analysts, argue that Hungary has got where it has *in spite* of the revolution, the opposition intellectuals maintain that it is only *because* of the revolution, because of the resistance, the refusal to 'accept realities', yes, and the bloodshed then, that Hungary's rulers now exercise their power in a relatively restrained, cautious, and tolerant fashion.

Emphasis falls on the word *relatively*. Generally speaking, those who publish regularly in *samizdat* will not be published officially and will be disbarred from official employment. Even with such an extensive second economy, this can make it very difficult for them to make ends meet. In addition, they may experience difficulties in staying in their state-owned apartments and in the education of their children. In this respect, too, the difference between Hungary and other Soviet-bloc states is one of degree, not of kind.

This is still a modest opposition by Polish standards. Hungary's 'democratic opposition' of intellectuals has not yet developed either a distinctive political strategy, such as KOR did in Poland, or those links with other classes—above all, workers—without which Solidarity would never have been born. Its impact has none the less been considerable. Probably the main effect so far has been to extend the limits of the possible in official culture. Editors of official journals, who themselves have anyway become bolder since the late seventies, can now argue that if they do not publish this author or that essay, he or it will 'go into *samizdat*'.

Moreover, the great social issues that the opposition opened up—the growing inequality, partly as a result of economic reform, the twenty to thirty per cent of Hungarians living below the poverty line—have been taken over by the official intellectual establishment. The best empirical studies of inequality are now being made by official and even Party sociologists, who naturally have all the resources to conduct the necessary research. In this sense, some of the opposition's best clothes have been stolen, and it has willy-nilly become part of the official cultural game. Though not in the maze, it is yet *of* the maze.

Coming from Poland, you expect the great divide to lie between opposition and collaboration, black and white, the craven and the brave. But here the needle on your Polish moral compass swings helplessly to and fro. Other fault lines cut across the canyon. There is, for example, the historic divide between 'populist' and 'urbanist' writers. The populists have traditionally celebrated the folk virtues of Hungarian village life, *la terre et les morts; Kultur* rather than *Zivilisation*. The urbanists were (and are) more cosmopolitan and often Jewish. (There are still as many as 100,000 Jews in Hungary.) Traditionally to be found on the left bank of the Danube, in the cafés of Pest rather than the hills of Buda, politically also 'on the left,' they have looked outward to Vienna and the West rather than inward to the Transylvanian strongholds of agrarian Hungarianness. They have been drawn to sociology rather than to ethnography, and to socialism rather than to nationalism. Such descriptions are, of course, historical caricatures. Yet it is curious to find that the question: Urbanist or populist? is still quite as important as the question: Officially favoured or dissident? There is even today a distinct group of populist writers, an intellectual party with one recognized 'leader'. Their great political theme is the fate of the Hungarian minorities in Yugoslavia, Slovakia, and, above all, in Romanian Transylvania. There, systematic cultural discrimination, and outright persecution by the dreaded Romanian security service (the Securitate), has dramatically worsened the position of the two million strong Hungarian minority in recent years.

In Poland during the 1970s there was a deliberate, difficult, and fruitful coming together of intellectuals from traditions that just twenty years before had been bitterly opposed: Jewish socialists sat down with Christian democrats, former Stalinists with Home Army veterans, hardened ex-revisionists with inspissated Thomists. In Hungary, this summer saw a first major attempt at such intellectual bridge building: a secretly organized meeting of some forty five intellectuals at a camp site in Monor, some thirty miles south-east of Budapest. The participants were carefully chosen to represent different traditions and groups—democratic opposition, populists, urbanists, independent writers, sociologists, reformist economists. 'The idea,' one of the organizers told me, 'was a kind of popular front.' They met for two days to discuss the position of the national minorities, the economy, efficiency *vs.* equality, the mounting social problems of poverty, alcoholism, welfare deprivation.

What emerged from Monor is not—or not yet—something one could call a united, let alone a popular, front. Thus far, one can detect no distinctive political strategy, no common programme for post-Kádár Hungary. But there was at least a common debate: economists explaining the imperatives of further reform to sociologists concerned about the resulting inequalities; populists and urbanists exchanging different views of Transylvania. Perhaps more than anything else it is the direct persecution of Hungarians in Romania that has catalysed this convergence: the kind of persecution that, as it were, *evades* the Hungarians in Hungary. Nicolae Ceauşescu as the godfather of Hungarian intellectual life—what an irony! Deeply unreliable rumour in Budapest has it that when Kádár went to see Gorbachev in September, the Soviet leader asked him: 'What's this I hear about your intellectuals getting together at Monor?'

The Lesson

14 October. Tomorrow, the European Cultural Forum—an official international conference to review part of the Helsinki agreements—will open in the gleaming conference centre next to the Novotel, all burnished metal and tinted glass. The airport metal detectors are being manoeuvred into place, to prevent any unofficial persons getting through. This is an event without precedent: the first Helsinki follow-up meeting to be held in a Soviet-bloc country, a French suggestion enthusiastically taken up by Hungary at the Madrid review conference that ended earlier this year. Tomorrow, delegates from the thirty-five states that signed the Helsinki Final Act will begin their fine speeches.

But today the talk is not of that. Today the talk is of an 'unofficial' or 'parallel' forum organized by the International Helsinki Federation for Human Rights, which links human-rights monitoring groups in ten Western countries. They have invited Western writers like Susan Sontag, Amos Oz, Hans Magnus Enzensberger, and East (or Central!) European writers currently living in the West—the Czech Jiří Gruša, the Hungaro-Yugoslav Danilo Kis—to come and discuss with their Hungarian colleagues, in a conference room at the Intercontinental Hotel, such modest themes as 'Writers and Their Integrity' and 'The Future of European Culture'.

By the standard of previous Helsinki follow-up meetings, in Madrid, Stockholm, or Ottawa, this is to be a truly inoffensive fringe group: this is no exile organization planning to surround the Novotel with placards demanding 'Freedom for Sakharov' or 'Independence for the Baltic States'. By Soviet standards, it is diabolical. Today, the diplomatic community vibrates to the echo of Czechoslovak and Soviet demands for the Hungarian government to ban it. So tomorrow the diplomatic niceties. Tomorrow the high-flown self-congratulatory Euro-rhetoric. But today the struggle.

I ask a senior Hungarian official for his response. The Hungarian government is committed to protecting the personal security of delegates to the (official) forum, he says. Like Western governments, it is very concerned about the threat of terrorism. But can't they be fairly sure that, say, well-known Western writers are not terrorists? 'Perhaps,' he replies, 'perhaps. But *what about the people who come with them?*' Aha.

Returning across the Danube, I find that the Intercontinental Hotel has cancelled the conference room booking. Another room booked in a different hotel has also been hastily withdrawn 'because the windows are being repaired.' (Some windows are indeed being repaired in this hotel, where I happen to be staying, but these windows are not in that room.) Next day, the Helsinki Federation organizers go to meet an official at the foreign ministry. A small group of us—journalists, participants, unofficial Hungarians—await their return in the near-deserted café of the Intercontinental.

Suddenly, the tables closest to us are occupied by burly, fat-faced men in sheeny jackets, with cheap Japanese watches and fists like Prague hams. They sip mineral water. Their eyes avoid ours, but their ears rotate in our direction, like radar dishes. František Janouch, an exiled Czech human-rights activist who has just arrived from Stockholm, springs up and starts taking photographs. Our neighbours bury their faces in their hams.

I begin to feel quite at home. We could almost be in Warsaw, or even Prague. It is no surprise to learn later this afternoon of a statement given to the organizers at the foreign ministry declaring that the unofficial symposium 'could disturb the atmosphere and work' of the official forum, and finding it 'incomprehensible why there is this private initiative.' But incomprehensible to whom? The statement is unsigned.

So have we found the limit after all? At last, a real, palpable limit to Hungarian tolerance, something we can hit our heads against, like a wall, a mirror, or a hedge?

No, we haven't.

For this very evening we all assemble in the spacious flat of István Eörsi (he who demanded censorship), its windows giving a marvellous view of the Danube. Eörsi himself is in West Berlin—the invisible host defies the anonymous statement. Here speaker after speaker gets up on the sofa and says everything that may not be said in the official forum: György Konrád, Susan Sontag, Miklós Haraszti, the Transylvanian philosopher Gáspár Miklós Tamás, Hans Magnus Enzensberger, speaking on censorship, *samizdat*, the persecution of the Hungarians in Transylvania, Solidarity, Charter 77—you name it, we hear about it. And the Hungarian authorities do nothing. For the next two days we meet in another private apartment and discuss those modest themes—writers and their integrity, the future of European culture—very much as planned. Most of the leading figures of the Hungarian opposition are here—including the independent publisher György Krassó, who was under house arrest until a week ago. In practice, no one is prevented from coming.

This is a beautiful loft apartment, with heavy brown-stained wooden beams and large studio windows looking across to the Buda hills, magical at twilight. The faded rugs, the Transylvanian pottery, the old glass-fronted bookcase (hallmark of Central Europe)—every detail speaks of an individual taste, of private and independent life. What a contrast to the antiseptic public interiors of the Novotel! As with the furniture, so with the speeches. There, the official Romanian delegate, after explaining that in his country 'more than 14,000 cultural establishments are used by some 270 million people every year,'[3] lauds the rich cultural freedom in which Romania's

---

[3] The population of Romania is 22 million.

Hungarian and German minorities can 'express themselves in their mother tongue.' Here, we learn the true story of increasingly harsh discrimination and persecution: Hungarian-language teaching abolished; Hungarian book and magazine publishing reduced to a trickle; Hungarian priests beaten and even killed by the Romanian Securitate; the Hungarian poet Géza Szőcs besieged in Koloszvar (Cluj), interrogated almost every day, telephone cut off, manuscripts confiscated and destroyed—'The candle is running low,' he writes to his friends in Hungary, 'and this is my last candle.'

There, at the official forum, the delegate from the Czechoslovak Socialist Republic proclaims—in Russian—the glories of a culture subordinated to the socialist state. Here, we listen to one of the many gifted Czech authors persecuted and expelled by that state. Here, too, we can read the answers of writers still in Prague to a questionnaire that asked them what that state—and the Budapest Cultural Forum— could do for their besieged culture. 'It is as if you were to ask what a cow can do for the flowers in a meadow,' writes Ludvík Vaculík. 'There is a simple answer: It could stop eating them. But can a cow do that? No way! For that reason there is no point in inviting a cow to some conference, seminar, or symposium about meadow flowers. The cow will gladly come, just for show, but anything it might say there is worth . . . a cow-pat.'[4]

It is impossible to summarize our debates. Memorable things are said by some of the Western guests—Amos Oz on the writer as smoke detector; Alain Finkielkraut defining both Europe and culture in ten minutes, as only a French intellectual can; François Bondy in praise of old ideas; Hans Magnus Enzensberger in search of a new one—as well as some unmemorable cant of the 'literature is freedom and freedom is literature' variety. But the real value lies in the East and Central European contribution. Here is Jiří Gruša, brilliantly sceptical about the writer as 'tale salesman' in the West *and* about the writer as disillusioned prophet in the East; Danilo Kis, with a scintillating anatomy of self-censorship; no Poles, alas (a great lack), but all the more Hungarians. If there is one central point that

[4] *A Besieged Culture: Czechoslovakia Ten Years After Helsinki.* Available from Charta 77 Foundation, Box 50041, S-10405 Stockholm, Sweden, and from the Helsinki Watch Committee, 36 West Forty-Fourth Street, New York, NY 10036.

emerges, it is perhaps the unimaginable *complexity* of censorship and self-censorship—as György Konrád remarks, we need a new science: censurology.

Yet as the second afternoon wears on, I feel a slight unease creep up behind me. A local writer delivers a short spiel. The local audience laughs appreciatively. I wait eagerly for the translation. It comes out something like this: 'Only the irrational is real, and Che Guevara, like Mohács, points to the "hope" of hopelessness, which is itself the irrational hopelessness of reason.' Well, ho ho. But surely we are back in the kingdom of the Periphrastic? And then, all the Hungarians are being so damn polite to each other. I know from private conversations that many of them are, for example, strongly critical of some of Konrád's larger and vaguer ideas. But do we hear this criticism here? We do not. Here it is all 'my friend' this and 'my friend' that. There is no unseemly controversy. This is the ultimate, the most understandable, and even morally defensible form of intellectual perversion: the *self-censorship of opposition*. And then of course we all know that the fact of this meeting's taking place will be bruited around the world (and *sotto voce* by Hungarian officials) as further proof of the Hungarian government's infinite cunning and 'liberalism,' whatever happens to the opposition when the limelight has moved on.

No, we are not yet in the maze. But we, too, are somehow *of* the maze.

Comprehension Test

You should now be able to interpret the following scene.

After the symposium, György Konrád invites you to a small evening party at his apartment. When you arrive, you are surprised to find yourself sat down, rather solemnly, between Susan Sontag and Danilo Kis, in a small circle in front of the leader of the populists, a writer called Sándor Csoóri, and a few of his associates. Konrád stands modestly aside, next to the tiled oven, and says, 'I would like my friends to tell you about Transylvania.' This they, or rather he—the leader of the populists—proceeds to do at length, with some chilling stories of Romanian persecution, slowly, almost ceremoniously translated (for, as befits a true populist, the leader speaks only Hungarian) by a member of his court.

What is going on?

Notes

a) The competent student will answer that this scene reflects the common and mounting concern among Hungarian intellectuals about the worsening position of their compatriots in Transylvania. This answer is good as far as it goes. The more advanced student of intellectual politics will suggest that György Konrád, himself so very obviously from the cosmopolitan, urbanist, democratic tradition, is here making a demonstrative gesture of friendship—or at least, common-frontship—to the populists, in the spirit of Monor. The student who is both advanced and cynical may further inquire why the populists seem to be making common front with the opposition. Could it possibly be that by so doing they hope to pressure the authorities into giving them their own literary journal? The really outstanding student, however, will conclude that if the author of this article had spent one more day in Budapest, met one more intellectual in one more café, he would probably have come up with yet another 'true' or 'real' reason, spied another distorted reflection in the mirrors, turned another corner in the maze.

b) Only one thing is certain: Nothing is certain. The hedges move daily. The Hungarian Party-state still has all the instruments it needs to punish the few outside the maze, if it wants to. There are no laws that curb its powers of censorship. There are, however, laws that could be used to gag writers, editors, and publishers—for example, the very elastic incitement paragraphs of the criminal code, as György Bence pointed out in an impressive paper prepared for the unofficial forum. During the official Budapest Cultural Forum, all has been sweetness and light—or almost all. But when you read this, the cultural forum will be drawing to a close, or already over. Will our hostess have suffered difficulties because she loaned her beautiful loft apartment for our meeting? We took no risk: She did. Will György Krassó be back under house arrest? An alert Western public opinion *can* make a difference in a state as careful of its Western reputation as Hungary is. It may even help ensure that the reputation is increasingly deserved. In other words, dear and patient reader: Their Country Needs You.

(DECEMBER 1985)

A Few Ideas . . . Nothing New!

This is the speech I delivered as a participant in the independent symposium described in 'A Hungarian Lesson'.

When I return from Budapest to Oxford, my neighbours will say that I have 'got back from Europe'. Britain is one of two European countries where people talk about Europe as a foreign land. The other is Russia. Now, it is patently absurd to exclude all English literature from our definition of European culture, just as it is absurd for Milan Kundera to exclude the whole of Russian literature from his definition of Europe, confusing Tolstoy with a T-42 tank. Yet there is a real sense in which Britain, even more than Russia, sits at an angle to Europe. Phrases that sound so natural in German—*Wir sagen ja zu Europa; Europa ist auf dem Wege zu sich selbst*—sound faintly ludicrous in English, as if someone were to remark: 'We say yes to the North Pole'; or, 'London is on the way to itself.' The waves of European rhetoric that have swept the Continent in recent years have largely passed by us. We have observed how French, German, Polish, Russian or Hungarian politicians and intellectuals have all declared their loyalty to Europe—but all meaning something rather different by it, and most of them meaning, in the first place, France, Germany, Poland, Russia or Hungary. When even representatives of the Soviet military start telling us that 'we Europeans must stick together,' we feel a strong temptation to stick apart. So I hope you will forgive me some initial notes of scepticism.

It seems to me obvious that European culture—in the sense of what European artists and intellectuals do—is still overwhelmingly a matter of national cultures. National, not in the frontiers of the nation-state but in the frontiers of linguistic, historical, and still also ethnic communities. This is almost a tautology. For historically, our sense of nationhood has been inextricably bound up with the sense

142

of cultural community: German has the word *Kulturnation*—and the thing still exists on both sides of the Berlin Wall, just as it does on both sides of the Hungarian state frontiers. To be sure, the sources of each writer's creative work are peculiar, individual and mysterious. There is no set of political conditions or state arrangements that is of itself conducive to the production of good writing, though there is for good reading. But for the vast majority of writers, their first reference group, the earth they cultivate and the air they breathe, their subject and their audience, remains their own people, their nation.

It seems to me equally obvious that this culture of national cultures is in a profound crisis, a crisis that it has brought upon itself. After two world wars begun by Europeans, after the genocides of Stalinism and nazism, after the Holocaust—above all, after the Holocaust—after everything that educated Europeans have done to educate Europeans, we are compelled to question our most fundamental ideas about what it is to be a civilized man or woman. Our studies in the so-called humanities have not only humanized, they have also dehumanized. Our culture—or cult—of nationhood has led to the extermination of nations. In our time, it is quite as meaningful to talk of European barbarism as it is to talk of European civilization.

That is why I am appalled by the easy arrogance with which many people in Western Europe—and particularly, in my experience, in West Germany—now habitually contrast 'European' values and behaviour with the allegedly naïve, inferior, and even (I have heard it said) 'primitive' values, behaviour and culture of the United States. Here we are again in what Kundera has called the kingdom of forgetting, but a more insidious and dangerous kind of forgetting, because it is not imposed from above (by the President of Forgetting, Gustav Husák), but grows as it were naturally and voluntarily from below. *Am Europäischen Wesen soll die Welt genesen* is not a refrain in which I wish to join. I think we are barely capable of healing ourselves.

Out of this experience of European barbarism there has emerged the demand—indeed, the necessity—for an explicit, public common definition of the basic values and standards of civilized behaviour. In Britain we have come to a similar point in our own national life and culture, although through much less traumatic experience. For three centuries the fabric of civilized life in Britain has been preserved by habits, traditions and manners rather than ideas, principles or rules. We had no written constitution or bill of rights. We just had this peculiar habit of somehow rubbing along together: *'die Philosophie des Durchmuddelns,'* as one German writer charmingly described it. Now the fabric is torn, the habits broken. We need ideas and explicit principles again: We need a bill of rights.

How much more does all of Europe need such a charter. I would like to read the Helsinki Final Act, and what has followed it, as such a charter: a charter that Europe has given itself, for itself, but also against itself—not against American values, not even primarily against Soviet values, but against the perverted values of European nationalism and European barbarism. But inevitably, such an agreement between states with different political systems stops precisely where it is most important to go on. It names those basic human rights and freedoms, but it does not go on to spell out what they mean, specifically, concretely, for each individual man or woman in each country. Where it leaves off, our task begins.

Moreover, by its very nature, no international charter can solve the problem of language. Historically, many of the most important words have meant very different things in different tongues: the word *Europe*, for example, and the word *culture*. And for many of the most important things we have no words. What emerges most vividly from Claude Lanzmann's extraordinary film about the Holocaust, *Shoah*, is the fact that the German executor executioners—the *Schreibtischtäter*—whom he interviews simply do not have the words to describe what they did. It is not just that they want to forget, to dissimulate, nor merely that they recall the bureaucratic euphemisms in which the Final Solution was originally wrapped: it is that they are, so to speak, physically incapable of finding the true words and attaching them to the deeds, as a paralysed man cannot tie his tie or lift a pen. If there is a specifically European task for writers, perhaps it is to find those true words and attach them with indissoluble glue to the deeds . . . to be not only, as Amos Oz put it yesterday, a smoke detector, but also an air conditioner—not merely sounding the alarm at the smoke of false meanings, but also pumping the fresh air of true meanings into our separate national and linguistic rooms.

A meeting like this may perhaps help us to find some of those shared meanings. But I must confess to scepticism (again) about the powers and sovereignty rights of the 'republic of letters'. György Konrád's vision of a literary *Ritterorden* is an attractive one, particularly for those who may presume to belong to it. But to me, there is also something suspect in the notion of a vanguard of intellectuals bringing enlightenment down from the mountain to raise the consciousness of the masses. A Fifth International of intellectuals—what a nightmare! I think our place is not on the mountaintop but down in those valleys where many people cannot even see the mountains.

Finally I would like, if I may, to say a few words about Poland. It's a great pity that we have no Polish writers or intellectuals participating in this meeting. This is a particular lack because it seems to me that Polish culture in recent years may be exemplary for the European culture we have been talking about in at least two respects. Firstly, in the last decade we have seen a major attempt by Polish intellectuals to overcome some of the great divides about which I spoke earlier—the divides born of European culture but threatening to devour it: between left and right, for example, or between Christians and Jews. In Solidarity, conservatives, liberals, and socialists, Christians and Jews, united on a common platform of those basic European values that it is our common task to define and to defend. It used to be said that Prussia 'went up' (*ging auf*) into Germany. We might say that in this coming together, Polish culture 'went up' into European culture. Secondly, and more familiarly, Poland is of course the best example of the successful defence, over the centuries, of national culture against state power. So if Poles will not speak here, then I would like to think that at least the epigraph for our meeting might be in Polish:

> *Ogromme wojska, bitne generaly,*
> *Policje—tajne, widne i dwu-plciowe—*
> *Przeciwko komuż tak się pojednaly—*
> *Przxeciwko kilku myślom . . . co nie nowe!*[1]

---

[1]'Colossal armies, valiant generals/Police—secret, open and of sexes two—/Against whom have they joined together? —/Against a few ideas . . . nothing new!' Cyprian Norwid.

East-West Divan

Prague

'Karel is out,' she says. 'You know, he works during the day. I mean, of course'—she blushes—'he does his real work at night.' Work: bricklaying. Real work: writing. 'You know, if you earn your living by writing, it's regarded as quite suspicious, and, well, almost unworthy.'

Now, here is a room full of writers, few of whom do anything so . . . unworthy. They sit around, feet in slippers, drinking wine and swapping jokes about Chernobyl. They have just produced the best journal of new writing in Czechoslovakia. It took about twenty minutes.

This is how it's done. Once a month, they meet for a small 'party' at somebody's flat. Instead of flowers or wine, the guests bring twenty copies of their latest text. (Most are carbon copies. It is a recognized fact that twelve is the largest number of legible copies achievable at one typing. Twelve is therefore the *samizdat* unit of reckoning—the writer's dozen.) The editorial meeting, then, has only one task: to decide the order of texts and type the contents page, also in twenty copies. This done, the texts are arranged in order in twenty blank cardboard folders, with the contents page on top, and—presto!—you have the Czech *Granta*. For the purposes of literary criticism, it is a journal called *Contents*. For the purposes of police search or legal defence, it is a miscellaneous collection of typewritten papers in a blank folder. If students want to sit up half the night typing further copies, that is their own business. (They do.) If Czech exiles in the West want to reissue *Contents* in print (they do), how can the writers prevent them? And if people want to bring these printed copies to Prague, what on earth can the poor writers do?

Early evening. A cellar beneath a ponderous red-brick nineteenth-century office building, now part of the ministry of culture. The cellar contains a grimy strip of carpet, two easy chairs (one with springs), an old office desk, a camp bed, a tin percolator, a typewriter and a piano that looks as if it first saw service at the Café Evropa in 1896. On the walls, a newspaper portrait of Stalin surrounded by his adoring subjects, *circa* 1951, and a black wire silhouette of a girl, *circa* 1963, with breasts that can only be described as 'proud'. A dirty T-shirt hangs from one nipple. Through a small skylight I see the rain splashing off the cobbles on the street outside, but in here it is dry and very warm, thanks to the huge coal-fired boiler in the next room.

My host, courteously ushering me to the chair with springs, starts to discuss the philosophy of Hayek. At one point he says: 'You know—but this is a *private* conversation, isn't it? You won't tell my friends?'

'No, of course not.'

'Well, you know, I have to say that I myself don't entirely reject *all* elements of socialism.'

When he left university, he knew there was no chance of pursuing an academic career in his subject and remaining honest. So he decided to become a stoker. It gives him time for his real work—philosophy. Income: small. Prospects: none. Spirit: unbroken.

'Now, would you like to hear my rags?' he asks after two hours' quiet argument. He sits down at the old piano and starts to pound out 'The Entertainer'. Then 'Bohemia,' 'our national rag'. I notice how, against the white keys, his fingernails are broken and black from shovelling coal. He's not really a good player—wouldn't pass muster in any jazz club in New York City—but endless practice has brought him up to an impressive tempo and his playing, here, is somehow electrifying. It has a kind of defiant ferocity. I see the music leap out of the basement skylight, like an escaping genie, force its way up through the pouring rain, giving a two-finger salute to the ministry of culture as it passes, and then up, up, high above the sodden city, above the smoke from his boiler's chimney, above the rain clouds, the two fingers turn the other way now, proclaiming V for Victory.

When you've spent a few days in this world turned upside down, among the writers turned bricklayer or window cleaner, between the philosopher-stoker and the poet-dustman, you inevitably start playing the 'If game'. Philip Roth does it in his novella *The Prague Orgy:* 'I imagine Styron washing glasses in a Penn Station bar-room, Susan Sontag wrapping buns at a Broadway bakery, Gore Vidal bicycling salamis to school luncheons in Queens—I look at the filthy floor and see myself sweeping it.' Anyone can play. Just insert your own favourite characters; end up with yourself. 'Me? Oh, I'd be cleaning lavatories. Sure. I wouldn't last five minutes under a dictatorship. Fascist or communist, they'd never publish *me*.' But what makes you so sure? Maybe they would, and maybe you (we, I) wouldn't. Maybe you (we, I) would still be (perish the thought) published writers. And then, what about all these official publishers and literary journals? Their former editors are all working as window cleaners, or in exile. But who edits them now? Somebody must. Window cleaners? It would be more fun if they did. But the answer is: writers, journalists, men of letters. Second- or third-rate, semi-literate, and corrupt writers, to be sure, but are there none such in our own literary establishments?

Here's the other half of the If game, the half we leave out because it's not so pretty. It would be invidious to name names. Let's be invidious: 'I imagine———— editing the *New York Review of Books,*———— taking over at the *TLS,*———— getting a rave review from———— , and———— being published after making his self-criticism on television.' And why not 'I look at this bookshop and see my books adorning its front window?'

What they all resent about Milan Kundera—and how!—is not, I think, his extraordinary success (perhaps that a little, too) but his stylized nightmare vision of a Prague from which, by definition, no good thing can come. No, they say, the Prague in which we live and work is *not* a 'Biafra of the spirit'—the Aragon phrase that Kundera takes as his theme. One well-known writer (the gentlest of men) tells me Kundera has to justify to himself 'the fact that he ran away' (but immediately adds, 'No, these are not the right words—"ran away," that's too strong'). And the self-justification, as for so many exiles, comes through depicting what you have left behind as hell—and painting how it was before as heaven. It wasn't heaven then. It isn't hell now.

I am determined to visit Václav Havel. It's not easy. He is staying at his remote farmhouse in northern Bohemia. It has no telephone. I am told the police will try to prevent my visit. I set off early in the morning in a hired car. After two hours' driving, as I pass through a small town, there are suddenly three police cars in front of me, lights flashing. I am guided onto the verge. *Damn!* Three cars seems a little excessive. And how on earth did they *know?* Then I notice that other cars are being waved down, too. This has nothing to do with me or Havel. We are all being stopped to make way for a bicycle race. I watch as gaggles of prune-faced youngsters come whizzing by. A *Tour de Bohème.* A banner in the window of the local toy shop says SOCIALISM—IS A CHILD'S SMILE.

Off again, winding up narrow lanes toward the Sudeten mountains, through the damp Bohemian pinewoods; turn a corner, there is the house—and there are the police: a Lada estate parked right across the drive, two uniformed officers, one in plain clothes. Their eyes follow me as I drive past inwardly cursing. Fortunately, however, I have about me my W.I.T.S, one of those marvels of Western technology that will confound the secret police and undermine the whole Soviet bloc. Activating my W.I.T.S, I become invisible and rematerialize inside the inner courtyard of the farmhouse.

Havel is a short, stocky man with curly blond hair; his moustache and lower face remind me of a friendly walrus. He is dressed entirely in shades of damask—slippers, cord trousers, and a T-shirt that declares TEMPTATION IS GREAT . (His latest play is called *Temptation.)* He is warm, intense, a concentration of nervous energy. He tells me the police turned up yesterday evening and have been there ever since. 'When this happens, it's usually because there is a Western visitor in Prague. Genscher or somebody.' He has been listening to Radio Free Europe and the BBC, trying to discover who it might be.

He talks about the nervous strain of writing under these conditions, when at any moment the police might walk in and confiscate a year's work. How he has crept out into the woods at night and buried parts of his typescript in the bole of a tree. How as a manuscript piles up, he writes faster and faster: the fear of a house search concentrates the mind far more effectively than any publisher's deadline. Just yesterday he was writing about this nervous tension. Then his wife came in and said, 'The police are outside again. I'm afraid they aren't our usual ones.' And so he got nervous about writing about the nervous strain of writing when . . .

This is nothing compared with the conditions under which he had to write in prison. There, except for one letter a week to his wife—maximum four sides, and only about 'personal matters', as the prison regulations specify—he was not allowed to write at all. The letters were his only opportunity to express himself as a writer, over a period of almost four years. If any part of a letter was unacceptable, the whole letter would be confiscated. The commandant of the prison camp at Hermanice took a sadistic delight in enforcing these instructions. This commandant was an old man, nearing retirement. His great days had been the 1950s, when he had more than a thousand political prisoners—bishops, professors, former government ministers—on whom to exercise his will. Things had never been as good since—worst of all in 1968, a little better after the invasion. But now, at last, he had some famous political prisoners to bully and abuse again: educated men—a writer, a journalist, a philosopher. His particular delight was censoring the writer's letters.

Havel started writing a 'cycle' of letters about his philosophical views. He mentioned the 'order of being'.

'The only order you can write about,' declared the commandant, 'is the prison order.' Then he decided Havel should not write about philosophy at all. 'Only about yourself.'

So Havel designed another cycle of letters on the subject of his moods: sixteen of them, two to each letter, one good, one bad, and he numbered them.

After eight, the commandant called him in: 'Stop numbering your moods!'

'No foreign words!' he ordered one week.

'No underlining!' the next. 'No exclamation marks!'

The book written under these conditions—for Havel conceived the series of letters to his wife as a book—is marvellous.[1] Much of it consists of his philosophical reflections, and in Havel's conception these were perhaps the most important part of the book. Yet for me, and I suspect for most of his readers, they are actually the least compelling passages: partly because, since he was not allowed to keep copies of his earlier letters, there is a great deal of repetition and

[1] Now published in English as *Letters to Olga,* (New York: Knopf, 1988)

recapitulation; partly because in order to smuggle his *pensées* past the commandant, he had to write in a fearfully convoluted and elliptical way. Instead of writing 'the regime', for example, he had to write something like 'the social-collective manifestation of the not-I.' Havel laughingly tells me that when he rereads some of his deepest passages today, he hardly knows what he was talking about.

What makes this book so compelling is the incidental detail of prison life—the elaborate rituals that surround the drinking of tea, toasting the New Year in a foaming glass of soluble aspirin—and the intense personal detail of his relationship with his wife: as a present, he makes her a piece of jewellery out of dried bread . . . 'I have tried to give it a touch of *Jugendstil*,' writes Havel.

Above all, the book is a self-portrait of the writer. There is Havel setting himself tasks for his four years in prison: '. . . Three. To write at least four plays. Four. To improve my English. Five. To learn German at least as well as I currently know English. Six. To study all of the Bible thoroughly . . .' There is Havel fretting about his health, fretting about old friends outside. And sounding through it all, again and again, there is his overmastering determination to remain a *writer*, though he has only four pages a week and each word he chooses can endanger the whole work. 'Last week's letter did not come off,' he writes—meaning it was confiscated.

Early in his imprisonment, in 1979, Havel writes several times about a 'Faust' play that he was mentally reworking. This is the piece that, seven years later, has its *première* in Vienna under the title *Temptation*. As with most of his plays, he has never seen it performed. He reads the reviews. Friends telephone from Vienna. And during rehearsals the actors call him with questions that show they have not *exactly* understood the piece. In this case, they ring up a few days before opening and ask, 'Oh, by the way, is there really black magic in Czechoslovakia?' Yet this is what he regards as his real work: writing plays. His political activity, his essays, his letters from prison, his role as a moral and political authority for thousands of Czechs and Slovaks (and by no means only those actively engaged in opposition)—an authority that no writer in the West enjoys; all that is secondary.

Since, unlike Havel, I can travel to Vienna, I go to see *Temptation*. His fears about the limited understanding of the Viennese company are justified. The director of the academic institute in which Havel's

Dr Faustka works, a deeply corrupt Party placeman, is played as if he were the manager of a department store in the Kärntnerstrasse. And yet, and yet . . . however much I make allowances for the Viennese factor, I still cannot avoid a deeper disappointment. The play, even as Havel has written it, is weak. And it is weak, it seems to me, for reasons directly related to his situation. For a start, the dramaturgy and the visual effects envisaged in his very detailed stage directions are stilted, and if not stilted, dated—all stroboscopes and smoke, *circa* 1966. Not surprising if you consider that he has been unable to work in a theatre for eighteen years. The dénouement is desperately predictable, and predictably political: the Mephisto figure (called Fistula) turns out to be working for the secret police. Despite some grimly amusing dialogue, which survives even the Viennese production, most of the action is so carefully plotted, and so obviously pointed, as to be quite schematic. It feels like a plan for a play rather than the play itself. Not surprising, again, when you consider that it was planned and re-planned through almost four years in prison.

So what of George Steiner's 'muse of censorship'? Here is a rather clear case, it seems to me, of an artist's work not enhanced but deformed and diminished by censorship and persecution. If he were a poet, it might be otherwise. But the playwright needs his theatre as a musician needs his instrument. Not merely the artist but the art has suffered. Yet at the same time, through that persecution and that censorship, or rather through his defiance of it, he has produced a volume of letters and a body of essays that will, I think, be read long after *Temptation* is forgotten. And what will then be known as his real work?

Paris

So here she comes, the fat whore, the tart, the harpy, flaunting her fancy clothes and waggling her bum. She has money. She has motor cars. She has sex. She has democracy. But she's lost her soul. She's deaf. She's blind. She doesn't know what she's got or how she's about to lose it. 'The West'? Mae West.

> Today [writes Kazimierz Brandys in his *Warsaw Diary*], the West is emitting cries of horror; the intellectuals are grumbling; the consciousness of impotence is everywhere.

They know already and are preparing themselves to be raped. All that matters now is that the rape not be a sexual murder but that it happen calmly, in some comfortable French bed. What should this up-coming state of affairs be called? Finlandization? Scandinavization? . . . But what if it's Czechoslovakization? In these preparations the French are, as always, in the intellectual vanguard. No one is able to spread their legs as aesthetically, to lie down for the act with such *esprit*, as the French intellectuals. An old suspicion of mine: how much money flows from the Soviet embassy to editorial offices in Paris?

Ah, there he blows: the Eastern prophet, the sage, the seer, righteous eyes ablaze, arms raised to high heaven as he denounces the whores of the rue de Babylone.

'You see, it's really very simple,' says Sławomir Mrożek looking out from his tranquil studio flat toward the Eiffel Tower. 'You are a Pole, an intellectual. You think of yourself as supremely Western and European: if only Poland were free, it would be a Western country; if only it were Western, everything would be all right. Meanwhile, European values are preserved in the West, to which you, unlike the Russians, indubitably belong. Then you come to the West, and the West knows you not. So after a time you get up on your hillock and rage, rage against the blindness of the West. Inwardly, you cry: "You may have your motor cars, your television, your bestsellers. But you have lost your soul. Your *soul*. If you only knew how great, how profound, how truly European I was, you would print me in a million copies. Since you don't, you will be eaten by the Russians."'

Part of this misunderstanding arises from what Mrożek calls the 'old-fashioned' idea of the moral value of culture and the role of the writer, which still persists in Prague or Warsaw. Eastern Europe, says Mrożek, is a very old-fashioned place, both materially (look at the trams) and socially (respect for the old, religion). This is just one more old-fashioned thing about it.

In the West, there are no more *Dichter*. No writer is regarded as a moral or spiritual leader, as Havel is in Czechoslovakia, or as Miłosz and Herbert are in Poland. Quite a familiar remark, this. It also comes as a question: Who was the last great intellectual authority in Western Europe? And the answer most often given—Kundera's answer, in his essay on 'The Kidnapped West'—is . . . Jean-Paul Sartre. Sartre, a moral authority! The author of *Les Mains Sales*. Yes, all right, he changed his mind. But when I was talking to Ivan Klíma in Prague about Western intellecuals' fatuous envy of the persecuted (*Verfolgungsneid*), Klíma exclaimed, 'You know, the man responsible for all this nonsense is Sartre.' Sartre, he said, had come to Prague in the early sixties, looked around for a day or two, and then given a speech to Czech writers in which he told them how fortunate they were. 'You have real subjects,' he said. 'We in the West no longer have any real subjects'—and so on. Sartre!

Anyway, Mrożek continues, literature in the West has become just another 'line of business' (he uses the Polish word *branża*), alongside television, films, video and windsurfing. A line of business where public relations and promotion are more important than the product itself—'The book of the film'; 'Now a Major TV Series'; 'Winner of the —————— Prize'.

'I don't regret this,' says Mrożek. 'I don't like it; I don't dislike it: it's just the way the world has moved on.' (Modernity has its advantages: as we talk, the phone rings and he stands up to listen in to the caller speaking to his answering machine; sometimes, he picks up; most often, he just turns down the volume.) But as Mrożek talks on in his dry, sardonic way, it's obvious that he does regret it. He speaks about the television discussion programme, with its basic assumption that there are two sides to every question, as the characteristic intellectual form of our time. On my left the murderer, on my right the victim. Two points of view—and of course the murderer is often more *interesting*. Orwell, he says—'Or-vell'—was one of the few people to refute this fallacy. Orwell understood that there are some things that are not open to discussion: some questions have only one side. An East European, says Mrożek, knows this from personal experience. Orwell's achievement was to understand it without that experience.

Mrożek's own situation is almost a reverse image of Havel's. Havel is deprived of theatrical experience—can never see his plays rehearsed or performed—but he still has what might be called *vernacular* experience: he lives in his own language. Mrożek has the theatrical experience but not the vernacular. He has lived abroad since 1963, in France since 1968. He can see his plays rehearsed and performed in English, French, German, Italian. But the Polish language of the street—changing slang, politics, contemporary allusions: all the essential stuff of most recent Polish prose—this he can absorb only at second or third hand. When his play *Ambassador* was (exceptionally) performed in Warsaw in the autumn of 1981, shortly before General Jaruzelski imposed martial law, the audience loudly applauded a scene in which the ambassador sits shivering beside a primitive coal stove. The Warsaw audience knew a political allusion when it saw one: who could not think of the bitter winter ahead, the shortage of heating fuel, for which Solidarity blamed the government, and the government, Solidarity? Were not they, like the ambassador, besieged by a foreign power? Except that Mrożek had never intended any allusion. Sitting in Paris, he had not thought what the Warsaw audience would think.

Yet there are striking similarities between a Havel play and a Mrożek play. Both favour settings that have a Kafka-like non-specificity: neither Eastern nor Western, not Prague, not Paris. Both cleave to the theme of the individual seeking to defend himself—by heroism, by compromise, or by humour—against the chicanery of impersonal powers. Both are fiercely intellectual: if you do not respond to the ideological argument in the dialogue, you have missed half the point. (As did the Viennese audience for Havel's *Temptation*. As did the audience for Mrożek's *Ambassador* when I saw it in West Berlin. Shift this theatre just a couple of miles to the East, I thought, across the Wall into East Berlin, and the play would be understood.) Yet it would be a foolish critic who attributed all these shared qualities to the common East European background. Another, equally cogent, explanation comes in two words: Samuel Beckett.

The exile's dwelling. Two tiny bare rooms up a narrow uncarpeted staircase. A broom-cupboard of a kitchen. Stools for chairs. A camp bed. And then the real essentials: cigarettes, tea, a telephone with a long flex, and books, books, books. Books to prop up the table, books to keep out the cold, books for food, books for drink, books for clothing.

Natalya Gorbanevskaya, whose dwelling I describe, is an extraordinary person. If you sat opposite her on the métro, you would probably take her for a student at the Sorbonne: a small, girlish figure in jeans and a chunky sweater, tousled hair, large spectacles, pulling at her cigarette with an air of distracted intensity. At second glance you might notice some hard-etched lines around the mouth and eyes, but you would never, never guess that she is in fact a fifty-year-old Russian poet, let alone that she spent the years 1969 to 1972 in a prison psychiatric hospital in Karzan, being treated for what Soviet psychiatry charmingly calls 'sluggish schizophrenia'—which is to say, being persecuted for her courage in political opposition. To enter a conversation with Natalya Gorbanevskaya is to feel yourself being seized by the hand and pulled helter-skelter down a steep, heavily wooded hillside—watch out for the Sinyavsky! jump over the Zinoviev!—screaming with a mixture of excitement and alarm, until you arrive, breathless but laughing, at a lake called Solzhenitsyn.

As we perch on our stools, eating the interesting omelette Natalya has volubly prepared in that tiny kitchen—cracking Kundera with one egg, tossing Brandys with the next—her running commentary rapidly moves on to familiar ground. The trouble with Kundera is that he excludes Russia from his definition of European culture. The trouble with Zinoviev is that he reinforces the false Western identification of the Soviet Union with Russia—which was in fact the Soviets' first victim. Zinoviev simply has no idea about the immortal soul . . . and she talks, very movingly, about the unbroken courage and decency of some of the women she met in prison, about the faith of persecuted Christians, not only the Orthodox, but the Baptists and the Evangelical sects as well.

I ask what was the greatest shock of her arrival in the West (she left Russia in 1975, and has lived in Paris ever since). Natalya's answer is quite surprising: 'You know, one of the few things I really looked forward to in coming to the West was having the opportunity to join in a real, authentic Orthodox mass.' If Mrożek's cartoon-Pole hoped to find those true European values preserved in the West, she looked forward to finding the true spirit of Russian Orthodoxy, the exaltation and the mystery, preserved in the free world. But she too was bitterly disappointed. She found that Orthodox services here had become social rites: People came less to worship than to meet each other, to see and be seen.

In Paris, Natalya is now deputy editor of *Kontinent,* the Russian literary and political review with which Solzhenitsyn is most closely identified, and her views on the West also have that prophetic ring: 'It's such an effort for the West to begin to understand. And it's so important: we may have so little time.' A French journalist of her acquaintance recently returned from Afghanistan, and he was so shocked to see what the Western press was writing about: Nicaragua. Nicaragua? 'Yes, that is the last battle, as it says in the "Internationale": the last battle against the evil empire.' People here just don't understand, she says, that this 'metaphysical evil' is spreading across the world: now in Afghanistan, now in Nicaragua. Yet the picture she draws in conversation is neither so solemn nor so starkly black-and-white as these lines in cold print might suggest.

Doesn't Solzhenitsyn, well, *exaggerate* a little? I ask. And what about his idealization of tsarist Russia? But of course he exaggerates! He has to, after sixty years during which the Russian people have been relentlessly drilled into believing the opposite; has to, if he's to make any impact at all. As for the West, the longer Natalya has been here, the more differentiated her picture has become. Even the French left has improved greatly in the last few years. They are quite stalwart, principled, and outspoken when they are in opposition. But when they come to power, it's a different story. Look at the French socialists. When they came into office, they granted French citizenship to the exiled Leonid Plyusch, another victim of Soviet 'psychiatry'—and immediately stopped listening to what he had to say.

For Natalya, too, the one great exception among Westerners is Orwell. The East European knows some truths instinctively, she says, echoing Mrożek. He is born to them—'like the aristocracy!' An aristocracy of suffering. By comparison Westerners are, well, plebeians. 'But the plebeian who has become an aristocrat through his own exertions is the most admirable of all.' Thus are rewarded all the Old Etonian Blair's exertions to become a true plebeian—with a Russian patent of nobility.

My lasting impression of Natalya Gorbanevskaya is of a great warmth, a warmth that seems to insulate me even against the bitter January wind howling down the Avenue Gay Lussac as I walked back to the métro. Here is a spirit permanently living at combustion point: exploding now into laughter, now into sympathy, now into anger—but if anger, then always, to adapt Orwell's remark about Dickens, *generous* anger.

Party time. A farewell party for Seweryn Blumsztajn, a veteran from the Polish class of '68 and one of the best-known Solidarity figures in the West, who has now decided to return to Poland. An expansive, grand old apartment belonging to an expansive, grand old lady—an Ottoline Morrell of the Russian emigration. Parquet floors, high rooms, tables overflowing with *kanapki*, vodka and wine, Polish and Russian intellectuals mixing as they never could in Warsaw or Moscow. Who's that scintillating in the far corner? Why, of course— Pani Natalya! And scintillating in this corner is the editor of *Aneks*. And there's the editor of *Zeszyty Literackie*, also scintillating. And the editor of *Kontakt*. And someone from *Kultura*. And someone from *Arka*. There must be more editors per square yard in this apartment than there are lawyers in Lincoln's Inn. Plus all the accompanying feuds, rivalries, scandals and affairs, all raised to boiling point by the pressures of exile.

For the first hour you might possibly recognize this as a literary party, as held in London or New York (or indeed Paris): the factional groups, the gossiping, this reviewer making up to that editor, more gossip, that editor making up to this author's wife, more gossip— except that here the volume, temperature, and gestic range are already several points higher. But two hours later you couldn't possibly. For by now everyone is crowded into one room, and *singing*. The exiled *chansonnier* Jacek Kaczmarski has given an impromptu concert: sharp, contemporary political ballads sung in an angry, rough-edged voice, to his own accompaniment on the guitar—the nearest we get to this in England is a stage performance of Brecht-Weill songs, and it's not very near. Now Sewek Blumsztajn himself is sitting in the middle of the room singing, in quick succession and apparently with equal delight, a Stalinist youth-movement song, violently anti-Church, and then the old religious-patriotic hymn 'Rota':

> We shall not yield our forebears' land
> Nor see our language muted
> Poles we are, our nation Polish
> By Piasts constituted.

A few, a very few, former comrades join in the first; everyone joins in the second.

Now, play the If game. Imagine, just try to imagine, that at a certain point in your London literary party everyone stops standing around getting quietly drunk in little groups talking about the decline of the *TLS*, forgets about their own private interests, schemes, feuds and resentments. Instead, all crowd into one room, sitting on the floor, the piano, each other, anywhere, and start singing, very loudly:

> Lilli bullero, lilli bullero bullen a la,
> Lero lero, lilli bullero, lero lero bullen a la,
> Lero lero, lilli bullero, lero lero bullen a la.

The film-maker Agnieszka Holland tells me that I must interview Blumsztajn about why he's returning to Poland, while she films us. I don't want to interview Blumsztajn. I want to go on enjoying this party. I hate doing interviews with a microphone to put people on their guard. I'm drunk, I have a stinking cold and a fever, and everybody in this room speaks better Polish than me. Why doesn't somebody else do it? No, she says, everyone else knows Sewek too well. They couldn't put the necessary, brutal, uncomprehending questions. That's what journalists are for. Anyway, this film will be used to help win support in the West if, as seems probable, he is arrested and imprisoned on his return to Warsaw.

Impossible to resist the moral half-nelson. So here I am, at two o'clock in the morning, sitting amid the broken glass in the glare of the film lights, with a head like a battered pumpkin, and asking feebly: 'Why are you returning to Poland?'

'Well,' says Blumsztajn, 'I am opposed to emigration.' All the crucial developments in Poland since the war have come from *inside* the country. It's still true today. That's why he feels he can be more useful there. And so on, in a well-rehearsed argument. I don't challenge it. I haven't the heart, let alone the head, to challenge it.

But the film-maker does. This is nonsense, she says. He can be more use here than he can there. And why is he leaving his wife behind? Isn't it simply that he puts being with his friends before his work and his family?

And she said they couldn't ask the brutal questions.

After a bit more of this I begin to feel like an umpire trying to separate two boxers, and taking all the punches to the head. By the end of round three the truth is plain, and indeed admitted with a sad smile. The guy's going back because he thinks he'll be happier there than here.

A few days later, Seweryn Blumsztajn did return to Poland. A great party of friends, Solidarity activists and sympathizers saw him off in Paris. At Orly airport he appeared at a press conference chaired by André Glucksmann. Another great party of friends, Solidarity activists and sympathizers awaited him at Warsaw airport. Everyone, in both places, was prepared to launch an instant volley of protest if he was arrested.

When he arrived at Warsaw airport he was immediately taken away by six policemen, who told him that his Polish passport was 'invalid' and had been 'misused', and then marched him straight back onto the Air France plane. The pilot was told that the plane would not be allowed to leave unless it had Blumsztajn on board.

It left. He was on board.

I sometimes wonder what happened to that film.

(AUGUST 1986)

Does Central Europe Exist?

1

Central Europe is back. For three decades after 1945, nobody spoke of Central Europe in the present tense: the thing was one with Nineveh and Tyre. In German-speaking lands, the very word *Mitteleuropa* seemed to have died with Adolf Hitler, surviving only as a ghostly *Mitropa* on the dining cars of the Deutsche Reichsbahn. Even in Austria, as ex-Chancellor Fred Sinowatz has remarked, 'until ten years ago one was not permitted so much as to mention the word *Mitteleuropa*.' In Prague and Budapest, the idea of Central Europe continued to be cherished between consenting adults in private, but from the public sphere it vanished as completely as it had in 'the West'. The post-Yalta order dictated a strict and single dichotomy. Western Europe implicitly accepted this dichotomy by subsuming under the label Eastern Europe all those parts of historic Central, East Central, and South-eastern Europe that after 1945 came under Soviet domination. The EEC completed the semantic trick by arrogating to itself the unqualified title Europe.

In the last few years we have begun to talk again about Central Europe, and in the present tense. This new discussion originated not in Berlin or Vienna but in Prague and Budapest. The man who more than anyone else has given it currency in the West is a Czech, Milan Kundera, with his now-famous essay 'The Tragedy of Central Europe' (first published in French in 1983 and in English in 1984). Subsequently, the Germans and the Austrians have gingerly begun to rehabilitate, in their different ways, a concept that was once so much their own. The East German leader, Erich Honecker, talks of the danger of nuclear war in *Mitteleuropa*. The West German Social Democrat Peter Glotz says the Federal Republic is 'a guarantee-power of the culture of *Mitteleuropa*'; whatever that means. And Kurt Waldheim's Vienna recently hosted a symposium with the

161

electrifying title ' *Heimat Mitteleuropa*'. A backhanded tribute to the new actuality of the Central European idea came even from the central organ of the Polish United Workers' Party, *Trybuna Ludu*, which published a splenetic attack on what it called 'The Myth of "Central Europe"'.

There is a basic sense in which the term *Central Europe* (or *East Central Europe*) is obviously useful. If it merely reminds an American or British newspaper reader that East Berlin, Prague, and Budapest are not quite in the same position as Vladivostok—that Siberia does not begin at Checkpoint Charlie—then it serves a good purpose. So also, if it suggests to American or British students that the academic study of this region could be more than footnotes to Sovietology. But of course the voices from Prague and Budapest that initiated this discussion mean something far larger and deeper when they talk of Central Europe.

The publication in English[1] of the most important political essays of three outstanding writers, Václav Havel, György Konrád, and Adam Michnik, a Czech, a Hungarian, and a Pole, gives us a chance to examine the myth—and the reality. Of course it would be absurd to claim that any one writer is 'representative' of his nation, and anyway, Havel, Michnik and Konrád are different kinds of writers working in quite dissimilar conditions.

Havel comes closest to general recognition as something like an intellectual spokesman for independent Czech intellectuals,

---

[1] The editions referred to in this essay are: *The Power of the Powerless: Citizens Against the State in Central-Eastern Europe* by Václav Havel et al., introduction by Steven Lukes, edited by John Keane, (London: Hutchinson, 1985).
The Anatomy of Reticence by Václav Havel, Voices from Czechoslovakia No. 1, (Stockholm: Charta 77 Foundation, 1985).
Antipolitics: An Essay, by György Konrád, translated from the Hungarian by Richard E. Allen, (New York: Harcourt Brace Jovanovich, 1984).
Letters from Prison and other Essays by Adam Michnik, translated by Maya Latynski, foreword by Czesław Miłosz, introduction by Jonathan Schell, (Berkeley, California: University of California Press, 1985).
Takie czasy . . . Rzecz o kompromisie by Adam Michnik, (London, Aneks, 1985).
KOR: A History of the Worker's Defense Committee in Poland, 1976–1981, by Jan Józef Lipski, translated by Olga Amsterdamska and Gene M. Moore, (Berkeley, California: University of California Press, 1985).

although there is a great diversity of views even within Charter 77 (as we can see from the other Chartist essays collected under Havel's title *The Power of the Powerless*). His 'political' essays are rich, poetic philosophical meditations, searching for the deeper meaning of experience, 'digging out words with their roots' as Karl Kraus once put it, but rarely deigning to examine the political surface of things. (He nowhere so much as mentions the name of any of the present communist rulers of Czechoslovakia. Magnificent contempt!) He shows a great consistency, from his seminal essay 'The Power of the Powerless', written in the autumn of 1978, through his 1984 address on being awarded an honorary doctorate by the University of Toulouse, to his open letter to Western peace movements, published in 1985 as *The Anatomy of a Reticence*. You hear in his writing the silence of a country cottage or a prison cell—for his part in the Committee for the Defence of the Unjustly Prosecuted (VONS), he was himself unjustly prosecuted and imprisoned from 1979 to 1983—the quiet voice of a man who has had a long time for solitary reflection, a playwright catapulted by circumstances and the dictates of conscience into the role of 'dissident' but not at all by temperament a political activist. Yet his contempt for politics is also more generally characteristic of Czechoslovakia, where most people find it hard to believe that anything of importance will ever again change on the immobile, frozen surface of Husák's geriatric 'normalized' regime.

Michnik, by contrast, has seen the earth shake in Poland. Though a historian by training, he has spent most of his adult life actively engaged in political opposition. A central figure in the Committee for Social Self-Defence-KOR and then an advisor to Solidarity, he, unlike Havel or Konrád, writes with the knowledge that he will be read for immediate political advice. Activists of underground Solidarity, students involved in *samizdat* publishing, look to him (among others) for practical answers to the question 'What is to be done?' This gives a sharper political focus to his work, but also makes it more controversial.

Like Havel, he is a hero to many of his compatriots. Unlike Havel, his views are fiercely contested. The KOR tradition, of which he is perhaps the most articulate spokesman (and certainly the most lucid essayist), now vies for popularity in Poland with views that may be characterized, with varying degrees of inaccuracy, as Catholic positivist (in the very special Polish usage of that term), Catholic nationalist, liberal, libertarian, or even neo-conservative. Astonishingly, the greatest part of his work has been written in prison and smuggled out under the noses of General Jaruzelski's jailers. (Besides almost three hundred pages of political essays, he has also produced a 285-page book of literary essays.) His style is often polemical, full of rasping irony—the rasp of an iron file cutting at prison bars—but modulated by a fine sense of moral responsibility and a keen political intelligence. Like Havel, he also displays a great consistency in his political thought, from his seminal 1976 essay 'The New Evolutionism' to his 1985 'Letter from the Gdansk Prison' and his most recent essay '. . . On Compromise', which has so far appeared only in Polish.

Konrád is different again. He is writing not in and out of prison but in and out of Vienna or West Berlin. We hear in the background of his long excursive disquisitions not the slamming of prison doors but the clink of coffee cups in the Café Landtmann or the comradely hum of a peace-movement seminar. In his book *Antipolitics* (German subtitle: *Mitteleuropäische Meditationen)* and subsequent articles, Konrád, a distinguished novelist and sociologist, has developed what I might call a late *Jugendstil* literary style: colourful, profuse, expansive, and ornate. *Antipolitics* is a *Sammelsurium*, an *omnium gatherum* of ideas that are picked up one after the other, briefly toyed with, reformulated, then abandoned in favour of other, prettier, younger (but alas, contradictory) ideas, only to be taken up again, petted, and restated a few pages later. This makes Konrád's essayistic work both stimulating and infuriating. Contrary to a widespread impression in the West, one finds few people in Budapest who consider that Konrád is a 'representative' figure even in the limited way that Havel and Michnik are. On the other hand, they find it difficult to point to anyone else who has covered half as much intellectual ground, in a more 'representative' fashion.

So Havel, Michnik and Konrád are different writers, differently placed even in their own countries, neither fully 'representative' nor exact counterparts. Yet all three are particularly well attuned to the questions a Western reader is likely to raise, and concerned to answer them. And all three are equally committed to the dialogue between their countries. Havel's *The Power of the Powerless* was written specifically as the start of a projected dialogue between Charter 77 and KOR. In discussing the richness of Polish *samizdat*, Michnik singles out the work of 'the extremely popular Václav Havel', and both Havel and the Hungarian Miklós Haraszti have appeared alongside Michnik on the masthead of the Polish independent quarterly *Krytyka*. Konrád refers constantly to Czech and Polish experience, and in one striking passage he apostrophizes a Pole identified only as 'Adam'—but the 'Adam' is clearly Michnik. So if there really is some common Central European ground, we can reasonably expect to discover it in the political essays of these three authors. If we do not find it here, it probably does not exist.

In the work of Havel and Konrád there is an interesting semantic division of labour. Both authors use the terms *Eastern Europe* or *East European* when the context is neutral or negative; when they write *Central* or *East Central*, the statement is invariably positive, affirmative, or downright sentimental. In his *Antipolitics*, Konrád writes of 'a new Central European identity', 'the consciousness of Central Europe', a 'Central European strategy'. 'The demand for self-government,' he suggests, 'is the organizing focus of the new Central European ideology.' 'A certain distinctive Central European scepticism,' Havel comments in *The Anatomy of a Reticence*,

> is inescapably a part of the spiritual, cultural, and intellectual phenomenon that is Central Europe . . . That scepticism has little in common with, say, English scepticism. It is generally rather strange, a bit mysterious, a bit nostalgic, often tragic and even at times heroic.

Later in the same essay, he talks of 'a Central European mind, sceptical, sober, anti-utopian, understated'—in short, everything we think of as quintessentially English. Or Konrád again:

> It was East Central Europe's historical misfortune that it was unable to become independent after the collapse of the Eastern Tartar-Turkish hegemony and later the German-Austrian hegemony of the West, and that it once again came under Eastern hegemony, this time of the Soviet Russian type. *This is what prevents our area from exercising the Western option taken out a thousand years ago, even though that represents our profoundest historical inclination* [my italics].

In this last passage, history has indeed been recast as myth. And the mythopoeic tendency—the inclination to attribute to the Central European past what you hope will characterize the Central European future, the confusion of what should be with what was—is rather typical of the new Central Europeanism. We are to understand that what was *truly* Central European was always Western, rational, humanistic, democratic, sceptical and tolerant. The rest was East European, Russian or possibly German. Central Europe takes all the *Dichter und Denker,* Eastern Europe is left with the *Richter und Henker.*

The clearest and most extreme articulation of this tendency comes from Milan Kundera. Kundera's Central Europe is a mirror image of Solzhenitsyn's Russia. Solzhenitsyn says that communism is to Russia as a disease is to the man afflicted by it. Kundera says that communism is to Central Europe as the disease is to the man afflicted by it—*and the disease is Russia!* Kundera's Central European myth is in frontal collision with Solzhenitsyn's Russian myth. Kundera's absurd exclusion of Russia from Europe (not endorsed by Havel or Konrád) has been most effectively criticized by Joseph Brodsky. As Brodsky observes, 'The political system that put Mr Kundera out of commission is as much a product of Western rationalism as it is of Eastern emotional radicalism.' But can't we go one step further? Aren't there specifically *Central* European traditions that at least facilitated the establishment of communist regimes in Hungary and Czechoslovakia, and traditions that those regimes signally carry forward to this day?

A superbureaucratic statism and formalistic legalism taken to absurd (and sometimes already inhuman) extremes were, after all, also particularly characteristic of Central Europe before 1914. That is one reason why we find the most exact, profound and chilling anticipations of the totalitarian nightmare precisely in the works of the most distinctively *Central* European authors of the early twentieth century, in Kafka and Musil, Broch and Roth. And then, what was really more characteristic of historic Central Europe: cosmopolitan tolerance, or nationalism and racism? As François Bondy has tellingly observed (in a riposte to Kundera), if Kafka was a child of Central Europe, so too was Adolf Hitler. And then again, I find myself asking: *Since when* has the 'Central European mind' been 'sceptical, sober, anti-utopian, understated?' For a thousand years, as Konrád seems to suggest? In 1948, when, as Kundera vividly recalls in *The Book of Laughter and Forgetting,* the most Central European of intellectuals joined hands and danced in the streets to welcome the arrival of heaven on earth? Or is it only since 1968?

The myth of the pure Central European past is perhaps a good myth. Like Solzhenitsyn's Russian myth, it is an understandable exaggeration to challenge a prevailing orthodoxy. Like the contemporary West German myth of the 20 July, 1944, bomb plot against Hitler (the myth being that the conspirators were true liberal democrats, proleptic model citizens of the Federal Republic), its effects on a younger generation may be inspiring. So shouldn't we *let good myths lie?* I think not. And in other moments, or when challenged directly, Havel and Konrád, among others, also think not.

In the late 1970s, the Czechoslovak historian J. Mlynárik (writing under the pseudonym Danubius) started a fascinating and highly fruitful discussion in Prague when he argued that the expulsion of the Sudeten Germans by the non-communist Czechoslovak government in the immediate aftermath of the Second World War was itself an inhuman and 'totalitarian' act—a precedent and path-breaker for the communist totalitarianism to come. 'Let us not forget,' the Czech writer Jiří Gruša movingly reminded us at the unofficial cultural symposium in Budapest last year, 'that it was we [the writers] who glorified the modern state' and that 'our nationalist odes may be found in all the schoolbooks of Europe.' Havel goes out of his way to underline the lesson of his fellow intellectuals' 'post-war lapse into utopianism'. And Konrád declares bluntly: 'After all, we Central Europeans began the first two world wars.' So if at times they indulge the mythopoeic tendency, there is also, in this new discussion of Central Europe from Prague and Budapest, a developed sense of historical responsibility, an awareness of the deeper ambiguities of the historical reality; in short, an understanding that Central Europe is very, very far from being simply 'the part of the West now in the East.'

Besides these historical ambiguities there are, of course, the geographical ones. Like Europe itself, no one can quite agree where Central Europe begins or ends. Germans naturally locate the centre of Central Europe in Berlin; Austrians, in Vienna. Tomáš Masaryk defined it as 'a peculiar zone of small nations extending from the North Cape to Cape Matapan' and therefore including 'Laplanders, Swedes, Norwegians and Danes, Finns, Estonians, Letts, Lithuanians, Poles, Lusatians, Czechs and Slovaks, Magyars, Serbo-

Croats and Slovenes, Romanians, Bulgars, Albanians, Turks and Greeks'—but no Germans or Austrians! As with the whole of Europe, the most difficult frontier to locate is the Eastern one. The reader may wonder why I have thus far talked so much of Prague and Budapest but not of Warsaw; of Havel and Konrád but not of Michnik. The reason is simple. Michnik never talks of Central Europe. His essays are full of illuminating references to European history and to the current affairs of other 'East European' countries, but in the whole corpus I have found not a single reference to Central Europe. And in this he is quite typical: the concept hardly surfaces in all the acres of *samizdat* produced in Poland over the last few years.

In the Polish part of old Galicia there is still more than a touch of nostalgia for the elegantly chaotic laxities of Habsburg rule—what Musil called the ' *kakanische Zustände*'. (At the offices of the Catholic weekly *Tygodnik Powszechny* in Kraków a portrait of the emperor Franz Josef hangs next to a row of popes.) For Michnik, as for most of the democratic opposition, it is self-evident that the small states between Russia and Germany contributed to their own destruction by the nationalistic rivalries of the inter-war years, and therefore that, were they ever to become independent again, they should co-operate as closely as possible—if not actually confederate. (The London-based Polish government-in-exile and the New York-based Council of Liberation of Czechoslovakia recently reaffirmed the 1942 Sikorski-Beneš declaration of intent to form a confederation of the Polish and Czechoslovak states.) But emotionally, culturally, and even geopolitically, the view eastward is still at least equally important to most Poles: the view across those vast eastern territories that for centuries were part of historic Poland. It is a lost half-mythical Lithuania that Czesław Miłosz celebrates in his poems and prose. And when Pope John Paul II talks of Europe he looks, with the eyes of a visionary and an exile, not just beyond the artificial, synthetic, truncated Europe of the EEC to Prague, Budapest and his beloved Kraków, but far, far beyond historic Central Europe, way across the Pripet marshes to the historic heartlands of Eastern Europe, to the Ukraine, to White Russia, even to the onion domes of Zagorsk; and when he preaches his European vision in Polish, he rolls an almost Lithuanian 'Ł '.

To say that Poland is to Central Europe as Russia is to Europe would be, no doubt, somewhat facile. But perhaps I have already said enough to indicate, however sketchily, just a few of the awesome historical, geographic, and cultural complexities, the rival memories and resentments that surround you, like a crowd of squabbling ghosts, the moment you revive the term Central Europe—let alone *Mitteleuropa*. If we treat the new Central European idea as an assertion about a common Central European past in the centuries down to 1945, as Konrád and Kundera seem to suggest we should, then we shall at once be lost in a forest of historical complexity—an endlessly intriguing forest to be sure, a territory where peoples, cultures, languages are fantastically intertwined, where every place has several names and men change their citizenship as often as their shoes, an enchanted wood full of wizards and witches, but one that bears over its entrance the words: 'Abandon all hope, ye who enter here, of ever again seeing the wood for the trees.' Every attempt to distil some common 'essence' of Central European history is either absurdly reductionist or invincibly vague. In this forest we find, with Stendahl, that 'all the truth, and all the pleasure, lies in the details.'

Fortunately, the new Central European idea is not only an assertion about the past. It is also, perhaps mainly, an assertion about the present. Put very baldly, the suggestion is that independent intellectuals from this part of the world *today* find themselves sharing a distinctive set of attitudes, ideas, and values, a set of attitudes they have in common but that is also, to a large degree, peculiar to them: just how common and how peculiar, they realize when they encounter Western intellectuals in Paris, New York, or California. This distinctive set of attitudes has, it is suggested, a good deal to do with their specifically Central European history—for example, the experience of small nations subjected to large empires, the associated tradition of civic commitment from the 'intelligentsia', the habit of irony that comes from living in defeat—but above all it has to do with their own direct, common, and unique experience of living under Soviet-type systems since Yalta. They are the Europeans who, so to speak, know what it is really about; and we can learn from them—if only we are prepared to listen. Central Europe is not a region whose boundaries you can trace on the map—like, say, Central America. It is a kingdom of the spirit.

'Compared to the geopolitical reality of Eastern Europe and Western Europe,' Konrád writes, 'Central Europe exists today only as a cultural-political anti-hypothesis (*eine kulturpolitische Antihypothese*) ... To be a Central European is a *Weltanschauung* not a *Staatsangehörigkeit*.' It is 'a challenge to the ruling system of clichés.'[2] (It is in this sense that Czesław Miłosz, too, has declared himself to be a Central European.) The Central European idea not only jolts us out of our post-Yalta mind-set, dynamiting what Germans call the *Mauer im Kopf*—the Berlin Wall in our heads. It also challenges other notions, priorities and values widely accepted in the West. What is more, it has something to offer in their place.

2

Such are the large claims for the *new* Central Europe. How far are they borne out by essays of Havel, Michnik and Konrád. How much do these major independent voices from Prague, Budapest, and Warsaw really have in common? And where are their most important differences? How might they change the way we look at 'Eastern Europe'? And at ourselves?

On a close comparative reading, I believe we can find important common ground—although we have to dig for it. The main elements of the shared intellectual subsoil are, it seems to me, as follows. First, there are the 'antipolitics' of Konrád's title. Havel also says, 'I favour "antipolitical politics" ' (in his 1984 Toulouse lecture),[3] and although Michnik does not use this term any more than he does the term Central Europe, the thing certainly pervades his writing.

The antipolitician rejects what Konrád calls the Jacobin-Leninist tradition and what Havel (following the Czech philosopher Václav Bělohradský) calls 'politics as a rational technology of power.' In *The Power of the Powerless*, Havel delicately criticizes those in Charter 77 who overestimate the importance of direct political work in the traditional sense. This I take to be a reference particularly to those former senior communists in Charter 77 who still conceive their activity primarily as a matter of seeking *power in the state*—and if not

[2] Quotations in this paragraph are from his essay '*Mein Traum von Europa,*' in *Kursbuch* 81 (September 1985).

[3] Quotations in this essay are from the translation first published in the *Salisbury Review* (January 1985), reissued by the Charta 77 Foundation as No. 2 in their Voices from Czechoslovakia series, obtainable from the Charta 77 Foundation, Box 50041, S-10405 Stockholm, Sweden.

power in the state, then at least a little influence on it. Konrád declares grandly: 'No thinking person should want to drive others from positions of political power in order to occupy them for himself. I would not want to be minister in any government whatever.' Since he is unlikely ever to be asked to be minister in Budapest, this hypothetical sacrifice may not seem too difficult.

But in the case of Poland, the statement 'We do not seek power in the state' has very recently had a real, immediate significance. There were some people in Poland in 1981 who thought that Solidarity *should* go for power in the state. This Solidarity's national leaders consistently refused to do. Of course, their main reason was a pragmatic calculation about what Moscow would tolerate. But there was also a theoretical and ethical underpinning from the dictionary of 'antipolitics'. 'Taught by history,' Michnik writes in his 1985 'Letter from the Gdańsk Prison', 'we suspect that by using force to storm the existing Bastilles we shall unwittingly build new ones.' And in his latest essay, he repeats: 'Solidarity does not aspire to take power in the state.' In the Poland of 1986 this is once again a purely hypothetical statement. But the antipolitical hypothesis— characteristic of KOR—still has to compete with other, now widely articulated views, which urge the pursuit of politics (albeit only on paper) in the traditional categories of left and right.

Michnik and Havel regard the categories of left and right as supremely irrelevant. Talking in his Toulouse lecture about the well-intended but uncomprehending questions of Western intellectuals, Havel exclaims:

> Or the question about socialism and capitalism! I admit that it gives me a sense of emerging from the depths of the last century. It seems to me that these thoroughly ideological and many times mystified categories have long since been beside the point.

'The very division "Left-Right" emerged in another epoch,' Michnik echoes Havel in his latest essay, 'and it is impossible to make a meaningful reconstruction of it in present-day Poland (and probably also in other countries ruled by communists).' Is the Jaruzelski regime left or right? 'To the vast majority of Poles "Right" and "Left" are abstract divisions from another epoch.'

In place of the old division between left and right, they offer us the even older division between right and wrong. This, they insist, is the truly operative distinction for those living under such a regime. Moral categories figure largely in the writing of all three authors (though less in Konrád than in Havel and Michnik). All three reassert the fundamental premises of Judaeo-Christian individualism. Reversing the traditional priorities of socialism, they begin not with the state or society, but with the individual human being: his conscience, his 'subjectivity', his duty to live in truth, and his right to live in dignity. 'First change thyself' might stand as the common motto of their work. But, they all insist, the attempt to live in truth and dignity does not merely have profound implications for the individual; it can slowly make a substantial impact on the communist state. For, as Havel puts it, 'the main pillar of the system is living a lie.'

Havel illustrates this with the now celebrated example of the greengrocer who puts in his shop window, among the onions and carrots, the slogan 'Workers of the World, Unite!' 'Why does he do it?' Havel asks.

> What is he trying to communicate to the world? Is he genuinely enthusiastic about the idea of unity among the workers of the world? Is his enthusiasm so great that he feels an irresistible impulse to acquaint the public with his ideals?

Of course not. He is signalling to the authorities his willingness to conform and obey. That is the meaning of his sign. He is indifferent to its semantic content. But 'if the greengrocer had been instructed to display the slogan "I am afraid and therefore unquestioningly obedient", he would not be nearly as indifferent to its semantics, even though the statement would reflect the truth.'

The mendacious tissue of ideology partly conceals the true nature of the power in question; more importantly, it enables the individual citizen to conceal from himself the true nature of his submission to that power. It is this canvas of ideologically determined lies that, Havel argues, really holds the system together—and keeps society in thrall to the state. Each of these tiny acts of outward semantic conformity—each in itself so trivial as to seem nugatory—is like one of the minuscule threads with which the Lilliputians bound down Gulliver; except that here, men and women are binding themselves.

By rendering this seemingly meaningless tribute, or even by not protesting against it, people

> *live within a lie*. They need not accept the lie. It is enough for them to have accepted their life with it and in it. For by this very fact, individuals confirm the system, fulfill the system, make the system, *are* the system.

The 'line of conflict' does not run simply between victim-people and oppressor-state, as in the conventional image, or just between different social groups, as in a more traditional dictatorship. 'In the post-totalitarian system, this line runs *de facto* through each person, for everyone in his or her own way is both a victim and a supporter of the system.' Except, that is, for the few who have decided to 'live in truth'—and in the West are so misleadingly known as dissidents.

Even these few voices have had an impact out of all proportion to their numbers. And if more people try to live in truth, to live in dignity . . . Well, look at Poland in 1980, at what György Konrád calls, in discussing Solidarity, 'the peaceful power of the plain-spoken truth.' Certainly that is Michnik's interpretation—'the politics of truth,' he writes, was one of the two principal traits of the democratic opposition to be taken over by Solidarity. (The other was non-violence.) So all three authors express the conviction that moral changes can have a seemingly disproportionate political effect, that consciousness ultimately determines being, and that the key to the future lies not in the external, objective condition of states—political, military, economic, technological—but in the internal, subjective condition of individuals. This is where Central Europe confronts Eastern Europe: in the autonomous sphere of culture, in the kingdom of the spirit.

If not in state or Party power structures then where, if at all, are these individual men and women 'living in truth' to combine? In *civil society*. Both Michnik and Konrád use the term; Havel certainly has the idea. 'In Poland,' Michnik writes in his 1985 'Letter from the Gdańsk Prison,' 'the structures of independent civil society have been functioning for several years—a veritable miracle on the Vistula,' and he entitled his account of Solidarity's first year 'The Promise of a Civil Society'. 'The antipolitician,' says Konrád, 'wants to keep the scope of government policy (especially that of its military apparatus) under the control of civil society.' To a historian of ideas, these usages of a term with such a long and chequered history might seem unforgivably vague. Yet the reader in Prague, Budapest, or Warsaw will understand exactly what is meant. 'You know, for us the struggle for civil society is a great daily drama,' a Hungarian sociologist recently remarked to me. A sentence that might equally well have been spoken in Prague or Warsaw, but hardly in Paris or London. Indeed, one could write the history of East Central Europe over the last decade as the story of struggles for civil society.

As the Hungarian philosopher and social critic János Kis has observed, from the mid-fifties until the late sixties (the key dates being, of course, 1956 and 1968), the 'general idea of evolution in Eastern Europe was that of reforms generated from above and supported from below.' Meaningful change would be initiated from within a ruling Communist party that had been enlightened by its own so-called revisionists. Socialism would acquire a human face. This idea was crushed in 1968, under the Soviet tanks in Prague and the police batons in Warsaw, but another has since emerged, gaining wide currency in the late seventies. Broadly speaking, this second 'general idea of evolution' is that meaningful change will only come through people's organizing themselves *outside* the structures of the Party-state, in multifarious independent social groupings. The operative goal is not the reform of the Party-state but the *reconstitution of civil society*, although of course, if the strategy is at all successful, the Party-state will be compelled to adapt to the new circumstances, if only by grudgingly accepting an incremental *de facto* reduction in the areas of its total control.

This strategy of 'social self-organization' or 'social self-defence' was outlined by, among others, Adam Michnik in his seminal essay 'The New Evolutionism', and it is, of course, in Poland that it has been most extensively pursued. In 1977, a year after its foundation, the Worker's Defence Committee (Komitet Obrony Robotników— KOR) formally renamed itself the Committee for Social Self-Defence KOR as a signal of this broader goal. In his history of KOR, Jan Józef Lipski gives a comprehensively detailed and scrupulous account of the very diverse kinds of 'social work' in which this involved KOR members—from *samizdat* publishing and journalism to support for private farmers and the first Free Trade Union committees. How much the birth of Solidarity owed directly to KOR and how much to other causes is a matter for historical debate, but there is no doubt at all that Solidarity was the child of this 'general idea of evolution'.

The biggest child, but not the only one. Strikingly similar ideas were advanced in Prague, for example by Václav Benda in his 1978 essay 'The Parallel Polis', and the family likeness of Charter 77 to KOR is unmistakable. The 'general idea' is the same. In Hungary, the distinction between reforms initiated 'from above' by the Party-state and changes coming from below, from a society aspiring to be 'civil', is much less clear. But here, too, the idea of the 'struggle for civil society' is one widely endorsed by independent intellectuals. It is therefore no accident (as Soviet commentators always remark) that we find the leitmotif of civil society in the essays of Konrád and Havel as well as Michnik.

Another common leitmotif is non-violence. The reasons given for the renunciation of violence are both pragmatic and ethical. Practically, because it has been clear since 1956 that violent revolt has no chance of success in the present geopolitical order. Ethically, because violence—and particularly revolutionary violence—corrupts those who use it. So also does the mental violence of hatred. Violence and hatred, lies, slanders, beatings and murders—these are the methods of the Jacobin-Leninist power holders. 'Let these methods remain theirs alone,' Michnik told me when we talked in his Warsaw flat in the fall of 1984—a few days after the murder of Father Jerzy Popiełuszko by state-sponsored terrorists from the Polish security service. 'We are not fighting for power,' he went on, 'but for the democratic form of our country; any kind of terrorism necessarily leads to moral debasement, to spiritual deformation.' And in his latest essay he repeats the formula so often used by Popiełuszko and by the pope: 'Vanquish evil through good' (*zło dobrem zwyciężaj*).

This is not merely preaching. As Lipski records, Michnik personally helped to save several policemen from being lynched by an angry mob in the small town of Otwock in May 1981. (He won the crowd's confidence by declaring, 'My name is Adam Michnik. I am an anti-socialist force.') Altogether, Solidarity's record of non-violence will more than stand comparison with that of any peace movement in Western Europe—and under incomparably greater provocation. Neither the Czechs nor the Hungarians have recently had the opportunity (or necessity) of putting the preaching into practice on anything like the same scale. But the commitment in principle is as emphatic with Havel and Konrád as it is with Michnik.

As Lipski points out, this is an area where 'the influence of Christian ethics' is most apparent. But, looking sideways at the Western peace movements, Havel and Michnik simultaneously bring forward another ancient and fundamental principle of Christian ethics: the conviction of the *value of sacrifice*. ('Greater love hath no man than this . . .') Referring to what he calls 'pacifist movements', Michnik says, 'The ethics of Solidarity are based on an opposite premise: that there are causes worth suffering and dying for.' Havel repeats the almost identical formula of Jan Patočka: 'There are things worth suffering for.'

Indeed, it is in their response to the Western peace movements that we find the most developed common position: In his 'Anatomy of a Reticence', Havel calls it the 'common minimum' of 'independent East Central European thinking about peace.' They begin by expressing an instinctive, 'prerational' (Havel) sympathy with people who appear to put the common good before their selfish interests. But they also begin with a healthy suspicion—nourished by Central European experience—of the peace movement's tendency to utopianism and 'the various much too earnest overstatements (which, at the same time and not accidentally, are not bought at a high cost) with which some Western peace-fighters come to us.' (Havel's rather contorted sentence repays a careful second reading.) They insist, against much of the Western peace movement, that

> The cause of the danger of war is not weapons as such but political realities . . . No lasting, genuine peace can be achieved simply by opposing this or that weapons system, because such opposition deals only with consequences, not with reasons.

Thus Havel. And from his prison cell, Michnik sent an almost identical message: 'Western public opinion has allowed itself to have imposed on it the Soviet pattern of thinking—arms are more important than people. But this is not true. No weapon kills by itself.'

The main 'political realities' in question are the division of Europe and the continued Soviet domination over half of it. 'It is an unobservant European,' declares Konrád, 'who fails to notice that the Iron Curtain is made of explosive material. Western Europe rests its back against a wall of dynamite, while blithely gazing out over the

Atlantic.' 'What threatens peace in Europe,' Havel agrees, 'is not the prospect of change but the existing situation.' The key to a lasting peace lies not in disarmament or arms control as such but in changing these political realities. In the long term, this must mean overcoming the division of Europe (which we describe in shorthand as Yalta) and moving toward what Havel calls 'the ideal of a democratic Europe as a friendly community of free and independent nations.' Hard to dissent from that; still harder to imagine its achievement. In the short to medium term, however, this means above all understanding the symbiotic connection between 'external peace' (between states) and 'internal peace' (within states)—for

> a state that ignores the will and rights of its citizens can offer no guarantee that it will respect the will and the rights of other peoples, nations, and states. A state that refuses its citizens the right of public supervision of the exercise of power cannot be susceptible to international supervision. A state that denies its citizens their basic rights becomes dangerous for its neighbours as well: internal arbitrary rule will be reflected in arbitrary external relations.

Such are the states of Eastern Europe, whose citizens, unlike those of West European states, do *not* enjoy 'internal peace'. Therefore—and this is a message both to the peace movements and to the governments of the West—the key to a lasting, genuine peace between East and West in Europe (as opposed to the present state of 'non-war') must lie in working toward greater respect for human rights and civil liberties in Eastern Europe. The struggles for disarmament and human rights do not merely go hand in hand (as a minority—and still only a minority—in most Western peace movements maintain). The struggle for human rights has an absolute, logical priority. Michnik: 'The condition for reducing the danger of war is full respect for human rights.' Havel: 'Respect for human rights is the fundamental condition and the sole genuine guarantee of true peace.'

So on the one hand, these Central European minds ('sceptical, sober, anti-utopian, understated') come up with a warning about the true nature of Soviet-bloc states that could warm the cockles of President Reagan's heart. Indeed, in his latest essay Michnik quotes with approval some of Reagan's remarks about the difficulty of reaching arms-control agreements with the Soviet Union. On the other hand they talk about respect for human rights as the *fundamental* condition and the *sole genuine* guarantee of *true* peace— to which a Western peace activist might well reply: And who is being utopian now? The message that combines these two aspects might be rudely summarized thus: The best thing that West European peace activists can do for peace is to support the democratic opposition in Eastern Europe.

This concludes my rudimentary short list of what seem to be important *common* positions, approaches, or leitmotifs in the political essays of Konrád, Havel and Michnik. Beyond this, however, as we move back up toward the surface from the common Central European subsoil, we find differences and inconsistencies that are quite as striking as the underlying similarities and consistencies. The three authors differ greatly in their analysis of the prospects for change in their own countries, in the lessons they draw from the history of Solidarity, and in their prescriptions for immediate political (or antipolitical) action in East Central Europe.

3

How might change come about in Czechoslovakia? In his writings, Havel does not give a clear answer to this question. He suggests that very gradually, indirectly, in convoluted and largely unpredictable ways, the pressure of individuals living in truth and dignity and associating in loose structures of 'social self-organization'. the 'fifth column of social consciousness', *must* eventually change the way the country is governed: but how and when, he cannot foresee. When we talked recently at his country house in northern Bohemia, he gave a slightly more concrete illustration of what he means. After Chernobyl, he said, people in Czechoslovakia were complaining openly and loudly on the streets. True, they did not organize protest demonstrations or sign petitions (that was left to some Austrian students who came to Prague specially for the purpose). But ten years ago most people would not have dared even to complain so openly in public, though of course they would have done so in private. And so perhaps in another ten years they *will* sign petitions. The evolution is so gradual as to be invisible to a casual visitor or to an angry young man engaged in the opposition. But coming back into society after four years in prison, he could measure the difference, as between two still photos, and he was favourably surprised.

To be sure, no one can predict how the regime will respond to this pressure from below. In the book he has just completed, a volume of intellectual memoirs taking stock of his first half-century, Havel describes how, in his view, pressure from below was decisive in the prehistory of the Prague Spring. But is there anyone inside the Party now who will respond to this pressure as Party intellectuals and reformers did then? Then there were still genuine, convinced communists and socialists inside the Party. Now there seem to be only cynics and careerists—and the younger, the worse. The 'fifth column of social consciousness' is at work, slowly, oh so slowly, like tree roots gradually undermining a house (my metaphor, not Havel's). But no one can be confident of their impact. They can be cut. The house can be shored up. Fortunately, the roots' main purpose is not to undermine the house. 'Dissident' man is, so to speak, a thinking root. His attempt to live in truth and dignity has a value in itself, irrespective of any long-term social or political effects it may or may not have.

As political analysis and prescription this is, indeed, 'sceptical, sober, anti-utopian, understated'—and present conditions in Czechoslovakia would lead us to distrust any analysis that was not. There are, however, also moments when Havel lifts off into a visionary, almost apocalyptic mode. 'It is . . . becoming evident,' he writes in his Toulouse lecture,

> that a single seemingly powerless person who dares to cry
> out the word of truth and to stand behind it with all his
> person and all his life, has, surprisingly, greater power,
> though formally disfranchised, than do thousands of
> anonymous voters.

Here he is closely following Solzhenitsyn, whose example he cites in the next sentence. Between the lie and violence, Solzhenitsyn wrote in his 1970 Nobel speech ('One word of Truth . . .'), 'there is the most intimate, most natural, fundamental link: Violence can only be concealed by the lie, and the lie can only be maintained by violence.' And he goes on to prophesy: 'Once the lie has been dispersed, the nakedness of violence will be revealed in all its repulsiveness, and then violence, become decrepit, will come crashing down.' The first part of this prophecy was realized in Poland in December 1981. But, alas, even in Poland, the second part has yet to be confirmed.

In his *Antipolitics*, Konrád draws a simple lesson from the apparent defeat of Solidarity by lie-clad violence. The Hungarians tried it in 1956, the Czechs and Slovaks in 1968, the Poles in 1980-1981: 'three tries, three mistakes,' says Konrád. Lesson: 'The national road to Eastern European liberation has not carried us very far.'

> 'Be careful,' I said to Adam [i.e. Michnik]. 'The third time around it has to work.' It didn't. Adam is awaiting trial perhaps. 'It's incredible,' he said: incredible that he was able to give a lecture at the Warsaw Polytechnic University on 1956 in Poland and Hungary. The lecture was first-rate: he didn't stammer at all; he was sharp, dialectical, and got to the heart of the matter. Then they said he fell madly in love with a great actress. Then they said he was arrested and beaten half to death. Then they said he was all right. What does it all tell us, Adam? You are thirty-five million, but you couldn't pull it off; now what?
>
> What would you say if I told you: 'Now let the Russians do it'?

Well, I think I can make a pretty good guess what Adam Michnik would say to that: (expletive deleted). But perhaps he will now give us his own answer, since he was unexpectedly released from prison in August. The 'it' the Russians should 'do', incidentally, is go home. This certainly seems a good idea, though not perhaps an entirely original one. To reduce Konrád's *Antipolitics* to a coherent argument would be to do some violence to the text. The peculiar (and peculiarly Central European?) quality of this book is, as I have suggested, the coexistence in a relatively small space of a remarkable diversity of formulations and arguments, as rich and multifarious as the nations of the dual monarchy—and as difficult to reconcile. For example, 'The Russians must be afforded tranquillity so they can reform their economy and administrative system,' but on the other hand, 'it would be fitting if credit-worthiness were reduced in proportion to the number of political arrests.' Yet three main pillars of argument may perhaps be discerned behind the ornamental profusion of the late *Jugendstil* façade.

First, there is the proposition already indicated above: national routes to liberation have failed; let us therefore try the international, all-European one: let us propose that American troops should withdraw from Eastern Europe: let us dissolve the blocs! 'To me, personally, that seems just lovely,' Václav Havel nicely comments on this not entirely new proposal, 'though it is not quite clear to me who or what could induce the Soviet Union to dissolve the entire phalanx of its European satellites—especially since it is clear that, with its armies gone from their territory, it would sooner or later have to give up its political domination over them as well.' *Basta!*

For Konrád, the 'who or what' that could induce the Soviet Union is the 'international intellectual aristocracy'. This is his second leitmotif. 'It appears,' he writes, 'that the intelligentsia—not the working class—is the special bearer of internationalism.' 'Dissidents—autonomous intellectuals—are the same the world over, irrespective of their political philosophies.' Therefore we should get together and produce the intellectual framework for going beyond the 'intellectually sterile operations of ideological war.' Incidentally, 'anyone who believes that two systems and two ideologies are pitted against each other today has fallen victim to the secularized metaphysics of our civilization, which looks for a duel between God and Satan in what is, after all, only a game.' (What would Adam say to *that?*) Hence his own 'plan to take down the Iron Curtain', which the Intellectuals' International should now place on the agenda of world politics. For it was 'our intellectual failings' that ultimately 'brought about the baleful situation in which our continent is cut in two.' Think right, and we'll walk happily ever after.

However, just in case the dolts in the Kremlin and the Pentagon can't see the light that the 'international intellectual aristocracy' is holding under their noses, Konrád has an interim fall-back position. This is the Hungarian way. While he has moments of stern fundamentalism ('The Hungarian nation . . . will not rest until it has won self-determination here in the Carpathian basin'), for the most part he writes in almost glowing terms about the present condition of Hungary, and in particular about János Kádár, whom he compares to the emperor Franz Josef. 'The best we can hope to achieve,' he writes,

> is an enlightened, paternalistic authoritarianism, accompanied by a measured willingness to undertake gradual

181

liberal reforms. For us, the least of all evils is the liberal-conservative version of communism, of the sort we see around us in Hungary.

In these circumstances, the task of the 'creative' or 'scholarly' intelligentsia is to engage in dialogue with the 'executive' intelligentsia, to help make the enlightened dictatorship still more enlightened. 'The intellectual aristocracy,' he declares, 'is content to push the state administration in the direction of more intelligent, more responsible strategies.' And he muses: 'Is a moderate, authoritarian reform possible on an empire-wide scale—an enlightened Party monarchy, a "Hungarian" style of exercising power?'

Now, these may indeed be realistic assessments and propositions for an independent intellectual wishing to act effectively in the peculiar circumstances of contemporary Hungary. But they find no echo at all in the work of Havel and Michnik. For Havel in Czechoslovakia, such a role for independent intellectuals is inconceivable. Where he lives, the intellectual aristocracy are working as window cleaners, stokers, and labourers. And even if it were conceivable, his conception of antipolitics hardly makes it desirable. For Michnik in Poland, such a role for intellectuals is entirely conceivable—and entirely unacceptable. A Polish Kádárism is his jailers' dream, not his. General Jaruzelski would sing hallelujahs to the Black Madonna if Poland's creative and scholarly intelligentsia were to accept the role sketched by Konrád. But they won't.

And for Michnik, the fact that Poland does not enjoy a Kádárite dispensation is a measure of success—not failure. Certainly, he would never endorse Konrád's formula of 'three tries, three mistakes'. Solidarity, for him, was hardly a 'mistake'. The fact that Solidarity was defeated by force does not demonstrate that Solidarity's fundamental strategy was wrong; it demonstrates that people without guns (and with a conscious commitment to non-violence) can be driven off the streets by people with guns (and the will to use them). And anyway, this was not simply a defeat. The imposition of martial law on 13 December, 1981, was 'a setback for the independent society' but 'a disaster for the totalitarian state.'

The point now is to sustain a genuinely autonomous, strong,

well-organized civil society. For Michnik, as for Havel, the key ingredient, as it were the basic molecule, of this civil society is the individual living in truth. Moral absolutism is the only certain guide in such times—such is the lesson he draws in his book of literary essays from the example of those like Zbigniew Herbert who were never ever morally 'compromised', even in the darkest times. On the other hand, just because individuals—and particularly intellectuals—do not accept the roles assigned to them in a would-be Kádárite dispensation, just because there is a strong and wholly independent civil society, there is a chance of positive political compromise with the authorities.

Most of Michnik's latest essay, '. . . On Compromise', is then devoted to exploring, through a vigorous and detailed analysis of the history of KOR and Solidarity, the question of the possible nature of such a compromise. His answers, too, are not always convincing. For example, he says at one point that 'no one among the activists of Solidarity today believes in dialogue and compromise with the authors of the December coup. Nor do I.' But if not with them, then with whom? He cautions that 'Solidarity should reject the philosophy of "all or nothing,"' but a few pages later he suggests that the precondition for any agreement with the authorities must be the recognition of the existence of an 'independent self-governing Solidarity' and that such an agreement must avoid the last vestiges of Newspeak that were present (and controversial) in the agreements negotiated by the Solidarity leadership in 1980 and 1981.

If that is not 'all', it is pretty close to it. Throughout Michnik's book, there is a palpable tension between the moral and the political argument. To discuss these problems in detail would require another essay. All I wish to emphasize here is that Michnik is wrestling with questions that do not even arise for Havel or Konrád and, consequently, that his answers are not answers for them. But if György Konrád is occasionally inclined to suggest, as a true internationalist, that the 'Hungarian way' might after all be the best way forward for neighbouring nations, Adam Michnik is not entirely disinclined to suggest the reverse. Poles should feel national pride, he writes, for

> it's the Poles who have showed the world that *something like this* is possible. Sooner or later these deeds will be seen to

have set an example. When other nations begin to follow this example, the Soviet order will be faced with its most serious threat.

In short, as soon as we move up from the common subsoil to ask the political question 'What is to be done?' we find that even these three writers, most keenly interested in the Central European trialogue, most open to other traditions and ideas, offer answers that are widely disparate, and in part contradictory—and their differences largely mirror those of their national circumstances. To say, as Konrád is inclined to, that these are merely different national 'strategies' or paths toward the same goal is to put an attractive icing over the cracks, but hardly to bridge them.

4

Besides these deep differences, moreover, there are some major limitations and omissions that are common to all three authors. In their domestic analysis, perhaps the most striking gap is their neglect of the entire material side of life—their contempt of economics. One may well insist—against Marx—that consciousness ultimately determines being, that ideas are ultimately more important than material forces; this hardly justifies completely ignoring the latter. Without the refinement of KOR's ideas there would have been no Solidarity (or, at least, a very different one)—but the midwife at Solidarity's birth was a vulgar increase in the price of meat. Much the most widespread, indeed the one almost universal, form of independent social activity in Eastern Europe today is work—or 'operating'—in the 'second economy'. Black-marketeering is the antipolitics of the common man.

Konrád makes a gesture in this direction when he advocates 'an amalgam of the second economy and the second culture'. But how? Tomáš Masaryk pointed the way forward to Czech independence (from the Habsburg 'Central Europe') with a twin commandment: 'Don't lie, don't steal.' But the qualities required for any kind of success in the second economy under a state socialist system are the precise opposite of those prescribed for the intellectual antipolitician. Don't lie, don't steal? Anyone who engages in any kind of independent economic activity anywhere in Eastern Europe will not survive five minutes unless he—well, shall we say, tolerates some terminological inexactitude—and unless—well, countenances unorthodox methods of procurement.[4] (A priest in Poland once told me that when people confess to him—in the secrecy of the confessional—that they have had to, well, use unorthodox methods of procurement, he instructs them that they should not regard this as a sin. In this godless system, it is a necessity. And how else would new churches get built to the greater glory of God?)

Neither Konrád nor Havel addresses this issue at all. Theirs are programmes for intellectuals. Michnik seems to assume that the economic demands of Solidarity-as-trade-union will naturally go hand in hand with the moral and antipolitical demands that mainly concern him. This assumption requires a little closer examination.

In their international analysis, perhaps the most important common weakness is their approach to what is still the most important regional power in Central Europe: Germany. True, they all recognize in a very general way that overcoming (or reducing) the division of Europe requires overcoming (or reducing) the division of Germany. So they're all for it. True, Konrád avers that the intellectual aristocracy should concentrate its mind on the issue of a peace treaty with Germany. But this really is not the significant level of German thought or action today. None of them begins seriously to engage with the real West German policies—the *Deutschlandpolitik* and the *Ostpolitik*—that are such a pivotal factor in contemporary European politics. The architects and executors of these policies, for their part, largely ignore such voices from below in Eastern Europe and see their real partners among the apparently all-powerful, in the ruling Communist parties and in Moscow, not among the apparently powerless, in opposition and in prison.

It is perhaps worth recalling that the original East Central European usage of the term Central Europe was developed and articulated by Tomáš Masaryk during the First World War in programmatic opposition to the German usage of the term *Mitteleuropa*, by Friedrich Naumann and others, as a justification for

---

[4] This applies even to the legal private sector, as Anders Åslund shows in his invaluable book *Private Enterprise in Eastern Europe*, (London: Macmillan/St Antony's, 1985).

imperial Germany's expansionist plans. To compare present German policies and visions to those of 1915 would obviously be quite wrong, and invidious. But it would be neither invidious nor unrevealing to explore the differences between the concept of *Mitteleuropa* as used by West German Social Democrats like Peter Glotz (particularly in the context of their 'second *Ostpolitik*') and the concept of Central Europe as it emerges in the work of independent East Central European intellectuals.

Another line of general criticism would be this (and I exaggerate deliberately): Konrád, Havel and Michnik are merely the latest scions of a tradition that has been present in Central and Eastern Europe since the Enlightenment: the Westward-looking, cosmopolitan, secular-humanist and rationalist element, what Thomas Mann contemptuously called the *Zivilisationsliteraten* (before becoming one himself). True, the *Zivilisationsliteraten* are now saying different things from what they were saying half a century ago: indeed, in crucial respects they are saying the opposite. But one thing has not changed: They have always been a tiny minority. They were a tiny minority before the First World War, impotent against the nationalism that tore that Central Europe apart. They were a tiny minority before the Second World War, impotent against the imperialism which tore *that* Central Europe apart.

And today? Why, even today, in a region largely and terribly purged of its two greatest minorities—the Jews, of course, and, yes, the Germans—nationalism still has a stronger appeal than Konrád's internationalism, even to many independent intellectuals, let alone to the general public. What is the greatest single issue (apart from declining standards of living and growing inequalities) for public and intellectual opinion in Hungary today? Is it human and civil rights? Is it democracy or 'the struggle for civil society'? No. It is the plight of the Hungarian minorities in Transylvania and Slovakia. I raised the idea of Central Europe with a highly intelligent and sophisticated Hungarian friend. 'Ah, yes.' He sighed. 'There could once perhaps have been something like a Central Europe. And you know, we rather blame *you* for the fact that it does not exist.' He referred to the Treaty of Trianon.[5]

And then the deepest doubts of all. Isn't all the common ground that I have attempted to describe ultimately no more than a side product of shared powerlessness? Isn't the existence of an imagined Central Europe finally dependent on the existence of a real Eastern Europe? Isn't antipolitics in the end merely a result of the impossibility of politics? Since you cannot practice the art of the possible, you invent the art of the impossible. Western Europe's moralistic criticism of American foreign policy has been characterized as 'the arrogance of impotence': Doesn't that description apply *a fortiori* to the moralism of antipolitics? Antipolitics is a product of living in defeat. How much would survive victory?

If I raise all these doubts and questions, dwell on the differences among the three authors, their inconsistencies and common limitations, I do so not because I regard what they have to say as marginal pie-in-the-sky—a view very widely held among those who shape Western policies toward Eastern Europe—but, on the contrary, because I regard it as relevant and important. Though still vague and half-articulated, the notions of antipolitics and Central Europe are, it seems to me, central both to understanding what *could* happen in Eastern Europe over the next decade and, potentially, to shaping that development.

Of course, we cannot entirely ignore the possibility of some large-scale geopolitical rearrangement with Moscow's agreement: a new Yalta, say, a negotiated Finlandization of Eastern Europe. But that is, to say the least, highly improbable. Nor can we wholly exclude the possibility of far-reaching reforms being encouraged by the Gorbachev leadership and carried forward by a new generation of communist leaders in Eastern Europe—economic reforms, initially, but with political implications recognized and deliberately accepted by those leaders.

[5] It will be recalled that the 1920 Treaty of Trianon, part of the post-war peace settlement whose main architects were Woodrow Wilson, Clemenceau and Lloyd George, stripped Hungary of more than two-thirds of its pre-1914 territory, including the Slovakia, in what then became Czechoslovakia; Transylvania, which went to Romania; and Croatia, to what then become Yugoslavia.

What is definitely probable, however, is the continuation of a slow, messy, piecemeal process of differentiation in which the peoples of Eastern Europe will gradually, in quite diverse and convoluted ways, come in practice to enjoy more and larger areas of *de facto* pluralism and independence—cultural, social, economic—areas partly conceded in a planned and deliberate way by their rulers, but mainly wrested from them by *pressure from below:* not the progress of a 'reformed' and thus revitalized communism, but the regress of a decaying would-be totalitarianism. The Ottomanization rather than the Finlandization of the Soviet empire.

If there is any truth in this prognosis, then it is obviously important to determine what shape the pressure from below will take. Will it be violent or non-violent, individual or collective, organized or disorganized? Now in practice, of course, there is a different and continually changing mix of ingredients in each country: here it is largely the pressure of individual expectations, there it is channelled through the Church, there again, the primitive threat of violent revolt. The formulation of antipolitics, in the broadest sense, is an attempt both to characterize and to shape this pressure from below. It is half description, half prescription. Its territory is the space between the state and the individual, between the power and the powerless. Its focus is the middle distance—beyond the immediate selfish concerns of the family nest maker, but well short of the horizon of full national independence. To an imperial system whose main instruments of domination are lies, violence, the atomization of society, and 'divide and rule', the antipolitician responds with the imperatives of living in truth, non-violence, the struggle for civil society—and the idea of Central Europe.

But this new Central Europe is just that: an idea. It does not yet exist. Eastern Europe exists—that part of Europe militarily controlled by the Soviet Union. The new Central Europe has yet to be created. But it will not be created by mere repetition of the words Central Europe as the fasionable slogan from California to Budapest, nor by the cultivation of a new myth. If the term Central Europe is to acquire some positive substance, then the discussion will have to move forward from the declamatory, the sentimental, and the incantational to a dispassionate and rigorous examination both of the real legacy of historic Central Europe—which is as much one of divisions as of unities—and of the true conditions of present-day East Central Europe—as much one of differences as of similarities. Happily, this process has already begun, in Prague, where the founding of an underground journal called *Střední Evropa* ('Central Europe') has catalysed a sharp debate between Catholic and Protestant intellectuals about the legacy of the Habsburg empire and the First Republic. But it still has a very long way to go.

If we look to the future, one crucial Central European issue, besides the articulation and enrichment of the domestic strategies of antipolitics, is surely that of minority rights. Can Central Europe be put together again, albeit only on paper, at the very point where it has most often, most horribly, and (from the point of view of the neighbouring empires) most successfully been divided—at the point where different nations, races, cultures, religions try (or fail) to coexist? Even today the most open, tolerant, and democratic intellectuals in Czechoslovakia and Hungary cannot agree a common statement on the position and treatment of the Hungarian minority in Slovakia. An interesting discussion has begun in the Polish underground press about attitudes to Germany and the German minority in Poland. At the moment the main focus of discussion is the question: Does the German minority exist? (Cardinal Glemp agrees with General Jaruzelski that it does not.) But perhaps the more important question is: Would it be a good thing if a German minority did exist? And what about a Jewish minority? And a Ukrainian minority? And *why not* a Hungarian minority in Slovakia? Provided, always provided, that each minority would enjoy those rights that we regard it as our Central European task to define.

Many of the obstacles to such a Central European dialogue are historical, emotional and intellectual. But others are simply practical. For this is a debate that the communist authorities have done everything in their power to discourage—or to channel in a chauvinistic direction. And a great deal is in their power. When we talk about the division of Europe or the Iron Curtain, we automatically think of the East-West divide, and usually of the Berlin Wall. But perhaps the most impenetrable frontiers in Europe are not those between East and West, and not even (thanks to a decade and a half of *Deutschlandpolitik*) the German-German frontier. For freedom of movement, and hence for genuine cultural exchange, perhaps the most impenetrable frontier in Europe today is that between Poland

and Czechoslovakia. That really is an iron curtain. Leading Polish, Czech, and Hungarian intellectuals meet more often in Paris or New York than they do in Warsaw or Prague. They read one another, if at all, in English, French, or German: with very few exceptions, their work is not translated into one another's languages. It is easier for the author of this essay to meet them than it is for them to meet one another. If they do have common ground, then by and large this has been arrived at independently. In the circumstances, we may be favourably surprised how much of it there is.

This common ground has a great potential importance for the part of Europe in which they live: Eastern Europe *in acta*, Central Europe *in potentia*. But does it have any broader relevance for intellectuals in the West? This, too, is part of the larger claim for the new Central Europe. In a negative sense, as a guide to the nature of totalitarian power and a source of ideological inoculation, it undoubtedly does. For example, no one who has honestly read and digested what Michnik and Havel have to say can continue to believe that there is any real structural symmetry or moral equivalence between American domination over Western Europe and Soviet domination over Eastern Europe. (I fear that danger remains for the casual reader of Konrád.) In this respect, they have undoubtedly had a beneficial impact on parts of the West European peace movement. But most of the *positive* ideas they advance are not strikingly new (though none the worse for being old), and where they are new, they are not obviously relevant to our Western circumstances. Attempts to interpret the activity of Western peace movements as part of the struggle for civil society, for example, are not very convincing; and most of us still think we know what we mean—in Britain or America—by the categories of left and right.

And yet I do believe they have a treasure to offer us all. At their best, they give a personal example such as you will not find in many a long year in London, Washington, or Paris: an example, not of brilliance or wit or originality, but of intellectual responsibility, integrity and courage. They know, and they remind us—vividly, urgently—that ideas matter, words matter, have consequences, are not to be used lightly—Michnik quotes Lampedusa: 'You cannot *shout* the most important words.' Under the black light of totalitarian power, most ideas—and words—become deformed, appear grotesque, or simply crumble. Only a very few stand the test, remain rocklike under any pressure; and most of these are not new. There are things worth suffering for. There are moral absolutes. Not everything is open to discussion.

'A life with defeat is destructive,' writes Michnik, 'but it also produces great cultural values that heal . . . To know how to live with defeat is to know how to stand up to fate, how to express a vote of no confidence in those powers that pretend to be fate.'[6] These qualities and values have emerged from their specific Central European experience—which is the central European experience of our time. But since we can read what they write, perhaps it may even be possible to learn a little from that experience without having to go through it.

The Russian poet Natalya Gorbanyevskaya once said to me: 'You know, George Orwell was an East European.' Perhaps we would now say that Orwell was a Central European. If this is what we mean by Central Europe, I would apply for citizenship.

(OCTOBER 1986)

---

[6]This quotation is from his introduction to a German edition of his essays reprinted in the Winter 1986 issue of the *East European Reporter*.

Pre-spring

Several Central European languages have a special word for the season just before spring: Vorfrühling *in German,* Przedwiośnie *in Polish,* Předjaří *in Czech. The pre-spring. Looking back from the spring of 1989, it now seems that the events of spring 1988, in Poland and Hungary, but perhaps even in Czechoslovakia, were something like a political pre-spring. Here, therefore, are three sketches from a pre-spring.*

Prague: the Yeoman and the Cardinal

It is twenty years since the Prague Spring. But no one has forgotten. Explicitly or implicitly, 1968 remains the central point of all political discussion in Czechoslovakia, as much for the ruling Communist party as for the democratic opposition symbolized by Charter 77; for disillusioned old communists but also for men and women who were not even born when the Soviet tanks crawled into Wenceslaus Square that August. Beyond the towering mountain range of 1968, Czechs and Slovaks look back to 1948, when the Communists took power in the February coup, to 1938, when democratic Czechoslovakia was betrayed by Britain and France at Munich, and to 1918, when the first republic of the Czechs and the Slovaks was conjured out of the ashes of the Austro-Hungarian Empire by Tomáš Garrigue Masaryk. Things happen for Czechoslovakia in years ending with eight. And in 1988? . . .

The major document of April 1968 was the 'Action Programme' of the Communist party of Czechoslovakia, adopted at the plenary session of the central committee and defining its task as 'to give a new shape to socialist development drawing on creative Marxist thinking and the knowledge of the international working-class movement, but relying on a correct understanding of the conditions of socialist evolution in Czechoslovakia,' etc., etc. The major document of this spring is a petition for freedom of the (Catholic) Church. Its thirty-one demands include the separation of Church and state, an end to the state veto on the appointment of new bishops, and greater freedom for religious publications. It has been signed, at the last count, by some 440,000 people, and not only Catholics—a staggering manifestation in a state where every form of public dissent has been so rigorously suppressed for almost twenty years. The contrast between the origins, the demands, and the very language of the two programmes is eloquent of the distance Czechoslovakia has travelled between that spring and this.

Although, as Václav Havel always stresses, the origins of the Prague Spring are also to be found in pressure 'from below', from non-communist intellectuals and society at large, the fact remains that it was led 'from above', and carried forward by intellectuals and journalists who were mostly still communists or, at the very least, socialists. Its enduring symbol is not a worker or a priest but the Party leader, Alexander Dubček. Its slogan: 'socialism with a human face'. This petition, by contrast, could hardly be less socialist or more 'from below'. It is the handiwork, not of any Party members or of some Prague intellectuals or of the Church hierarchy, but of one devout Moravian peasant, Mr Augustin Navrátil.

I went to visit Mr Navrátil in his remote Moravian village of Lutopecny, near Kroměříž. A portly, rubicund lady in shabby working clothes was sweeping the path as I arrived at the modest red-brick house. 'He's on the allotment,' said Mrs Navrátil, mounting her bicycle to fetch him. While I waited, I admired the cows, hens, and rusting farm machinery in the yard at the back of the house, the large devotional pictures in the roughly furnished living room, and the books: Christian texts, of course, but also the legal code of the Czechoslovak Socialist Republic, *Teach Yourself French*, and Mark Twain in translation. And here he was in person: a thick set figure in gardening clothes, with an intense, straight gaze and a mighty handshake. There have been Navrátils living in this part of Moravia for more than three hundred years, he told me. One of his great-grandfathers had been a judge. Yeomen rather than peasants, then, in English terms. His education had begun under the wartime German 'Protectorate': an education in German (most of which he had forgotten) but also in good and evil (which he had not). The

Communists took away his family land. For his living, he works at a local railway station. As a Catholic, he first became active in protest against the removal by local authorities of one of the countless crosses and crucifixes that still adorn the fields of rural Moravia.

Without more ado, he plunged into a detailed recitation of his last ten years' activities, while his wife plied me with homemade sausage. His first petition, he told me, was made in 1976 and had seventeen points; his second petition, in 1984-85, had twenty points; the latest, launched at the end of last year, has thirty-one. I should note particularly the number of points. The first, which was a local affair, organized with a friend, collected some 700 signatures before he was incarcerated in a psychiatric hospital. The next time, he sent the petition first to the ministry of the interior, and all other conceivable ministries, with a covering letter asking: Is it legal to circulate this? He did the same with several open letters about issues of religious freedom and persecution. None of the bureaucrats, he says, dared give him a straight answer: They referred him from one office to the next and then back to the first. Only the secret police declared themselves '*kompetentní*'. They had him interrogated, detained, and then put into the psychiatric ward of a prison hospital, where he was nightly threatened by other inmates: 'We'll kill you before morning.' When his case finally came to trial, the judge cited the diagnosis: 'paranoia querulans'. His remaining at liberty would, it was claimed, be a danger to society. After almost a year in detention, he was released—only to be beaten up by 'unknown assailants' at his railway station.

At this point Mr Navrátil broke off to tell me how much letters from abroad had helped him in captivity. They had put pressure on the authorities and they had kept his spirit up. He had received letters from Holland, Germany, England, Scotland—yes, particularly from Scotland. And he would like to ask me, if I could, to express his heartfelt thanks to all those who had written—and particularly to those in Scotland—and to tell them how much it had helped. The global emphasis on Scotland might have seemed, in other circumstances, a trifle comical; but he gave his message so warmly and sincerely, and with such a moistening in his eyes, that I'm not sure my own eyes were entirely dry.

Then, in a sudden change of mood, he leaped up and produced his duplicator: a home-carpentered affair, the size of a large book, with a silk screen, black ink and roller. 'You see, I'm *permitted* to process this,' he said, and produced a certified notarial copy of a letter from the ministry of culture (I have it before me as I write) solemnly affirming that 'the citizen does not require a permit . . . to employ duplicating equipment for his own use.' I could not detect even the faintest Schweikian glint in his eye as he went on to explain how he distributed these duplicated texts to all and sundry. And here they are: open letters, petitions, open letters in connection with the petitions, letters from the prosecutor, an annotated list of the vacant dioceses, on pink paper, on blue paper, on tissue paper—anything he thinks of interest is hand-typed by his wife and then hand-duplicated by him, on his wonderful Heath Robinson machine. And here, at last, is the latest petition, on coarse, yellowy paper, with a copy of the open letter of 4 January, 1988 from František Cardinal Tomášek, archbishop of Prague, urging the faithful to support the petition, assuring them that to sign and circulate it is not illegal, and concluding 'I recall most emphatically that cowardice and fear are unworthy of a true Christian.'

Augustin Navrátil had earlier made personal contact with the cardinal, himself from Moravia and a man who seems to stand more upright and speak more firmly with every passing year. Mr Navrátil tells me that he personally discussed the text of this petition—should we call it the Thirty-One Articles?—with the cardinal. He now goes up to visit him in Prague about once a fortnight, he says. The cardinal's public endorsement was of course crucial to the extraordinary success of the petition, which since January has been displayed and signed in churches. Yet the Cardinal was as surprised as anyone by the scale of the response.

As I prepared to leave, Mr Navrátil thanks me ceremoniously for my visit and tells me that I am the first foreigner ever to have visited his house. He also introduces me to the cows, who are charming. His is, I think, a wonderful story: the tale of the yeoman and the cardinal. He has developed to a high degree that art, common to many oppositionists in Eastern Europe but perhaps most characteristic for the Czech lands, of embarrassing the authorities by taking them strictly at their word. He also has that quality of divine stubbornness that one finds in the lives of much better known resisters to communist oppression: in Poland's Cardinal Wyszyński, in Grigorenko or Bukovsky.

Where it will lead is, of course, another question. The 'new' Party leadership of Miloš Jakeš is clearly in the business of assuring that no spontaneous 'Spring' does bloom in this anniversary year. At a plenary session of the central committee twenty years almost to the day after that which launched the 'Action Programme', Mr Jakeš squealed against 'anti-communist forces' aided by 'certain Western mass media' causing trouble 'behind the mask of religious motives.' At the end of March, a wholly peaceful candle-lit demonstration for religious freedom in Bratislava was brutally broken up by riot police. But the authorities' touch is uncertain. At the same time as the water-cannon are turned on the Catholics, what one might almost call the 'old' opposition, grouped in the rainbow coalition of Charter 77, is more active than ever. This January, some of them launched a new monthly called *Lidové Noviny* (roughly, 'People's News'), specifically designed to appeal to a more general public, with short news articles, photos, cartoons, and even a monthly song. Most articles are signed, and the editors give their full names—yet they are all at liberty. Each issue carries a calendar of the month's events in 1968. The January number has on its masthead a cartoon of a sad-looking 1988 baby with a large gob-stopper in his mouth and a huge ball and chain attached to his ankle. The ball is marked '1968'.

Ay, and there's the rub . . . One may enjoy the spectacle of the Czechoslovak Party leadership being unsettled by Moscow, of all places. Most specialists agree that a Soviet reassessment of the Prague Spring was only stopped on the insistence of the Prague leadership. A Soviet journal recently published a relatively friendly account of a meeting with Václav Havel. *Repentance*, the Soviet cinematic allegory on Stalinism, has been showing in Prague cinemas to an electrified response. None the less, the fact remains that the overall political conditions for a peaceful, evolutionary change, with state and society in some sort of controlled dynamic interplay, are almost as unfavourable in 1988 as they seemed favourable in 1968. For a start, there is the present leadership. 'When will *perestroika* have succeeded?' asks the Prague joke. 'When Bil'ak's widow visits Štrougal in prison to tell him how Jakeš had been shot at Husák's funeral.' But even if the old gang is replaced—after 1988—by newer, more flexible, and realistic men, the possibilities of constructive compromise (or *modus vivendi*) between authorities and society still seem small.

Unlike in 1968, this society will not now lightly trust its communist rulers. Yet the whole divided history of the Czech and Slovak lands, and the memory of their common defeats ('38,'48,'68), still make it difficult to imagine how this society can really agree and effectively pursue its own common 'action programme', as opposed to supporting one formulated by the Party 'from above'. This petition for the freedom of the (Catholic) Church is an inspiring thing. But just look for the moment at the state of that Church. Only three out of its thirteen dioceses have bishops: two of those, in Slovakia, are old and compromised, the third—Cardinal Tomášek—is a leader, and increasingly outspoken, but he is eighty-nine years old. Priests are paid by the state, closely supervised by a local Party secretary for religious affairs, and dependent on him for the annual renewal of their state licence to preach. (There is, however, a thriving catacomb church of banned priests.) The religious orders were brutally dissolved in the 1950s. The Church has virtually no property of its own. There are no seminaries worth the name. It is infinitely worse off than the churches (both Protestant and Catholic) in East Germany, let alone in Poland. Far from intervening, like them, for the universal human rights of the whole society, this Church is struggling to defend its own.

Then there is the division between Protestants and Catholics, which has in Czechoslovakia an almost Irish politico-historical accretion: Catholicism, associated with Habsburg Counter-Reformation and empire, but also with post-1948 resistance; Protestantism, with Masaryk and independence, but also with post-1948 collaboration and so forth. Within Charter 77 there are still deep divisions between Catholics and Protestants, old communists, democratic socialists, and liberal-conservatives in search of a past. Agreement on anything beyond a basic human-rights strategy is hard to achieve. In the country at large, Czechs are still Czechs and Slovaks remain Slovaks. Economic stagnation, slowly sinking standards of health and welfare provisions, and worsening pollution are cumulative irritants for a wider public. People obviously find it absurd, embarrassing and distressing that Czechoslovakia, once an advanced European industrial democracy, is slowly sinking away from most of Europe while its ridiculous rulers gabble the kind of prefabricated nonsense that even the Kremlin has abandoned. But where is the common focus for these diverse discontents? And where the strategy for change?

Whether for good or ill, we cannot know the future—as Raymond Aron once unshallowly remarked. Particularly in Central Europe, change is likely to come from the corner where we least expect it. We spend our time looking at the names from the headlines, **at** the powerful and the famous. We think they make history. But meanwhile, behind our backs, there is this irrepressible old yeoman toiling up in the slow train from Kroměříž, with his home-duplicated Thirty-One Articles in his battered leather bag—and *he* makes history.

(APRIL 1988)

Gdańsk: Inside the Lenin Shipyard

' *Cicho!* Quiet!' shouts a tired and earnest-looking worker. 'The boss wants to sleep!' And sure enough, here is Lech Wałęsa lying flat on the floor, his unmistakable moustaches framed by an improvised pillow and his feet up on a chair. Negotiations are at a critical stage. Riot police surround the shipyard. All Poland watches. But within five minutes Lech is sound asleep. His steward carefully, almost tenderly, draws the curtain to protect 'the boss' from the bright afternoon sun. Around the wooden tables of the strike-committee room, beneath the crucifix, workers and their intellectual advisors sit drafting texts, listening to the latest news from Radio Free Europe on a short-wave transistor radio, and chewing dry bread. Others sleep under the tables, exhausted and oblivious.

Look at the main blue-grey gate, festooned with flowers, flags and images of the pope and the Black Madonna; look at the young workers perched atop it, stripped to the waist but never shedding their red-and-white armbands; half-close your eyes and you might just imagine that you were back in August 1980, with Solidarity about to be born. Not just Wałęsa, but many of the faces around him are familiar. Here is the melancholy-humorous face of Tadeusz Mazowiecki, the Catholic editor he asked to advise him in August 1980 and who has been doing so ever since. There are the four-square features of Andrzej Celiński, a sociologist advising then as now.

Yet everything is changed, changed utterly. Then, a vast cheerful crowd of wives and well-wishers milled around before the gates, passing in food and donations through the bars. In their midst stood

a crude wooden cross, with pinned to it some lines from Byron's
'Giaour' in the translation by Adam Mickiewicz:

> For Freedom's battle once begun,
> Bequeath'd by bleeding sire to son,
> Though baffled oft is ever won . . .

But whoever wrote this dedication had omitted the word *bleeding*.
Now, in place of the wooden cross there are the soaring metal crosses
of the Solidarity monument; but around it there is an eerie
emptiness, with only the riot police and their blue marias visible
some hundred yards away. Then, the gate constantly opened to
admit strike-committee delegates from all over Poland, as well as
Western journalists, ample food and sundry visitors. Now, Western
journalists have to evade the police cordon and scramble in through
obscure back corners of the vast yard. Scant food and messages are
smuggled in by the same precarious routes.

On the eighth day of the 1980 strike there were many thousands of
workers occupying the yard, not to mention the hundreds of
delegates from other striking factories across the land. A deputy
prime minister was soon to open direct and public negotiations with
the 'Inter-Factory Strike Committee'. On the eighth day of this strike
the number of workers inside the yard has dwindled from thousands
to hundreds. No Inter-Factory Strike Committee. No deputy prime
minister. No direct or public negotiations.

Some of these strikers were here in August 1980. But most of those
that now remain are very young, in their late teens or early twenties.
Their formative experience was martial law rather than 'August' or
the five hundred days of above-ground Solidarity. They interrupt
Wałęsa's speeches with the hard, rhythmic chants characteristic of
the post-martial-law period: ' *Sol-i-darność! Sol-i-darność!*'; '*nie ma
wolności bez Solidarności*' ('there's no freedom without Solidarity').
He can barely restrain them. Unsurprisingly, some Polish official
sources hint that Wałęsa planned this strike. So far as one can
determine, this is the opposite of the truth. He certainly did not start
it, and he almost certainly did not want it. These workers started the
strike themselves. If the Nowa Huta steelworkers came out, they say,
how could they—in the birthplace of Solidarity—do less?

They hung five demands from the gate: a 15 to 20,000 złoty pay
rise to compensate for the price rises; restoration of the independent

self-governing trade union 'Solidarity' in the shipyard; the release of all political prisoners; the re-employment of all those sacked for political reasons; and no reprisals against the strikers. In conversation, they mention some of the underlying material and social grievances that were already there in 1980 and, indeed, are chronic. 'I've waited fourteen years for a flat,' says a blond, moustachioed welder. 'When I go to the accommodation department [flats are allotted through the shipyard], they say: "Do you belong to the (official) trade unions? Do you belong to any (official) organization? No? Well that's too bad." ' The injustice hurts as much as the material deprivation. His mate says simply: 'Forty years of socialism and there's still no toilet paper!'

Many Western governments and observers agree with the Polish government (and the IMF) that the wage demands are unrealistic and irresponsible. Indeed, real wage cuts are a necessary (though by no means a sufficient) condition for economic recovery or reform. But Solidarity leaders and advisors see this, too. Even the strikers partly see it. When Wałęsa asked them whether they would abandon the wage demand if they got a genuinely independent trade union in the works, they shouted back, 'Yes.' (What that union would then do is another question). For those that remained on Monday there was essentially only one demand: the restoration of Solidarity in the shipyard where it was born. But the irony is this: inflationary pay rises are precisely what the authorities are prepared to concede. For several years now, wages have leap-frogged ahead of prices, as frightened managers bought off potential discontent. This happened against last month with striking transport workers in Bydgoszcz. It has happened in the neighbouring yards, with large pay rises granted to preempt solidarity strikes. It has happened here, where management has agreed to a 15,500 złoty rise. The one thing the authorities refuse is the one thing that strikers really want: the restoration of Solidarity.

Sitting in the sunshine near the gate, an older striker, a technician, points up the contrast with 1980. Today, he says, the *external* conditions are better but the *internal* conditions are worse. In 1980 there was a real fear of Soviet invasion. With Gorbachev, that has disappeared. 'The problem of the Eastern border', as he rather quaintly puts it, is no longer there. What is more, he notes with pleasure the reaction of the American, British, and West German governments. This helps. On the other hand, there was in 1980 a real hope of a genuine agreement with the authorities. He mentions the goodwill of the then Gdańsk Party secretary, Tadeusz Fiszbach. There was hope of an historic compromise. But today . . .

Today the authorities wage what Wałęsa calls psychological war. There is the police siege. There was the news from Nowa Huta, where the strike was broken up with gratuitous violence, not just by police but by a special anti-terrorist brigade. And then, every few hours, the management radio broadcasts a communiqué from the managing director. It explains that in the light of these developments, the national bank has said it cannot extend any more credit and the finance ministry has said it cannot give any more subsidies, and therefore he has asked the industry minister for a decision on the future of the yard. In short, a threat of permanent closure. But there have also been fraught and tortuous negotiations: between the Church-appointed mediators (Tadeusz Mazowiecki and the lawyer Władysław Siła-Nowicki) and the management inside the shipyards; between the bishop of Gdańsk and the head of the Gdańsk police; and, at the highest level, between the Church and the authorities in Warsaw. But no one can square that circle: strikers who want Solidarity, authorities who will talk about everything except Solidarity.

And Wałęsa? Wałęsa insists that he is not the leader of the strike. Formally speaking, he is not even on the strike committee. 'I'm an advisor to both sides,' he jokes. But of course he's 'the boss', in fact. When I first described the August 1980 strike, I saw a 'funny little man with a droopy moustache and ill-fitting trousers' (see the *Spectator*, 30 August, 1980). Today, Wałęsa is a portly figure, with neatly trimmed hair and moustache, a rather smart sports jacket (though still with the Black Madonna and Solidarity badge on the lapel), well-fitting pin-striped trousers and, somewhat incongruously, leather house slippers. He chews vitamin C tablets and has a doctor in attendance, a charming elderly lady professor in a white coat. He is calm and authoritative, summoning advisors like a king. In 1980 he was surrounded by an excited crowd of blue-overalled workers wherever he went—he was one of them. Today, the young strikers treat him almost with awe—he is twice their age, and a world celebrity. But he has not lost the gift of the gab. On Monday afternoon he lifts their spirits and stiffens their morale with a characteristic quick-fire speech. 'There aren't so few of us,' he says. 'It's enough . . .'

It looks like intransigence. But it isn't, for Wałęsa is a natural politician of something close to genius and he knows exactly what he's doing. He knows perfectly well that he can't get Solidarity back with three hundred lads and a prayer. But as the national leader and worldwide symbol of Solidarity, he cannot be seen to settle for less. So he encourages the negotiations—'Panie Tadeuszu,' he exclaims to Mazowiecki, 'you're the man for negotiations, you're for wisdom'— at least partly playing for time to see whether, after all, against all the odds, other big factories will come out again in solidarity as they did in 1980. Meanwhile, he'll keep ahead of the crowd so that he can be sure to lead them out the only possible way: that is, in a dignified voluntary withdrawal, without agreement. Just for a moment on Monday afternoon it looks as if the miracle might happen: 'Ursus is out', someone shouts, and indeed that is the news they hear from Radio Free Europe. But it is at best only half-true, and by evening Wałęsa and his advisors can see—as they expected—that history does not repeat itself. So on Tuesday they march out, arm in arm, Father Jankowski to Wałęsa's right hand, Tadeusz Mazowiecki to his left, and off to St Bridget's Church for a thanksgiving mass. In front of them someone carries the wooden cross that has stood just inside the yard gates. It bears the words *'God, Honour, Country'*, and under- neath: '1970, 1980, 1988, . . .'

(MAY 1988)

Budapest: Death to Nero!

Crouched uncomfortably beneath the massive horse of Árpád, the legendary ninth-century Magyar chieftain, in his triumphal nineteenth-century cast-iron reincarnation, I look out across the vast crowd filling Heroes' Square. Amid the upturned faces, banners proclaim: 'Down with the Ceauşescu dictatorship' and 'Ceauşwitz Endlösung.' Small placards bear the names of Transylvanian villages that the Romanian dictator proposes to raze to the ground in his mad programme of 'systemization'. At seven in the evening a recording of church bells sounds across the dusky square. We are told the bells are ringing across the frontier in the persecuted Hungarian settlements of Transylvania. 'Forty-four years after the war there is once again a dictator in Europe who wants to murder hundreds of thousands of people,' declaims a speaker. 'Death to Nero!' chants the crowd. This is the first authentically Hungarian demonstration 'for decades,' they are told a little later. 'Hungarian! Hungarian!' they chant back. In the distance I spy a banner that says, in English, 'Where are the Great Powers *Now?*'

An Englishman cannot go for long in Hungary without being reminded that it was the Western powers that dismembered Hungary after the First World War, giving Transylvania to Romania and other parts to Czechoslovakia and Yugoslavia. Territorially, things changed little after 1945. The Hungarians in Romania remain the largest national minority in Europe west of the Soviet border. They probably number some two million today. Resentment and concern about their lot was universal, and often virulently nationalistic, in inter-war Hungary, subdued or suppressed after the war, but has become acute again in recent years, as the Ceauşescu regime has descended into grotesque, corrupt misery, with ludicrous Dacian nationalism in place of bread.

All Romanian citizens suffer acute economic deprivation and political repression, but the Hungarians—like the smaller German minority—bear an additional burden of systematic racial discrimination and persecution. Not 'genocide', as the Hungarian speakers hysterically proclaim, but something very nasty that does indeed recall the policies and ideologies of pre-war fascism. For several years now, I have found this almost the first topic of conversation in Budapest. But officially, the Kádár regime said almost nothing about it. The new Hungarian leadership of Mr Károly Grósz promises to do more. One of the first things it has done is to allow this demonstration organized by the nationalist, or 'populist', wing of the Hungarian intelligentsia. It is the first time an East European state has officially permitted (and even discreetly encouraged) a demonstration explicitly directed against the government of a neighbouring, allied 'socialist state'. And the result is the largest independent demonstration in Hungary since the revolution of 1956.

As dusk turns to night, the crowd, perhaps some forty thousand strong, marches off to process past the Romanian embassy with flaming torches. The embassy building, protected by Hungarian riot police, is completely dark and silent, with shutters down. Only one shutter is raised a few inches, and as the torch-lit procession goes past, we see the flash of a camera from the window behind it. 'Where are you hiding? Come out there, Romanians!' someone shouts, to the accompaniment of whistles and cat-calls. But the organizers have repeatedly appealed for dignified silence, warning against the danger of Romanian-inspired 'provocations', and this appeal is supported by the great and literally silent majority of the crowd, who hush the rowdy minority away. 'By our silence,' a speaker declares through a megaphone, 'by our silence we demonstrate that we are Europeans and not barbarians.'

(APRIL 1988)

The Prague Advertisement

*This essay is a contribution to the permanent symposium
Czechoslovakia 88.*

Symposium

'How will you mark the anniversary?' I asked Václav Havel earlier
this year. No need to say which anniversary.

'We shall hold a symposium,' he said. It would discuss the
significance, not just of the Prague Spring and the Soviet invasion,
but of all those 'years of eight' which have been turning points for
Czechoslovakia and the whole of Europe in the twentieth century:
1918,1938,1948,1968. Interested Western scholars, intellectuals and
writers would be cordially invited. Perhaps I would be kind enough
to prepare a paper? They would try to hold the meeting quite openly.
They would inform the authorities.

In early November, a few days before the date of the planned
meeting, Havel himself went to the prime minister's office and
explained the project to an official deputed to receive him. This man
said neither yes nor no. But actions speak louder than words. On 10
November, as we, the Western guests, began to assemble in Prague,
virtually all our Czechoslovak hosts—scholars and members of the
country's main independent groups—were locked up or placed
under house arrest. Havel was in hiding.

Advertisement

A lady with a red flower would meet us at breakfast, we were told.
She would lead us to the meeting place. So there we sat, on Friday, 11
November, in the faded Jugendstil splendour of the Hotel Paříž, a
score of academics, writers, human rights activists, and

parliamentarians from Western Europe and the United States, waiting for the lady. Several prominent Western guests, including Marion Gräfin Dönhoff of *Die Zeit* and the eminent dean of Copenhagen University, Ove Nathan, had been refused visas on the grounds that the gathering was 'illegal'—although by what law the Czechoslovak representatives could not say. Our hosts were in prison. Plain-clothes police swarmed around the hotel. I anticipated arrest, expulsion.

Then in through the glass doors came not a lady with a red flower, nor yet a policeman with handcuffs, but . . . Václav Havel. He walked quickly to our table, sat down, and formally declared the meeting open. Within seconds, three plain-clothes men were behind him. 'Well, in this moment I am arrested,' said Havel. But before they hurried him away he managed to repeat, with quiet emphasis, that he had declared the symposium open.

Sally Laird of *Index on Censorship* photographed the scene. More secret police moved in to confiscate her film. As we argued with them we noticed a large, muscular woman in a tight-fitting leather jacket sitting in the foyer, with not just one flower but a whole bouquet. She moved toward us and theatrically distributed unmarked envelopes. Inside, we found the most extraordinary poison-pen letter it has ever been my privilege to receive. Typed and photocopied, with the text in English, German, French, and Italian, it read as follows:

ADVERTISEMENT

I am warning you that the action called symposium CZECHOSLOVAKIA 88 is illegal and its performance would be contrary to the interests of Czechoslovak working people and consequently illegal. In this connection your efforts to take part in this action would be considered as a manifestation of hostility to Czechoslovakia and in virtue of this we should have to draw relevant consequences against your person.

'I am warning you . . .' but the document was unsigned. Kafka! thou shouldst be living at this hour.

Someone asked the lady with the bouquet to identify herself. She said she ensured order in the hotel. In subsequent conversation we tentatively identified her as a secret police officer who had watched over the Havel family, presenting herself as 'Lieutenant Novotná', which is to say something like 'Lieutenant Smith'. Briefly detained in a police car the next day, three of us were again handed a crumpled copy of this fantastical 'Advertisement' (the German text, incidentally, was headed *Achtung*) by another plain-clothes man. We asked him whence it came. From the City Council of Prague, he said. But, we insisted, who is this mysterious 'I'? He pointed to himself, adding helpfully, 'Police!', as if, sitting in a police car, we might not have realized.

By this time we were visiting such few of the Czech and Slovak symposium participants as were still at home—usually under house arrest—and the families of those in prison. Earlier we had attempted to reconvene the meeting in a private flat, as had been done successfully in the case of the independent cultural symposium in Budapest in 1985.[1] But here, police in front of the door had simply prevented any Czechs from getting in.

We had drafted a strong statement of protest against this 'blatant violation of the Helsinki Final Act', a statement sent directly to all the delegations at the Vienna Helsinki review conference, but which also came back within hours to most Czechoslovakia, via the BBC, Radio Free Europe, and the Voice of America. We had briefed our ambassadors. We had laid flowers on the grave of the philosopher and founding father of Charter 77, Jan Potočka. Among our group was Max van der Stoel, who, as Dutch foreign minister in 1977, had been the first visiting Western politician to meet with Patočka in his capacity as leader of the human rights movement. Following that meeting, Patočka had been hauled in for eleven hours of interrogation, at the end of which he collapsed and died. Now, on his first visit to Prague since that time, van der Stoel spoke movingly at Patočka's grave. Patočka is dead, he said, but we all know that his spirit, and the spirit of freedom, live on in Czechoslovakia. The ceremony was filmed by an independent video team.

Then we had marched up to the headquarters of the central committee and delivered a letter of protest addressed to the Party leader Miloš Jakeš. A clever-looking official at the door assured us—in fluent Russian—that he would pass the letter on to 'Comrade Jakeš', but regretted that there was no one to receive us on a Saturday. And who was he? What was his name and position? 'I just work here,' he replied, *glasnost* glinting from his glasses. Two photographers took

[1]See 'A Hungarian Lesson', above p. 130 & ff.

pictures of us from across the parking lot. Then we marched down to the main secret police office in the Old Town, demanding to know why and where our hosts were imprisoned. Once again, the officer at the door explained that no one was working over the weekend—at which point a man in plain-clothes pushed through our group to enter the building, somewhat undermining the general contention.

Now, as we paid our individual visits, I was interested to observe the surveillance techniques of the police. Perhaps naïvely, I had not realized before how they use nicely dressed young couples, boy and girl walking arm in arm. And then I was glad to note that they, at least, have no shortage of hard currency. Three of us alone, myself and the Parisian scholars Pierre Hassner and Aleksander Smolar, were honoured with the attentions of at least two foreign cars, a blue Ford Sierra and a red Fiat Uno. Spying the latter after one of our calls, and feeling tired and hungry, we thought to ask our narks for a lift home ('home' in this case being, aptly enough, the Hotel Jalta). As we walked towards the car, the driver started the engine and pulled slowly away. We pursued them down the road.

Amusing for us—but no joke for our Czech friends sitting in prison. In theory, the Czechoslovak authorities' handling of this 'action' was relatively sophisticated. Earlier this year they received harsh criticism in the Western press, and a drubbing at the Vienna review conference, for breaking up an East-West peace seminar, and expelling all the foreign participants. Now they would allow the foreigners to stay, but lock up all the Czechs—initially for forty-eight hours and then, in some cases, immediately again for part of another forty-eight-hour period (thus abandoning all but the barest shreds of legality). We, meanwhile, would be allowed to go where we pleased. We would have what the Germans call *Narrenfreiheit*, jester's freedom. All doors would be opened to us, and the police would politely usher us into empty rooms. Better still, we would bring suffering to the innocent. For if we were foolish enough to visit anyone not already well known to the police, those people would surely feel the 'consequences' with which we were merely threatened.

In practice, this exercise in damage limitation did not go quite as planned: because of Havel's *coup de théâtre*; because of the black comedy of 'Lieutenant Novotná'; because we made our own protest dramatically, *urbi et orbi*; and because West German television managed to film Havel's arrest through the window of the restaurant, and to get the film out. It was shown on the television news in several Western countries. People in Slovakia saw it on Austrian television. At the Vienna review conference, Western ambassadors lined up to deplore the Czechoslovak authorities' action.

It was, indeed, a prime-time 'advertisement' for the present regime in Prague.

Commentary

On Monday, 14 November, the following commentary, signed 'Václav Dolezal,' appeared on page two of *Rudé Právo*, the central organ of the Czechoslovak Communist party:

ATTEMPT AT PROVOCATION

Fourteen days after the provocative demonstration of anti-socialist forces [i.e., the unofficial Independence Day demonstrations on 28 October] the same group of people attempted another form of provocation. It took advantage of co-operation with organizations for psychological warfare of the North Atlantic Pact. Western broadcasting stations took an active part too. What was up?

In the past weekend days, the so-called Charter 77 wanted to organize a 'symposium' called Czechoslovakia 88 in Prague. According to the foreign press, some twenty persons representing various official and unofficial Western structures, many of which take extreme anti-Czechoslovak positions, were to come to participate in the action, under the cloak of tourism.

The interest of these 'also-tourists' was not devoted to inspecting the cultural glories of our capital, but rather to encouraging the so-called dissidents to develop even more anti-socialist activity. They failed to achieve this goal. They wanted to use materials prepared beforehand to discredit our social system and to blacken our homeland in the countries of our neighbours. According to the foreign press, these materials, often glorifying the pre-1938 political structures, describe our previous political positions from subjectivist positions and sometimes antagonistically. A series of organizers of this provocation have been detained.

A similar action with the same political intentions was organized by émigré and other centres in Vienna on Sunday. The intention behind both the mentioned actions was a single aim: to defame the efforts of our Party and society for reconstruction, but also to complicate the Vienna meeting [i.e., of the CSCE] and, at variance with the Final Act of the Conference on Security and Co-operation in Europe, to interfere in the internal affairs of the CSSR and to infringe Czechoslovak sovereignty.

I fear my translation does scant justice to the full semantic absurdity of the original. As I read it, I remembered the lines that Auden wrote following the Soviet invasion twenty years ago:

> The Ogre does what ogres can,
> Deeds quite impossible for Man,
> But one prize is beyond his reach,
> The Ogre cannot master Speech.
> About a subjugated plain,
> Among its desperate and slain,
> The Ogre stalks with hands on hips,
> While drivel gushes from his lips.

But the ogre that Auden had in mind was the Soviet Union, and that ogre is changing. He has begun to master speech. So in Prague his dwarfs are left bewildered, lost. The drivel still gushes, or dribbles, from their lips. But it lacks even the force of consistent absurdity. The materials for our symposium 'glorified the pre-1938 political structures', splutter the dwarfs, who dare not even sign their own names. Yet they themselves are now making obeisance to the great architect of those 'structures', Tomáš Garrigue Masaryk, in an attempt to gain some patriotic legitimacy. And the people laugh at them in the streets.

I asked the receptionist in a hotel for a copy of *Rudé Právo*. 'Why on earth do you want to read that?' she said. I explained that I had heard there was this commentary about our symposium. 'Oh, I must read it,' she cried, but when she reached the sentence about 'organizations for psychological warfare of the North Atlantic Pact' she could go no further. She was just doubled up laughing.

The Permanent Symposium

On Sunday most of the Western participants departed to Vienna, for the 'parallel' symposium organized by a formidable company of exiled Czech and Slovak intellectuals, and for a widely reported press conference arranged by the International Helsinki Federation. On Monday virtually all our hosts were out of prison, although some of them had to walk several miles home after being released in the early hours when there was no transport of any kind. They swapped tales about their latest prison experiences. How the ordinary prison guards were angry with the secret police for disturbing their settled routines. How the interrogations were perfunctory and absurd.

Havel himself had at one point been interviewed by our charming 'Lieutenant Novotná'. She marched in and announced, 'I have come to debrief you.' I suggested to him that after the liberation she should really be sent to work in the theatre, what with her looks and her proven aptitude for the theatre of the absurd. He said he might write her a part in one of his plays.

Havel and the others were of course exhausted by their days in prison. But they were also buoyed up by the international support. They were moved by news of the ceremony at Patočka's grave, encouraged by the protests they heard via Western radio stations, and delighted with the way in which we had interpreted Havel's opening words. We had understood this as an invitation to continue the meeting as best we could. I think it was Pierre Hassner who first observed that since Havel had formally opened the meeting, it could not end until he formally closed it.

The meeting thus continues. It has become a permanent symposium. As I left, Havel asked that those who write something relevant to the theme should, wherever it appears, mark it as 'a contribution to the permanent symposium Czechoslovakia 88.' Until, of course, we can all gather again in Prague, to close the meeting.

Czechoslovakia 88

What does this tragicomedy tell us about the subject of our aborted discussion, Czechoslovakia 88? It tells us, obviously, that the present regime in Czechoslovakia is still going backward where Hungary,

Poland, and, most important, the Soviet Union are going forward—although not uniformly so. Indeed, after the removal in October of Lubomir Štrougal as prime minister, the present government looks more reactionary than ever. As one Czech historian commented to me, between interrogations, it is a bitter irony that in 1988, in the age of Gorbachev, they have finally achieved the government that Brezhnev hoped for twenty years ago, after the invasion. Yet this is a Brezhnevite government without Brezhnev, a regime whose time has gone.

For this episode also tells us that the regime that has imposed the grotesque abnormality of 'normalization' in Czechoslovakia for two decades is now profoundly unsettled, confused, and wavering. It is unsettled from the East, for if Gorbachev is behaving like Dubček, and Poland and Hungary almost like free countries, then how on earth do they justify their continued immobility? By reference to the great socialist model of the German Democratic Republic? Or perhaps Bulgaria? It was interesting to note that both the Polish and the Hungarian press reported Dubček's speech in Bologna on 13 November reaffirming the continued relevance of the Prague Spring. There have been signs that senior Gorbachev advisors, at least, can barely restrain their desire to reassess the Prague Spring in the direction of Dubček's plea. Gorbachev's close political ally Aleksandr Yakovlev was in Prague the day after our meeting, and *Rudé Právo* carried a front-page photograph of him looking pensive between the beaming figures of Jakeš, Vasil Bil'ak, the veteran reactionary, and their ideological watchman, Jan Fojtík. It might have been captioned: '*Que diable allait-il faire dans cette galère?*'

Secondly, the regime is unsettled from below—by the new flowering of independent initiative and civil courage inside Czechoslovakia. This is of course partly inspired by the impact of Gorbachev, the examples of neighbouring Hungary and Poland, and the new East-West détente. But it is also the result of internal processes of political and economic decay, on the one hand, and intellectual and social emancipation on the other. The political leadership is now of Brezhnevite biological antiquity, while, on the other side, a new generation is thrusting forward, a generation impatient with the compromises and evasions of their parents. I heard of one girl who took part in the largely spontaneous demonstration in Wenceslaus Square on Independence Day, 28

212

October. On 21 August, 1968, she had confronted the Soviet tanks in the same square—as a three-week-old baby in a pram.

The authorities now face opposition and protest not merely from the old front line of Charter 77, not only from intellectual *samizdat*, but from thousands of young people who have found the courage to speak out, and from the no less than 600,000 people who have now signed the petition for religious freedom initiated by a simple Moravian farmer earlier this year. On the twentieth anniversary of the Soviet invasion, thousands of young people demonstrated in the centre of Prague, chanting 'Dubček!' and 'Freedom!'

Then, in mid-October, the authorities suddenly found themselves confronted with a serious, explicitly political opposition platform: the manifesto of a Movement for Civil Liberties, entitled 'Democracy for All'. Although many of the first signatories of the manifesto are Chartists, it differs fundamentally from the original Charter 77 programme by attempting to spell out a concrete programme for systematic, political change. This programme goes far beyond that 'socialism with a human face' which Dubček nostalgically recalled in his Bologna speech. Dubček summoned Machiavelli and Gramsci as his intellectual ancestors. But the patron saints of this manifesto are rather Montesquieu and Keynes. It is a somewhat baggy document, as you would expect from a coalition of independent persons and groups with widely differing political views. But the central common ground is plainly stated: liberal democracy, the rule of law, a mixed economy.

Then, in another attempt to gain some patriotic credibility, the authorities suddenly declared that the seventieth anniversary of Czechoslovakia's independence on 28 October, 1918, could be celebrated as a national holiday. (Canny shopkeepers hedged their bets by putting in their windows the slogan 'Long live October!'— which could refer either to Russia's revolution in 1917 or to Czechoslovakia's independence in 1918. Only a few risked putting out a picture of Masaryk.) Then the authorities locked up virtually all the front-line opposition leaders, to ensure that there would be no genuinely patriotic manifestation. Yet that is what they got none the less, with a largely spontaneous and mainly young crowd, again chanting 'freedom', and being pursued down the narrow streets by rather ineffectual water-cannon.

The new interior minister, František Kincl, is a professional policeman, and police tactics have toughened. The round-ups of oppositionists in connection with 28 October, and again in connection with this symposium, are the worst in years. As I write, many people have been, or are about to be, hauled in for interrogation about the 'Democracy for All' manifesto. An attempt is clearly being made to deter others from joining them. Worst of all, the prime mover of the petition for religious freedom, Augustin Navrátil, has been confined to a mental hospital with a diagnosis of 'paranoia querulans'—and this at a time when even the Soviet Union seems to be desisting from the abuse of psychiatry for political purposes.

Yet at the same time the regime is making half-hearted gestures of reform and relaxation. Extraordinarily frank accounts of the country's economic stagnation have appeared in the official press. The Slovak minister of culture had an article in *Rudé Právo* saying that it was an unhealthy condition for there to be two cultures in the country, and they should seriously consider what were the reasons behind the emergence of Charter 77. Official theatre groups can take slightly more licence. Confronted with the formation of an independent Helsinki group, and anticipating another unofficial demonstration on human rights day, 10 December, the authorities have proposed the formation of an official human rights committee on the same date.

As de Tocqueville taught us long ago, this inconsistency, this wavering between increased repression and half-baked reform, is characteristic of an *ancient régime* in its last years. How long the twilight period will last, and how the transition will come about— whether fast or slowly, peacefully or less so—is of course very hard to say. It is rumoured that younger men such as the Prague Party secretary, Miroslav Štepan, will shortly step up into more prominent positions. They too have had a part, albeit a junior one, in the grimy business of 'normalization'. By most accounts, Štepan's political generation is composed largely of opportunists, careerists, and cynics. But this is not necessarily a disqualification. In Hungary, Károly Grósz and his contemporaries are hardly the world's purest idealists. Yet they are making what are, with all due caveats, really striking attempts at political and economic reform, out of insight into necessity. One man's cynic may be another man's realist. Nor is it entirely clear that what Czechoslovakia needs above all at this moment is another decent, limited idealist like Alexander Dubček.

What is more, it is possible to argue that when the moment of change comes, Czechoslovakia might actually be better placed than Poland and Hungary, because its once powerful economy, although seriously run-down, is still in a less catastrophic state, and relatively free of the crippling burden of hard-currency debt. Yet this cuts both ways. For without their deep economic crisis, and concomitant dependency on the West, would the Polish and Hungarian leaderships ever have felt compelled to launch such radical reforms? Here is a crux of the East European dilemma. You can have economic crisis and political reform (Poland, Hungary). You can have no economic crisis and no political reform (GDR, Czechoslovakia). You can even have economic crisis and no political reform (Romania). But can you have political reform without economic crisis? Maybe Czechoslovakia will yet be the first to achieve that feat, as Milan Šimečka optimistically suggests in a paper prepared for our symposium. Maybe.

The World

What happens will depend mainly on developments inside Czechoslovakia, in the Soviet Union, and elsewhere in Eastern Europe—in that order. But it will also depend on us. 'The world sees you!' the crowd chanted at the police during the 28 October demonstration. But does it really?

In 1988, as at all those turning points which were the subject of our symposium—1918, when Britain, France, and the United States gave Masaryk the international licence to create an independent Czechoslovak state; 1938, when, at Munich, Britain and France sold that independent state down the river; 1948, with the communist coup; and 1968, with the Soviet invasion—in this 'year of eight', too, the fate of this small country in the centre of Europe still crucially depends on the attitude of the Western as well as the Eastern world.

Now the current line being peddled to the West by the Jakeš crew goes roughly like this: 'We really want to press ahead with our own *perestroika [prestavba]*, with economic restructuring above all. But for this we need order and stability at home. *Ordnung muss sein.* Therefore you must give us credits and technology while understanding why we have to lock up dangerous criminal elements' ... such as the country's most famous playwright Václav

Havel. A feeble line, you might think. Yet strangely enough there are signs that some Western governments are half-prepared to swallow it. This applies to Austria and to some extent to West Germany, both of which have a particular interest in a stable setting for their own national rapprochements, with Hungary and the GDR respectively, and a history (even a philosophy) of promoting economic ties irrespective of political circumstances.

More surprising is the case of France, whose foreign minister earlier this year made the extraordinary statement that Czechoslovakia's human rights performance was improving (an assertion he subsequently modified), and whose president, François Mitterrand, has chosen Prague of all places, and this of all times, to pay a state visit—scheduled for early December. One might understand his regal reluctance to follow in Mrs Thatcher's wake to Poland or Hungary, but this is carrying the personal competition a bit far.

To offer such high-level political recognition or economic support to the present regime in Czechoslovakia is not just morally questionable. It is also politically short-sighted. It ignores a prime lesson of recent East European (and not just East European) history: the longer fundamental reforms are delayed, the more difficult they are to implement, and the less likely they are to occur peacefully. Such an approach is thus likely, in the longer term, to achieve the opposite of the desired effect.

There is a time to praise and a time to scold; a time to finance and a time to refrain from financing; a time to travel and a time to wait. With the Czechoslovak regime in its present, repressive yet unsettled state, this is the latter time. It is a time for watchful waiting and for strictly conditional encouragement. Encouraging the old guard to depart. Encouraging the new guard, when it comes, to try to behave as befits a deeply civilized country, in the heart of Europe, in the late twentieth century.

To Be Concluded

There are now reasons to believe that, for once in the history of Czechoslovakia, this sea-change may occur before the calendar turns up another 'year of eight'. It almost seems a pity to spoil the pattern. But they have waited long enough.

So I look forward to hearing Václav Havel formally close our permanent symposium, in the Slovanský Dům, Na Přikopě 22 (first floor), Prague 1—and well before 1998.

(NOVEMBER 1988)

Reform or Revolution?

This long essay is an exercise both in contemporary history and in prognosis. The latter is necessary folly. Folly, because we cannot know the future. Necessary, because developments in East Central Europe may be of crucial importance, not merely for the people who live there, but also for the fate of *'perestroika'* in the Soviet Union, and hence for us all. To read analyses of developments in the 'Soviet bloc' over the last forty years is to appreciate just how foolish it is to make any predictions about this region. As I write, I have before me a Penguin Special entitled *The Break-up of the Soviet Empire in Eastern Europe*. It was published in 1965. Yet we are all, governments and private citizens, condemned to make our dispositions on the basis of guesswork about the future. The detailed analysis of attempted reforms in Poland and Hungary, on pp. 192–217, has to some extent been overtaken by the dramatic and encouraging developments sketched in a final essay (below, 'Refolution' pp. 274), written just as this book goes to press in spring 1989. Yet all the deeper dilemmas identified here remain. In any case, the reader must bear in mind that the 'present' of this essay is the summer and early autumn of 1988.

Forty Years On

Eight years after the birth of Solidarity, occupation strikes once again spread across Poland. The workers' first demand is: Solidarity. On the twentieth anniversary of the Soviet invasion, ten thousand Czechs march through the streets of Prague, chanting 'Dubček!' and 'Freedom!' With official permission, some 40,000 people demonstrate in Budapest—against the policies of a neighbouring socialist state. Without official permission, more than half a million Czechs and

Slovaks sign a petition for religious freedom. The Protestant churches in East Germany try to praise the recent policies of the Soviet Union but are censored by the state. The Polish government spokesman invites himself to visit Radio Free Europe. A Hungarian politburo member says he has 'no arguments in principle for the one-party system.'[1]

These days one is mildly disappointed if, on opening a Polish or Soviet journal, one finds that some great, immovable forty-year-old taboo has *not* been casually broken. It would be amusing, although perhaps a little cruel, to compile a small anthology of statements from Soviet and East European experts of the form 'what is unthinkable is . . .' or 'one thing is certain . . .'

It is not just individual taboos that fall like ninepins. Whole concepts have crumbled. Normalization, for example. After the imposition of martial law in Poland, most serious Western analysts concentrated on the 'prospects for normalization' in Poland, where normalization might be defined as the attempt to return an East Central European country, initially by the use of force, to Soviet norms. The comparison was with Hungary after 1956 and Czechoslovakia after 1968. This line of analysis was entirely reasonable at the time. But what relevance has the concept today? Not only has the Jaruzelski team's original vision of normalization— Kádárism à la Polonaise—failed, as the best analysts predicted it

[1] Imre Pozsgay, quoted in BBC, *Summary of World Broadcasts—Eastern Europe* (hereafter SWB-EE), 24 May, 1988, C/14. The exact wording of the translation transcript is: 'I have no principled arguments on the side of the one-party system.'

The author would like to thank Ivo Banac, Archie Brown, Włodzimierz Brus, Norman Davies, Charles Gati, Elemér Hankiss, Philip Hanson, Pierre Hassner, Tony Judt, Leszek Kołakowski, Miłowit Kuniński, Zbigniew Pelczynski, Jacques Rupnik, George Schöpflin, Aleksander Smolar, and Rudolf Tökes for their comments on an earlier draft of this essay.

would.[2] The very idea of what is normal seems to have changed.

Old concepts crumble, but where are the new? Besides the novelty, intricacy, and fragility of internal developments in each country, and the central uncertainty about the nature, pace, and durability of change in the Soviet Union, there is the problem of divergence. To generalize about Eastern Europe was always a difficult and questionable exercise—even at the height of Stalinist *Gleichschaltung*—but it becomes ever more difficult and questionable as individual countries become increasingly different, not just from the Soviet Union but from each other. The historian Joseph Rothschild calls his new political history of East Central Europe since the Second World War *Return to Diversity*. A knowledge of each country's pre-war, or pre-Yalta, history is now quite as necessary as a general understanding of the Soviet-type systems.

Eastern Europe today resembles a landscape on whose commanding heights vast uniform concrete blockhouses were built some forty years ago. There they stand, still inhabited, still hideous, from the wooded hills of Thuringia to the great Hungarian plain, and on their terraces the familiar fat-jowled proprietors still sit at lugubrious leisure, with their black, curtained cars and their prefabricated lies. But look again: strange things have happened. Here, a whole wing has fallen to the ground, rusty steel roads jutting out of crumbled concrete. There, the blockhouse has incongruously acquired a baroque frontage or a romanesque interior, repainted in the pre-war national colours, while the strains of a patriotic march sound from the hall. There again, cottages in half-remembered versions of traditional styles shoulder up the hill towards it, while around the corner a private entrepreneur has built himself something altogether more modern and luxurious. And who is that

[2] See, for example, Włodzimierz Brus, 'The Prospect of "Normalization" in Poland', in W. Brus, P. Kende, Z. Mlynář, *'Normalization' Processes in Soviet-Dominated Central Europe* (1982), Study No.1 of the Research Project on 'Crisis in Soviet-type Systems', directed by Zdeněk Mlynář; Jacques Rupnik, 'The Military and "Normalization" in Poland', reprinted in Paul Lewis, ed., *Eastern Europe: Legitimation and Political Crisis* (New York: St. Martin's, 1984); and pp. 299–303 in my own *The Polish Revolution: Solidarity* (London: Jonathan Cape, 1983). Two interesting references to the Polish authorities' dream of Kádárization are to be found in Adam Bromke, *Eastern Europe in the Aftermath of Solidarity* (Boulder, Colorado: East European Monographs, distributed by Columbia University Press, 1985), p. 41.

man in a black soutane being ushered obsequiously across the terrace? And since when have blockhouses had spires?

Gorbachev

Let us start with Mr Gorbachev—which is not, however, to start at the beginning. Faced with this bewildering East European vista, most Western news commentators have taken refuge in a formula as simple as it is facile. Every new development in Eastern Europe is treated as a function of, or alternatively as a challenge to, Soviet *glasnost* and *perestroika*. Yet in truth, a serious analysis of Hungary or Poland's present dilemmas could almost as well begin in the Middle East[3] as in Moscow. Of course Gorbachev's impact has been large: it has also been complex, ambiguous, more indirect than direct, and the 'Gorbachev factor' has played into political scenes that, at least in Hungary and Poland, already had powerful dynamics of their own.

The most radical and basic speculative question about Moscow's approach to its 'external empire'[4] might be called the TITO question: Troops In, Troops Out? In what circumstances might Soviet troops once again march into an East European country? Under what conditions might they march out?

Is the so-called Brezhnev Doctrine of limited sovereignty within the socialist commonwealth, so eloquently presented by Mr S. Kovalev in *Pravda* of 26 September, 1968, still valid twenty years after the Warsaw Pact invasion of Czechoslovakia? At least two senior Gorbachev advisers have declared, on the record, that they regard invasion as unthinkable in present circumstances.[5] In purely theoretical terms, the 'new thinking' in Soviet foreign policy would at least demand a different ideological justification of such an action,

---

[3] The Middle East—which produced the oil, which earned the petrodollars, which Poland and Hungary borrowed, which created the debt, which precipitated the crisis, which compelled the reform.

[4] 'External empire' meaning the six member states of the Warsaw Pact, as opposed to the 'internal empire' of the non-Russian republics of the Soviet Union.

[5] Oleg Bogomolov, quoted in the *Financial Times*, 27 June, 1988, p. 17; Viatecheslav Dashitchev in *Der Spiegel*, Number 27, 1988, p. 126. Bogomolov was also quoted in the *Washington Times*, 8 July, 1988, as saying, 'The Brezhnev Doctrine is completely unacceptable and unthinkable ...'

in terms of 'all human' rather than class interests. (The Soviets could say the ozone layer is threatened by pollution from Czech industry.) Two leading Soviet legal scholars argued in a recent article that the principle of 'peaceful coexistence' must, in the context of the 'new thinking', be extended to relations between states with the same political and social systems.[6] Gorbachev himself has emphasized the right of socialist states to find their own paths to socialism, notably during his visit to Belgrade.

On the other hand, in discussing the 'priority area of relations with the socialist countries' the theses for the extraordinary Party conference in Moscow in May 1988 declared: 'Our internationalist links are built on the basis of mutual benefit, a balance of interests and common responsibility for the fate and prestige of socialism and the enhancement of its role in world development.' Official Soviet commentaries on the twentieth anniversary of the invasion of Czechoslovakia (20–21 August) were largely unrepentant, although this can be explained by their concern not to embarrass the Husák-Jakeš regime in Prague. During his visit to Warsaw in June, Gorbachev declined to renounce the Brezhnev Doctrine, despite a direct public challenge to do so from a Polish intellectual.[7]

These statements are important, not least for their direct impact—simply as statements—on Eastern Europe. But they do not get us (or Soviet leaders) much further in determining what they would actually do were an East European country to blow up in their faces. Nobody can know that, not even Mr Gorbachev. This question can only be answered in practice. All we can say is that in response to the

---

[6] The article from the March 1988 issue of *Soviet State and Law* is summarized and analyzed by Theodor Schweisfurth in the *Frankfurter Allgemeine Zeitung*, 13 May, 1988, pp. 9-10.

[7] The question was posed by Marcin Król, editor of the independent monthly *Res Publica*, at Gorbachev's meeting with selected intellectuals in the Royal Palace on 14 July. In his speech on the seventieth anniversary of the October Revolution, Gorbachev also spoke of the damage that could be done to relations between socialist countries 'by a neglect of the common interests of socialism on the international scene' (quoted from the official translation appended to *Soviet Weekly*, 7 November, 1987, p. xvi).

three major post-war East European challenges, the Soviet Union has each time hesitated longer—days with Hungary in 1956, months with Czechoslovakia in 1968, more than a year with Poland in 1980–1981. It has gone to increasing pains to disguise its intervention—unilateral in 1956, multilateral (Warsaw Pact) in 1968, Polish 'internal' in 1981. It now has stronger reasons than ever for hesitating and fudging, since an invasion would also be a blow to reform inside the Soviet Union, and since relations with the West are so important for that reform. The nature of the East European challenge has in each case been a matter of definition: What is 'reform' and what 'revolution'? What helps 'the fate and prestige of socialism' and what harms it? What—to use the favoured Western policy term—is 'stability' and what 'dangerous instability'?

All Soviet leaders since Stalin (except the transitional figures of Andropov and Chernenko) have faced a major East European challenge. There are strong reasons for believing that this challenge will come sooner rather than later to this Soviet leader. Politically, it is therefore of the first importance that the West should prepare itself for such a crisis: analytically, psychologically, and by planning possible responses. One part of the response is precisely the matter of definition. In the past, major Western powers—and particularly West Germany—have too often adopted a restrictive, indeed almost a Soviet, definition of 'stability,' treating as symptoms of 'dangerous instability' phenomena such as strikes and street demonstrations, which are an entirely normal part of political and public life in our own countries. Of course a strike in a socialist state self-evidently *is* a more important thing than a strike in a liberal democracy. But there is a strong tactical case for the West now to say (while firmly warning the Soviet Union of the disastrous consequences of the use of force, whether direct or camouflaged): 'So [name of country] has fifty thousand people on the streets? There are strikes every week? They have independent political parties? So what! This is normal. This is fine. It's reform, not dangerous instability. We call it *glasnost* and *perestroika*.' But that is a political argument. Analytically, there is little more of interest to be said on this subject, beyond registering the Soviet statements and signs.

It is more pleasant to speculate about troop movements in the other direction. In mid-July, the Hungarian Party foreign-affairs spokesman said on television that Soviet troops could be withdrawn from Hungary 'in the foreseeable future'.[8] This is a possible development to which immense attention has been paid in the West—mainly because of the 'militarization of thought' about East-West relations that is the common weakness of American cold war thinking since the 1950s and European peace-movement thinking in the 1980s. Plainly, any quantitative reduction or qualitative transformation of the military confrontation in Central Europe is bound to have an impact on the East European polities. Plainly, a physical withdrawal of Soviet troops—the very bearers and symbols of domination—would have more political impact than any changes in the structure of force, armaments, or military doctrine, although some of these might actually be more important for the military balance. But what exactly this political impact would be it is exceedingly difficult to say.

Any implicit argument suggesting, 'Soviet troops brought communism to Eastern Europe forty-five years ago, so if Soviet troops go, communism will go,' contains an obvious, childish fallacy in its conclusion, as well as a small oversimplification in its premise.[9] Yet it is far from obvious that such a half-articulated hope would not be raised in many a patriotic breast were the invaders to depart. In the short term, the new Hungarian Party leader, Mr Károly Grósz, might well gain some popular credit for such a move. But in the

[8] Géza Kótai, quoted in SWB-EE, 14 July, 1988, B/6. According to this transcript, his actual words were: 'There is understanding on the plane of Soviet policy, *vis-à-vis* the Hungarian endeavours, that we should be affected in the first stage, according to the schedule, meaning we, Hungary, would be affected by this in the foreseeable future. This is our objective, this is our endeavour . . .' However, the Warsaw Pact summit in Budapest a few days later offered no further hints in this direction. Károly Grósz, the new Hungarian Party leader, reportedly denied the story on his visit to the United States in late July. In effect, Mr Kótai's remarks may therefore be little more than a verbal flirt, mainly for domestic consumption.

[9] An over-simplification, above all, in the case of Czechoslovakia, although at the time of the February 1948 coup, Stalin's emissary to Klement Gottwald 'pointedly suggested that Gottwald should ask the Soviet government for military assistance; Soviet troops were already massed on the Hungarian border.' See Karel Kaplan, *The Short March: The Communist Takeover in Czechoslovakia 1945–1948* (London: Hurst and Co., 1987) p. 175 and passim. An equally differentiated account of the communist takeover in Hungary is to be found in Charles Gati, *Hungary and the Soviet Bloc* (Chapel Hill: Duke University Press, 1986)

medium to longer term, would not expectations be raised that he could not satisfy?

In general, the domestic effect of any Soviet military reductions will probably be to put that emphasis more nakedly, and even harshly, on the question of changing the political, economic, and social system that came with, or was at least partially restored by, those troops. Increased military 'stability' can mean reduced political 'stability'. This is patently not an argument against careful disarmament. It is just an argument for keeping our eyes open. The two halves of the TITO question are intimately related: Troops Out now can increase the danger of Troops In later. But any real political change in Eastern Europe is bound to be accompanied by some reduction in political 'stability'—otherwise it will not be real.

The countries of East Central Europe[10] at present divide into two categories: those whose regimes are rhetorically embracing the Gorbachev example, for their own purposes, and those whose regimes are still resisting, while their peoples wistfully embrace, the Gorbachev example. The Jaruzelski team in Poland and the new leaders in Hungary are not simply taking leaves out of Mr Gorbachev's book. Rather, they are taking his licence to pursue national strategies that are deeply different and highly specific, but in some respects also more radical or 'advanced' than those currently being debated in Moscow. The Jakeš-Husák regime (mutton dressed as lamb) in Czechoslovakia and the Honecker gerontocracy in the GDR are not simply resisting *glasnost* and *perestroika*. They are also

[10] Meaning Czechoslovakia, Hungary, Poland, and the GDR. Since the terms 'Eastern' and 'Central' Europe are so variously used, it is perhaps worth justifying this further distinction. The term East Central Europe combines the criteria of post-1945 Eastern Europe and pre-1914 Central Europe. By post-1945 Eastern Europe one means the formally independent member states of the Warsaw Pact, apart from the Soviet Union. The term Central Europe is, of course, more problematic, but for the period before 1914 it may be taken to mean those countries that, while subsumed in one of the three great multinational empires (Austro-Hungarian, Prussian-German, or Russian), none the less preserved major elements of Western traditions: for example, Western Christianity, the rule of law, some separation of powers, a measure of constitutional government, and something that could be called civil society. The western Ukraine and the Baltic states are thus excluded by the first criterion, while Bulgaria is excluded by the second. Romania is a borderline case, but one at present so eccentric that I shall touch upon it only incidentally.

defending national strategies that have kept them in power and their societies in relative quiescence (or 'stability'?) for nearly twenty years.[11]

It is probably wrong to suggest that Mr Gorbachev wholly deplores these latter regimes. Although, like Mrs Thatcher, he cannot always resist the personal itch to preach his own solutions, his general message has been: You must solve your own problems in your own way. The last thing he wants is a new Prague Spring to complicate his own. It is also wrong to imply that he is an entirely comfortable patron for Hungary and Poland. Economically, Brezhnev's Soviet Union was in many ways a 'softer' partner. Gorbachev's hard-nosed approach to Soviet-East European trade, his insistence on the delivery of better-quality goods, his desire to revitalize Comecon integration, his penchant for Soviet-East European joint ventures (favourably mentioned in his book *Perestroika*): none of this necessarily helps economic-reform programmes whose success or failure is measured in hard currency.

The general position is, however, as clear as it is extraordinary. For the first time in decades, the primary limits to political change in Eastern Europe are not external but internal. The ultimate limits are of course still external, even if no one knows exactly where they lie. But the barriers up against which the enterprise of economic and political liberalization in Poland and Hungary is currently pushing are internal Polish and Hungarian barriers. Comparisons with Yugoslavia, a socialist state without the external Soviet limits, are increasingly apt.

Moreover, even if the Soviet Union is not directly pressing recalcitrant regimes to change, the indirect effect of the Gorbachev example is to increase the pressure from their own populations for change. This is demonstrably the case in the GDR and Czechoslovakia. There is a partial parallel here between the impact of Gorbachev's 'second de-Stalinization' and that of Khrushchev's first de-Stalinization. But whereas the lessons of Khrushchev's de-Stalinization were first articulated inside the ruling parties of Eastern Europe, now we find that independent social movements, the churches, non-Party intellectuals, young people, and just crowds

---

[11] One should also note that the GDR has enthusiastically supported Soviet 'new thinking' in *foreign* policy.

welcoming Mr Gorbachev are the first to spell out the lessons—and not afraid to do so—leaving the ruling parties embarrassed and straggling behind.

There is a swelling conviction in both Czechoslovakia and the GDR that their old, weary, wooden Brezhnevite leaders cannot last for more than another year or two. People looked with keen interest at Hungary's palace revolution in May, when an extraordinary Party conference kicked János Kádár upstairs (to the newly created post of Party chairman) and expelled his whole inner circle, not merely from the politburo but from the central committee as well.[12] But when the change in Party leadership comes in Czechoslovakia and the GDR, there will not simply be a populace eager to follow the Party's new Gorbachevite line. Here too, albeit on a smaller scale than in Poland or Hungary, there will be non-Party intellectuals, the churches, independent social groups, the oppositional rainbow coalition of Charter 77 in Czechoslovakia, ecology, peace and human rights activists, and the refuseniks in the GDR, all advancing their own programmes for change. Each case will be different: Czechoslovakia, because of the legacy of 1968; East Germany, because of West Germany. But in both, the real trial is still to come. In Poland and Hungary, by contrast, the trial is already on.

Ottomanization

Finlandization is the crude metaphor that has been used in the West—but also by independent East European intellectuals—to describe the direction and outer limit of desirable and conceivable change for East European countries. Finlandization, or self-Finlandization, is held up as a nightmare for Western Europe but a dream for Eastern Europe. The metaphor is not wholly useless to describe a condition in which an East European state would, like Finland, enjoy almost complete autonomy in its domestic social,

---

[12] With one exception: György Aczél. For a detailed analysis see George Schöpflin, Rudolf Tökés and Iván Völgyes, 'Leadership Change and Crisis in Hungary', *Problems of Communism*, Sept.–Oct. 1988.

economic, and political life, while perforce remaining compliant to the Soviet Union in military and foreign affairs.[13]

The term is, however, almost wholly useless to describe the process by which an East European country might get from here to there. Does it mean that the East Europeans should first give the Russians a bloody nose in a winter war? Obviously, it cannot mean that; but would the Finns enjoy even their present measure of autonomy had it not been for their brave military resistance in 1939–1940? Does it mean achieving a new status in the context of an international settlement, a 'new Yalta'? In all the Soviet 'new thinking' about foreign policy—a fundamental re-examination of Soviet positions in many parts of the world—there has been no hint of Soviet interest in such a basic renegotiation of the status quo in Europe. The vagueness of the metaphor is amply illustrated by the fact that when applied to Western Europe, it means the precise opposite of its putative meaning for Eastern Europe. For Western Europe it means a process of increasing dependence on the Soviet Union, for Eastern Europe, a process of diminishing dependence.

I have in the past offered an alternative metaphor, almost equally crude, but slightly better in indicating the nature of the process, though not the end result. This is the metaphor of the Ottomanization of the Soviet empire. I mean by this, in a very loose analogy to the decline of the Ottoman Empire, a long, slow process of imperial decline in the course of which one would see an unplanned, piecemeal, and discontinuous emancipation, both of the constituent states from the imperial centre and of societies from states. This would occur not by planned reform from the imperial centre, in the context of sustained growth and comprehensive modernization, but

---

[13] Note, however, that Finland itself seems to be edging as close to Western Europe as it can; see the article Daniel Vernet in *Le Monde* (9 July, 1988). A fairly representative East European usage of the term 'self-Finlandization' can be found in Ferenc Fehér, 'Eastern Europe's Long Revolution Against Yalta', in *East European Politics and Societies* (an excellent new journal), Vol.2, No.1, 1988, p. 34. A useful reminder of how the Finns actually resisted Finlandization is the chapter by James H. Billington in Cyril E. Black, ed., *Communism and Revolution* (Princeton: Princeton University Press 1964), pp. 117–144.

mainly by unco-ordinated independent action, whether individual, collective, or national, by pressure from below or from outside, in an overall context of growing relative backwardness in relation to much of the developed world, and specifically to Western Europe. In a phrase, Ottomanization means *emancipation in decay*.

It is tempting to pursue the historical analogy. The Ottoman Empire, after all, also started out as an ideological empire: 'the divinely protected well-flourishing absolute domain of the House of Osman.' It liquidated much of the old ruling class in several of the territories it conquered and replaced them with a new and initially functional ruling class drawn mainly from lower social strata. These Ottomans had their own language, the Osmanlica; the communist *nomenklatura* has its Newspeak. There was one great sociopolitical divide: between the Ottomans and the *reaya*, or 'flock'. Like communism, the Ottoman system assumed its functionaries to be angels: selfless servants of the cause, with no need for petty human checks and balances. As a result, they could behave like devils. This new class degenerated into what the historian Peter Sugar calls 'ossified functionalism', with the growth of corruption, the assertion of local and self-interests, and the rise of an entrenched bureaucracy.[14] The Ottoman Empire was imprisoned in a rigid, archaic economic and fiscal system, incompatible with the demands of the modern industrial economy emerging around it and incapable of competing with the West. And then there is the parallel originally suggested by Hugh Seton-Watson: that the final collapse of the empire might result from the rise of a power in the East. Let China be to the Russian empire what Russia was to the Ottoman Empire!

All this is tempting; but the temptation must be resisted. For a thousand historians will at once reach for their pens to point out the numerous respects in which the decline of the Ottoman Empire cannot possibly be compared with that of the Soviet empire. Someone else will add, for good measure, that the Ottoman Empire finally fell apart in war, not in peace: 'Is it war you want?' they will indignantly ask. So let me stress again that this is not a detailed

[14] See Peter F. Sugar, *Southeastern Europe Under Ottoman Rule, 1354–1804* (Seattle: University of Washington Press, 1977), *passim*.

historical analogy, just a crude metaphor, 'good enough for government work' as I believe they say in the State Department.[15]

The metaphor of Ottomanization stresses, in very general terms, the overall context of imperial decline and the unplanned, piecemeal, and discontinuous nature of that process. It allows both for attempts at reform from the centre (Gorbachev as Selim III) and for attempts at revolution from the periphery, for the partial failure of each, and it recognizes, in the long run, the dialectical relationship between reform and revolution. Indeed, even in the mere forty-five years of the Soviet external empire we have already seen several turns of that dialectic: the reforms introduced by János Kádár were an attempted response to the Hungarian revolution of 1956, just as the Jaruzelski reforms have all been an attempted response to the Polish revolution of 1980–1981. This metaphor therefore invites us not to think of revolution as the end of reform, or of reform as the definitive alternative to revolution, but rather of both as part of a very long-term historical process—whose final outcome is, to be sure, almost impossible to conceive, since most previous empires ended in wars, but this empire has nuclear weapons.

Beyond this, we have to look in detail at individual countries that are, as you would expect in the course of Ottomanization, increasingly different. In what follows I shall look briefly at some symptoms of decay and contours of emancipation, taking most of my examples from Poland and Hungary. I shall then pose the question of reform or *transformation:* that is, whether in either of these pioneer countries there seems any chance that the disparate elements of emancipation in decay can be combined, partly at the wish of the present political leadership and ruling class, into a new sociopolitical

---

[15] Recent events in Transcausasia and the Baltic republics could lead one to ask how far the metaphor of Ottomanization might also be applied to the internal empire. A reasonable answer is probably 'not yet'. But how would the growth of international tensions inside the Soviet Union directly affect the East European process? One can imagine its cutting both ways: negatively, by prompting a backlash against Gorbachev's reform programme or by underscoring the need for tighter imperial control (lest, say, Poland become an example for Lithuania); positively, by giving the Soviet leaders more than enough to handle at home, thus increasing the temptation to let East European states work out their own problems in their own ways.

system: either into some 'viable'[16] system short of liberal democracy as we know it, in Western, Northern, and Southern Europe, or simply into a Central European variant of liberal democracy.

Decay

Why should anyone in Eastern Europe ever support a socialist state tied to the Soviet Union? Forty years ago there were perhaps three main reasons for doing such a curious thing. First, there was the reason of force. Secondly, there was what presented itself as the force of reason: that is ideology. Thirdly, there was the hope of emancipatory modernization. The reason of force had two sides. In Eastern Europe it was Soviet armies that defeated Nazi Germany; Soviet power could subsequently be said to protect the new territories of Poland and the restored territory of Czechoslovakia against a revanchist Germany. For that, some felt they had reason to be grateful. On the other side of this coin there was simply *force majeure*. The Soviet Union was self-evidently the single dominant power in the region. It, or its fraternal Communist parties, had the guns, the ammunition, the soldiers, the police, and the will to use them. If you resisted, they would crush you. There was no alternative. Not a noble reason for supporting a state, but a powerful one.

Soviet power came as 'the wheel of history'. It brought a future that was both inevitable and sublime. Many reasons led sensitive and educated men and women to embrace those incredible, utopian claims of ideology: from the experience of social injustice, racial prejudice, and bigotry under pre-war regimes to the indescribably terrible Central European experience of war, occupation, and Holocaust. These reasons cannot be summarized or synthesized, for they are not only reasons but motives, drives, compounds of fear and longing, 'of eros and of dust': hunger for power, lust for destruction, vulgar ambition, but also desperate responses to such suffering as the human spirit simply will not acknowledge to be senseless.

[16] I use the term 'viable' in the sense very usefully explored by Włodzimierz Brus in his 'Socialism—Feasible and Viable?' *New Left Review*, No. 153 (September/October, 1985), pp. 43–62 (a review essay on Alec Nove's *Economics of Feasible Socialism*.)

Literature and biography, rather than philosophy or history, are here the only ladders to *Verstehen*.[17]

The more rational part was the hope of emancipatory modernization. In, say, 1948 it was by no means wholly irrational to believe that some version of Soviet socialist planned economy could pull most of Eastern Europe out of its historic backwardness and dependency and, particularly in the case of its developed parts such as the Czech lands or Silesia, even out-perform the capitalist economies. Nor was it entirely absurd to imagine that a socialist state could achieve a standard of social justice and 'social rights'—universal equal provision of employment, housing, health care, education, and so forth—far superior to the miserable standards of much of pre-war Eastern Europe, and perhaps even superior to those achieved in capitalist states.

Up to the mid-sixties it remained possible to believe that something of this was actually happening. Growth rates were high, even allowing for statistical exaggeration. Western scholars wrote seriously about 'convergence'. Khrushchev talked publicly of 'burying' the West. The Czechoslovak leader Antonín Novotny worried privately about Czechoslovakia's economic problems of success.[18] As for 'social rights', there was already one great structural inequality—automatically privileged status for the *nomenklatura*—but it none the less really looked as if there could be jobs, housing, basic health care, and basic schooling for all. A certain rudimentary social security was an indisputable fact. So was the social advancement of a whole generation of workers and particularly peasant children, who found themselves, for the first time, in a modern apartment with running water and inside lavatory, or even in a lace-curtained office, with a potted plant and a plastic Lenin.

[17] Czesław Miłosz's classic account, *The Captive Mind*, should be supplemented by the earthier observations of the other greatest living Polish poet, Zbigniew Herbert, in Jacek Trznadel, *Hańba Domowa* (Paris: Instytut Literacki, 1986).

[18] Thus, for example, Zbigniew Brzezinski's book of 1965, *Alternative to Partition*, contains a section on 'the ideological neutrality of industrial development', and statistical tables to show that Poland and Italy, Hungary and Austria, Czechoslovakia and Sweden were all developing pretty much in the same way. For 'convergence' see also Zbigniew Brzezinski and Samuel P. Huntington's book of 1964, *Political Power: USA, USSR*. The reference to Novotny comes in a reminiscence by Vasil Bil'ak, published in the Slovak paper *Nedelna Pravda*, 4 March, 1988.

But what is there today? Growth rates have slumped since the mid-seventies, with an absolute decline in national product in some years, not only in Poland but also in Hungary and Czechoslovakia. Eastern Europe's total share of world trade is shrinking. Poland, Hungary, and the GDR are among the world leaders in per capita hard currency debt.[19] The model plants of Stalinist modernization—those Lenin steelworks, Lenin mines, and Lenin shipyards—are now mostly sheer liabilities. Even the most advanced and West German subsidized-GDR has fallen dangerously behind with essential investment, not merely in the industrial plant, but in basic infrastructure: roads, railways, waterways, telephone lines, and so forth.

The Soviet Union offers less than before in hidden or open subsidy and next to nothing in providing a model for economic reform, management techniques, or technology.[20] Only by dint of their ties with Western Europe are some of these countries just barely clinging to the coat-tails of the revolution of high technology that is transforming the industrial West and Far East. The historical reckoning is drastic: 'We have lost four decades'; 'We are returning to the starting point of 1945–1946.' These are not the judgements of dissidents but almost casual asides from senior members of the government economic-reform teams in, respectively, Hungary and Poland. If one considers the added dynamism that West European economies may acquire in the mid-1990s through the completion of the EC internal market, it seems fair to say that—barring radical change—Eastern Europe once again faces the prospect of growing relative backwardness vis-à-vis Western Europe.

If this is the objective reality, the subjective reality for the individual citizen is even grimmer. The economists tell us that material standards of living have stagnated or declined, with open inflation in Poland and Hungary. But the quality of life is felt to have

[19] A very useful overview is the Economist Intelligence Unit's *Eastern Europe and the USSR: Economic Structure and Analysis* (London: Economist Intelligence Unit, 1988), especially the chapter by Lászlo Számuely, pp. 7–14.

[20] Even the highly conformist editor of the East German communist youth movement (FDJ) paper *Junge Welt* observed recently that although the Soviet Union deserves great historical respect for having defeated Hitler, 'as far as technology and progress are concerned, it is no model for us' (quoted in *Die Zeit*, 27 June, 1986).

233

sunk still further, because of pollution, because of the shortfall in basic investment—painfully visible in housing, hospitals, and schools—and because the members of the younger generation compare their situation not with their own countries' recent past, but with the situation of their contemporaries in Western Europe, whither they travel in growing numbers.[21]

In international forums, and notably at the Vienna Helsinki review conference, Soviet and East European governments still advance their notion of 'social rights', with the clear implication that whereas people in the West may enjoy more individual or civil rights, people in the East enjoy more social rights. But in much of Eastern Europe those very 'social rights' (to adopt the questionable terminology) have been eroded to an unprecedented degree, in both quality of things provided by the state and equality of access to them. Poland, where hospitals lack the simplest medicines, where children go to school in three shifts, for want of classroom space, and where a young couple can now expect to wait twenty years for an apartment, is obviously an extreme case. But even a good hospital in central Prague resembles an English hospital in, say, the early 1960s.

In addition, there is the injustice: not just the formal injustice of separate, better-supplied hospitals for the *nomenklatura* and the police, but the informal injustice of corruption and graft, when in practice you have to pay illicitly (preferably in hard currency) for the surgeon to perform an operation, for the nurses to look after you in the hospital, for extra tuition to remedy your child's inadequate schooling, and even for the apartment that is theoretically yours by right.

Current projects of economic reform will certainly result in a further erosion of these 'social rights', including violation of the ultimate taboo of full employment, as loss-making factories are closed. Unemployment of about 100,000 (some two per cent of the working population) is now officially projected for Hungary. Even for those in employment, there is the frustration of senseless work and a real feeling of exploitation. For the younger generation of worker and peasant children, moreover, there is little prospect of the kind of social advancement that their parents' generation enjoyed.

---

[21] One should also mention the impact of radio and television—not only the West German television received in most of East Germany, but also the Austrian television received in parts of Hungary and Czechoslovakia.

Solidarity, it has been well observed, was to some extent a product of blocked social mobility. Not only social but actual physical life expectancy has declined in some countries. In Hungary, average male life expectancy has reportedly declined from sixty-seven to sixty-three over the last eight years. The statistics for suicide, alcoholism, and drug abuse also show change for the worse.[22]

Of course the picture is not uniformly grim. Of course many young people in Eastern Europe have a rose-tinted picture of the West. But that itself is a reality that their governments have to confront. The general feeling is, I think, nicely captured in an exchange between Teresa Torańska, a Polish journalist of the younger generation, and Julia Minc, one of the old Stalinists she interviewed for her splendid book *Oni*. Julia Minc has been defending the Afghan government, 'which is trying to build socialism':

> *Torańska:* What is socialism?
> *Minc:* A higher standard of living for everyone, free education and social security.
> *Torańska:* Like in the West?[23]

Ah yes, socialism! The end of ideology and the bankruptcy of socialism in Eastern Europe have been proclaimed so often that one has to say more precisely what one means. In what senses is ideology more dead and socialism more bankrupt in Eastern Europe in the 1980s than it was in the 1970s? By then, of course, no one believed that heaven would be built on earth. Regimes sought their popular 'legitimation' in nationalism or consumerism as much as or more than in socialism. Popular ignorance of and indifference to the ideology had already attained impressive dimensions. Generally, one would rather people learned things than not; yet there is something

[22] The context of the Hungarian official estimate for unemployment is explained below (p. 266). The Pope and Father Jósef Tischner have both written eloquently about the problem of 'senseless work'. The reference to Solidarity as a product of blocked social mobility comes from an unpublished paper by Aleksander Smolar; the statistic for Hungarian life expectancy I owe to George Schöpflin. For some telling details on suicide, sickness, pollution, poverty, and inequality in Poland, see George Kolankiewicz and Paul G. Lewis, *Poland: Politics, Economics and Society* (London: Frances Pinter, 1988), esp. pp. 30–32, 42–43, 58–64.

[23] Teresa Torańska, *Oni* (London: Collins Harvill), p. 24.

glorious in the capacity of millions of human beings to spend billions of hours being inculcated with Marxism-Leninism and to emerge knowing nothing, but *absolutely nothing*, about it. In 1985 Radio Budapest sent two of its reporters to Marx Square to ask passers-by who Karl Marx was. The transcript notes:

> *Another voice:* He was a Soviet philosopher; Engels was his friend. Well, what else can I say? He died at an old age.
> *A female voice:* Of course, a politician. And he was, you know, he was what's his name's—Lenin's, Lenin, Lenin's works—well, he translated them into Hungarian.
> The reporters then went to Engels Square.
> *Q:* Who was Engels?
> *A:* He was an Englishman, and he screwed around with communism.[24]

But this is light relief. There are three serious ways in which ideology has further decayed in the 1980s. It remained generally true in the 1970s that although virtually no one had any use for official Marxism-Leninism, most people in Eastern Europe would probably endorse some variant of something called 'socialism', or even if they reacted against the term (because it was poisoned by official usage), they had internalized some of what might be regarded as core values of socialism: egalitarianism; belief in full employment; social ownership of the means of production; a large welfare role for the state. Evidence for this assertion came from sociological research, opinion surveys and, not least, from the demands made by the worker-activists and leaders of Solidarity in Poland. Yet there are now signs that even this is beginning to erode, under the impact of the economic and social crisis indicated above. At least among younger and better-educated people (students as well as skilled workers) in Poland and Hungary, not just the Soviet-type system but some basic core values of socialism, such as equality or social ownership, are increasingly questioned. It is still unlikely that in a free and secret ballot you would find a majority for returning heavy industry to private ownership. (Apart from any theoretical preferences, this would involve many people's voting themselves or their relatives out of a job. There is still widespread passive

[24] Quoted from Radio Free Europe Research, Hungarian SR/6, 16 May, 1985, pp. 39–41.

attachment to the old habit of 'they pretend to pay us, and we pretend to work.') But it may soon be right to talk, in this more fundamental sense, of a popular rejection of socialism *tout court*.[25]

Secondly, socialism has virtually disappeared from the language of opposition. Of course KOR and Charter 77 had already, in the late 1970s, taken a decisive step beyond the revisionist hope of 'socialism with a human face'. Yet Adam Michnik ended his seminal essay on the 'New Evolutionism' in 1976 with a sentence beginning, 'Every act of resistance permits and allows us to build the foundations for a structure of democratic socialism . . .' and much of the vocabulary of the opposition in Poland, Hungary, and Czechoslovakia was unmistakably of the left.

This is no longer true. The small refounded Polish Socialist Party (PPS) and the dwindling 'Eurocommunist' faction of Charter 77 are the exceptions that prove the rule. If asked 'How do you recognize a leftist opposition intellectual in East Central Europe today?' the unkind answer might be: 'The leftist intellectual is the one who says that the categories left and right no longer have any significance in East Central Europe.' The right does not say that; and by now it is certainly possible to talk of a 'right' opposition. Indeed, for good or ill, the fashion in oppositional thinking, whether in Poland, Hungary, or Czechoslovakia, is now for liberal, libertarian, conservative, or revived pre-war nationalist/national-democratic/populist argument and/or rhetoric.

[25] Byron once said that while the English do not have the word *longueur*, they have the *thing* in great profusion. One might say the same about Solidarity and socialism. The word did not appear in the Solidarity programme of autumn 1981; but the thing was there in some profusion. Clearly, in all of East Central Europe there is still a strong current of egalitarianism and a deeply ingrained habit of looking to the state as provider. But the *trend* is away from this. For evidence see, for example, the article by Lena Kolarska-Bobinska in the special Central and East European issue of *Social Research*, Vol.55, No.1, Spring/Summer 1988. According to a report on the latest in a fascinating series of surveys of Polish attitudes, 'Poles '88', thirty to forty per cent of respondents were in favour of permitting private ownership *without any limitation* in the retail trade, restaurants, services, agrarian wholesale, and housing construction. A majority was still against the reprivatization of hospitals, social security, banks, and heavy industry. But would an opinion survey even in Mrs Thatcher's Britain show a majority for the reprivatization of hospitals, social security, or even of heavy industry? (see Władysław Adamski and others, 'Konflikty i Reformy', in *Polityka*, 23 July, 1988.)

Thirdly, there is the change in official ideology. It has been customary to observe that although the leaders of socialist states might not privately believe a word of their own official doctrine, they cannot publicly abandon it, since this is the only fundamental legitimation they possess for their continued monopoly of power. Historical necessity must stand in for charisma, divine right, or the ballot box. Yet in Poland and Hungary the ideological pretence has been dropped to an extraordinary degree. The new Hungarian leader, Károly Grósz, has said that it is only because of 'bad luck' *(pech)* that Hungary has ended up with a one-party system.[26] I cited at the beginning of this essay the remark of the most outspoken reformist in his politburo, Imre Pozsgay, that he had only a practical argument: the need for political stability.

In Poland, the Jaruzelski regime has not entirely abandoned ideological self-justification, and the most vaunted 'reformist' in the politburo, Mieczysław F. Rakowski, believes in the leading role of the Communist party more fervently than many a 'hard-liner'.[27] Yet the defence of martial law—still an obsession with this group—was conducted in almost entirely non-ideological terms. The government adopted what might be called a neo-brutalist tone: If we had not done it, the Russians would have. In any case, we have the guns and you do not: So what are you going to do about it? Come and get us! We know we're a minority government. We know we're hated. But we're going to pull this nation up by its bootstraps whether it likes it or not. History will prove us right. That, in effect, was the message of the likes of Rakowski, the government spokesman Jerzy Urban, and the *Polityka* columnist Daniel Passent. As for economics: in both countries, the superiority of capitalism is more or less openly acknowledged.

Threadbare as the ideological legitimation had already become, its nearly total abandonment in favour of arguments of *raison d'état*,

[26] Cited from Charles Gati, 'Reforming Communist Systems: Lessons from the Hungarian Experience', in William E. Griffith, ed., *Central and Eastern Europe and the West* (Boulder, Colorado: Westview Press, 1989).
[27] This is vividly apparently from a remarkable leaked document by Rakowski, entitled (in Polish), 'Reflections on Some Aspects of the Political and Economic Situation in the Polish People's Republic in the Second Half of the Nineteen Eighties.' (Hereafter Rakowski, 'Reflections . . .') The sixty-page typescript is signed and dated 'Warsaw, 8.6–10.10. 1987.' Rakowski has privately confirmed that it is genuine. All translations are my own.

expediency, or efficiency is a significant development. In the short term, this redounds to the popular credit of the leadership: 'At least they are calling a spade a spade.' But in the longer term, one wonders. If Václav Havel is correct when he writes that the quotidian canvas of ideologically determined lies plays an important role in preserving the system, then the very public rending of this canvas cannot be without consequences.

The hope of emancipatory modernization has faded. Ideology is not only dead by almost officially buried. This leaves the reason of force—and only in its coercive aspect. For while Soviet leaders may still believe that Eastern Europe owes the Soviet Union a 'blood debt'[28] for liberation from Nazi occupation, I doubt if there is now a single human being anywhere in Eastern Europe who does not feel that this 'debt', insofar as it ever existed, has long ago been paid, with multiple compound interest. General Jaruzelski may still wheel out the old line about the Soviet Union's protecting the Polish frontiers against German revanchism, but most young Poles have an increasingly positive view of the Federal Republic and certainly do not believe for an instant that the Red Army is there to protect them against the West Germans.[29]

---

[28] For Soviet claims of the 'blood debt' at the time of the invasion of Czechoslovakia see Karen Dawisha, *The Kremlin and the Prague Spring* (Berkeley, California: University of California Press, 1984).

[29] According to the series of sociological surveys entitled 'Poles, '80,'81,'84', and, most recently, ' '88', the percentage of respondents who saw a threat to the independence of the Polish state from the Federal Republic fell from a mere 10.7 per cent in 1980 (when the figure for the Soviet Union was 49.6 per cent!) to 4.7 per cent in 1984 (USSR: 23 per cent), although a further 4 per cent in 1980 and 2.9 per cent in 1984 saw a threat from 'Germans'—without specifying which Germans! (See Jan Powiorski, 'Polacy '84 . . .' in *Krytyka*, Warsaw, No.27, 1988, p. 63.) I do not yet have figures from 'Poles '88'. Matthias Rust is probably the first German since the Second World War to be a popular hero in Poland. One of the surrealist 'Orange Alternative' groups in Poznań calls itself the 'Matthias Rust Commando': 'On 8 March this particular Matthias Rust landed outside a bar in Półwiejska Street, in the form of a group of women displaying banners proclaiming "We, Polish women, support the government," and the like. The group . . . quickly swelled to some one hundred people and proceeded down the road shouting, "Thank you for the price rises" and "Long live the government"' (*Obserwator Wielkopolski*, No.119, March 1988. Quoted in *Uncensored Poland News Bulletin*, No.12, 1988).

The fear of Soviet invasion and internal repression remains. It was reinforced throughout East Central Europe by the example of Poland's 'state of war'. Yet at the time of writing, in the summer of 1988, even these fears have diminished. For reasons outlined above, it is rational to assume that the danger of Soviet invasion has at least temporarily receded. But it is also broadly true to say that the level of internal repression has decreased, even in Czechoslovakia and the GDR.

Very nasty things still happen. In May, 'anti-terrorist' forces broke up a peaceful strike at the Nowa Huta steelworks in Kraków with gratuitous violence. Also with gratuitous brutality, Hungarian riot police dispersed a small, peaceful demonstration in Budapest on the thirtieth anniversary of the judicial execution of the leader of the 1956 revolutionary government, Imre Nagy. The prime mover of the petition for religious freedom in Czechoslovakia, Augustin Navrátil, has been committed to a psychiatric hospital. Germans are still imprisoned or shot just for trying to walk from Germany to Germany.[30] But in general the risks of speaking your mind have become more calculable and less extreme, although they still differ greatly from country to country. Adam Michnik says that this is not 'socialism with a human face' but 'totalitarianism with the teeth knocked out'. The metaphor is only half apt. Yes, this is a further symptom of the decay of a once-totalitarian system. But the teeth—the instruments of coercion—are still there and, indeed, in the case of Poland, more numerous and sharper than ten years ago. What is different is that the present heads either have less will to use them or more desire not to use them, or indeed—for reality is complex and messy—a bit of both.

Yet this is surely the least irreversible of the trends of decay. One can hardly imagine a successful revival of ideology. A recovery of state-directed emancipatory modernization seems scarcely more probable. But one can all too easily imagine the recovery of force in states that still possess formidable apparatuses of repression. This

---

[30] However, it does appear that at the moment, thanks to consistent West German pressure, the East German border troops do not, as a rule, 'shoot to kill'. For Augustin Navrátil, see above, 'The Yeoman and the Cardinal', p. 192. His confinement to a mental hospital was reported in the *Frankfurter Allgemeine Zeitung* of 2 July, 1988.

might take new forms: the murder of Father Popiełuszko in Poland four years ago was more reminiscent of El Salvador than of 'classical' totalitarian repression. It might be an autonomous response to domestic unrest or unwilling compliance with a conservative backlash in Moscow. Yet even if there were to be a reversion in Poland to the systematic use of force, one can already say, with confidence, that this would not stem but rather hasten other processes of decay.

At the time of writing, the net result of all these different sorts of decay—imperial, regional, and national; economic and social; ideological and political—is that, in Hungary and Poland at least, there are more and larger spheres in which the state does not in practice intervene, or intervenes ineffectually, more opportunities for the individual citizen to speak and act for him or herself (but also more need to fend for yourself), more *de facto* pluralism, than at almost any time in the last forty years.[31] How, then, do people speak or act in these expanded spheres? What are the contours of emancipation?

Emancipation

A comprehensive map of the opposition in East Central Europe today would resemble nothing so much as one of those kaleidoscopic multi-coloured maps of ethnic groups in this region before the war. In both Poland and Hungary, groups or grouplets whose identities or programmes arise from specific post-war realities overlap or combine with groups raising almost every flag, slogan, aspiration, or prejudice of the pre-war political spectrum (except communism): populists, reform economists, radical sociologists, smallholders, Lutherans, Catholic 'base groups', evangelical sects, democratic opposition, democratic youth, democratic academics, Solidarity, Fighting Solidarity, national democrats, liberal democrats, liberal Catholics and conservative Catholics, Christian socialists, Jews, anti-Semites, advocates of workers' self-government, apostles of free enterprise, syndicalists and monetarists, self-styled 'crazy liberals', 'neorealists', 'neopositivists': You name it, we have it. And this is merely the surface of explicit opposition. One could produce another

[31] Excepting of course, a few weeks in 1956 and, for Poland, sixteen months in 1980–1981.

rich catalogue of official or semi-official projects for 'reform'. Hungarian political scientists have coined the delightful term *paradigm ecstasy.* [32]

Here I shall merely indicate four dimensions that every cartographer of emancipation must bear in mind. The first might be called a popular rediscovery of the national past: a widespread and passionate interest in history,[33] pre-war national traditions, forgotten authors, ethnic minorities past and present (Jews, Germans, Ukrainians, Hungarians in Transylvania and Slovakia), and regional ties ('Central Europe', Germany, Lithuania, and the Ukraine). To subsume all this under the label 'nationalism' would be crass over-simplification. Much of it is simply the quest for what is regarded in the West as a 'normal' cultural continuity: an identification with national symbols, traditions, and even myths, as benign in moderation as it is dangerous in excess. The lack of normal access to the national past was a form of deprivation; the recovery of it is a form of emancipation. Tradition, said G.K. Chesterton, is the democracy of the dead. But does the recultivation of tradition necessarily conduce to the democracy of the living? What about the authentic, national un- or anti-democratic traditions? And cannot nationalism act—or be used—as a substitute for democracy?

This fear is particularly acute among the 'democratic opposition' in Hungary. Why, they ask, did the new Party leadership, as one of its first acts, permit an independent mass demonstration against the Ceauşescu regime's persecution of the Hungarian minority in Transylvania? Partly, of course, to give vent to a burning popular concern and gain social credit for so doing. But also, perhaps, because if you let people shout about national rights in Transylvania, they may be less inclined to think about civil rights in Hungary. Certainly, it was a strange affair, this torch-lit demonstration in Heroes' Square in Budapest. The speeches were an uneasy mixture of somewhat stilted liberal sentiments (universal rights, the poor Romanians

---

[32] For *paradigm ecstasy*, see Rudolf L. Tökes. 'The Science of Politics in Hungary in the 1980s', in *Südosteuropa*, Vol.37 (1/1988), p. 15 and *passim*.
[33] The observation about the interest in history is repeatedly made in regular series of reports about Polish *samizdat* in the leading underground weekly *Tygodnik Mazowsze*.

suffer too) and purple patriotic rhetoric.[34] My overwhelming impression was of a lonely crowd: men and women with slightly bewildered faces mouthing half-forgotten hymns and just beginning to rediscover, for good or ill, what it means to be a nation; a spectacle at once pathetic, moving, and disturbing.

'All we want is freedom and democracy for the Hungarians in Transylvania,' said a speaker at one point. Loud applause. Then, almost as an afterthought, '. . . and freedom for ourselves.' Still louder applause. If I were the new Hungarian Party leader, Károly Grósz, I would not be at all sure that I could separate the national from the democratic cause. It is a short step from asking why the Hungarian government is not doing more for the Hungarians in neighbouring socialist states to asking why you have the kind of Hungarian government that cannot do more. To some extent, the Jaruzelski government faces a comparable dilemma on the burning national question of the Katyn massacre and the other 'blank spaces' of Soviet-Polish relations. If you cannot make or obtain a clear statement of the truth, it may be safer to say nothing.

A second dimension is the revival of religion, not just in Poland, but also in Czechoslovakia, East Germany, and even, on a very small scale, in Hungary. This, too is exceedingly complex, whether one considers social roots, confessional forms, or political implications. Why do so many young people in Eastern Europe, often brought up in a wholly atheistic environment, at home as well as at school, turn to religion, or at least to the churches? Is it simply because nature abhors a value vacuum such as the collapse of socialist ideology has left? Is it the search for comfort amid material decay, misery, and hopelessness?

> Change and decay in all around I see;
> O Thou, who changest not, abide with me.

Part of the larger rediscovery of the past? The impact of the Polish pope? Divine intervention? All of the above? Religious participation can be a channel for basically secular, social, and political aspirations: as it is in part of the Church-protected peace and human rights movement in the GDR. But it can also be a substitute for social and political activism. The surge of church-going in Poland after the

[34] See above, 'Death to Nero', p. 202. One should note that the Romanian refugees in Hungary were also represented at the demonstration.

imposition of martial law had elements of both. Like the rediscovery of national history, the religious revival cuts several ways, and it is very difficult to say which cut goes deeper.[35] This is a nice analytical problem for the scholar but a hard political dilemma for the authorities.

A third important dimension is what has come to be known as the reconstitution of 'civil society' in East Central Europe. There is already a substantial literature on this subject,[36] yet the concept remains woefully imprecise, partly because of the variety of earlier uses (notably by Hegel), but mainly because it is currently used to describe two different things: (A) the entire range of social associations, ties, and activities independent of the state, from glee clubs to Charter 77, from *samizdat* to breviaries, and from private farmers to homosexuals;[37] (B) more narrowly, and more politically, the products of that strategy of 'social self-organization' that was, broadly speaking, adopted by the democratic oppositions in Poland, Hungary, and Czechoslovakia in the mid- to late 1970s. For them, the reconstitution of 'civil society' was both an end in itself and a means to political change, including, eventually, change in the nature of the state.

(B) is a sub-category of (A). The growth of (A) will generally be unplanned, or at least not part of an overall political strategy, yet the emergence of non-political social associations and bonds has been facilitated by, and is deliberately included in, the strategy of (B). It might just be possible to call (A) simply 'society', except that in Poland the term 'society' (*społeczeństwo*) has come to be used precisely for those organized or civilly active parts of society (whether workers, farmers, or intellectuals) that, since August 1980, can meaningfully be talked of in opposition to the powers that be

---

[35] Even in the most political churches, there is an extraordinary jumbling of national, social, and religious issues. At the last 'Mass for the Fatherland' I attended at Father Popiełuszko's church in Warsaw, the preacher ended up exhorting the faithful to fight the good fight against alcoholism, robbery, abortion, and communism—in that order.

[36] See, for example, John Keane, *Democracy and Civil Society* (London: Verso, 1988) and John Keane, ed., *Civil Society and the State* (London: Verso, 1988), especially the essay by Z. A. Pelczynski.

[37] The example of homosexuals is not imaginary. An association of homosexuals is currently applying for registration in Warsaw.

(*wladza*). So while elsewhere people say 'civil society' but mean society, here people say 'society' but mean civil society.

In Hungary, 'civil society', even in sense (A), was almost totally destroyed by Stalinism and János Kádár's counter-revolution after 1956, but it has been slowly, quietly reconstituted. A rudimentary measure of this is the number of independent clubs and associations: more than 13,000 in the 1930s, sinking to as few as 1,000 in the 1950s, but up again to more than 3,500 by 1981.[38] However, in the last year or two, and most dramatically in recent months, we have seen a sudden flowering of civil society in sense (B): the more or less spontaneous combustion of debating clubs, associations, and lobbies of different social and intellectual groups, most of whose members are consciously agitating as *citizens* concerned, not merely with their individual or group interests, but with the state of the nation. The appeal for the demonstration in Heroes' Square was signed by no fewer than twelve such groups, and two of these were alliances: The Hungarian Democratic Forum for 'populists' or nationalists, the Network of Free Initiatives for the rest.

Probably the most notable of these new groups are the Democratic Union of Scientific Workers (i.e., academics) and the Alliance of Democratic Youth (FIDESZ) (mainly students), both founded in the spring of 1988. These are the first independent unions to be launched in Eastern Europe since the banning of Solidarity. The differences between this ferment and Poland in 1980 are obvious and legion. Yet I must say that listening to a gloriously discursive meeting of the new academics' union (only academics would try to write footnotes to a demonstration) or talking to the marvellously fresh and bright student activists of FIDESZ, I felt almost as if I were back in Poland in the autumn of 1980.

In Poland, the situation is both worse and better. When, in the mid-1970s, the democratic opposition first embarked on the strategy of 'social self-organization' and 'change from below', it never imagined a mass movement like Solidarity. It did, on the other hand, imagine that it might find some partners, albeit reluctant ones,

---

[38] Excluding sports clubs. Quoted in a paper by Elemér Hankiss for the Woodrow Wilson Center European Alumni Association conference on 'The European Question' in May 1988. (The papers from this conference are due to be published in book form.) The number of private foundations also rose from nil in 1977 to 380 by 1986.

within the system, and that the result might even be some new, explicit or implicit, 'social contract'. In the late 1980s, civil or self-organized society exists in Poland on a scale no one then dreamed of. There is a fantastic landscape of independent clubs, associations, periodicals, publishers, and the like, and this, together with the existence of something called 'the opposition', is accepted by more realistic members of the *nomenklatura*, and even of the secret police, as a lasting feature of Polish life. In his long memorandum, written in 1987, Mieczysław F. Rakowski noted that 'in practice we have recognized the opposition as a lasting element on the country's political map.'[39]

Earlier this year, the authorities felt themselves compelled by the depth of the economic crisis and popular discontent to start talking privately with this opposition again, very gingerly exploring the notion of an 'anti-crisis pact'. In recent weeks, they have been compelled by a wave of strikes to start talking directly and publicly with the man whom they have so often said was no longer a 'partner' for them: Lech Wałęsa. But, as I write, in mid-September 1988, there is still nothing remotely resembling a 'partnership' between the authorities and the 'society' represented by Solidarity. There is no 'historic compromise' or 'social contract'.

This seven-year stalemate has had many demoralizing effects. Not the least important is that it has confined 'civil society' largely to the realm of words. Written words—in *samizdat* journals too numerous to list, legal independent Catholic journals like *Tygodnik Powszechny*, *Znak*, or *Więz*, internal university publications, *samizdat* books from publishers like *Krąg*, *Nowa*, or *cdn*, political programmes, long and short, moderate and extreme; spoken words—in sermons, hymns, lectures, legal and illegal seminars, worker education groups, theatres, cabaret, unofficial cassettes; audio-visual words— wonderfully funny tapes from the satirist Jacek Fedorowicz, wonderfully serious tapes about Friedrich von Hayek, passed around on the country's now numerous videocassette recorders; words, words, words.

For many, this is still exhilarating—for writers, in particular. But most people are not writers. Although it is wrong and patronizing to assume that workers or peasants are not interested in words, ideas,

---

[39] Rakowski, 'Reflections . . .', p. 40.

free debate, worship or drama, these give no immediate answers to their most pressing concerns: wages, housing, health care, pollution. Even a student or academic may tire eventually of words if they are wholly disconnected from any visible results. The defensive message of much of the underground press is summed up in the title of a journal I noticed the other day: *Jesteśmy*, which means simply 'We Are.' The contemporary Polish version of Descartes is 'I print, therefore, I am.'

What is more, the virtual abandonment of ideology by the authorities, combined with the relative freedom of speech, even in censored publications, has resulted in a curious devaluation of language. Solzhenitsyn's 'one word of truth' really mattered when it was spoken amid a forest of lies, and when those in power seriously sought to compel public endorsement of the lies: But when you can say anything you like and those in power will even publicly agree with you (but then do nothing about it), words, however true or noble, lose some of their value.

Partly in response to this impasse, many bright young people have turned their attention to the most recent and dynamic form of social emancipation: the fourth dimension. This is private enterprise. Of course most classical definitions of civil society assume an economic foundation, with private ownership, property rights guaranteed by due process of law, free exchange, and so forth. In a sense, therefore, the pursuit of private enterprise is the logical complement of the pursuit of civil society. But in practice, the engagement in private enterprise has so far been seen rather as an alternative to the pursuit of civil society in the narrower, more political sense indicated above.

I suspect that few people in the West (and perhaps also in the East) have really woken up to the sheer scale of private economic activity in Poland and Hungary. In his excellent book of 1985, *Private Enterprise in Eastern Europe*, Anders Åslund suggested that the economic activity of the legal private sector in Eastern Europe was likely to continue to fluctuate around a very low level, as it had done ever since the 1950s. But in a recent paper, the Anglo-Polish economist Jacek Rostowski argues convincingly that 'Åslund's Law' no longer holds for Poland; and the same is clearly true for Hungary.

All figures are extremely speculative, but Rostowski estimates that private economic activity (legal and not so legal) now accounts for somewhere between thirty-eight and forty-five per cent of personal money incomes in Poland. Total private-sector employment accounts for nearly one third of the labour force. Two fifths of new housing construction can be classified as private. In 1986 and 1987, hard currency remitted from abroad by individual Poles was almost equal to the hard-currency trade surplus earned by the whole socialized sector.[40] For Hungary, private economic activity is estimated to generate at least thirty per cent of household incomes. Although the share of the labour force is much smaller (no private farmers), it is growing, and estimates of the private share of housing construction go as high as eighty-five per cent. In both countries, the role of the private sector is already visible, both in the city centres and the countryside: here a bar, boutique, or software firm, there a smart new villa or farmhouse.

In many ways, the dramatic growth of private enterprise in the 1980s is a classic example of emancipation in decay, or Ottomanization at the social level. Private enterprise is stepping in to fill the holes left by the decaying state-provider: literally so, in the case of private dentists. It flourishes by providing what the public sector cannot, whether housing, services, consumer goods, or medical care. The variety of people who have turned to private enterprise is at least as wide as that of those who have turned to religion. So is the variety of motives. With religion, it is not always the pure love of God; with private enterprise, it is not always the pure love of money. Those involved range from people using private enterprise as a means to support opposition publications to secret policemen, who keep an official eye on private firms but also an unofficial hand in the till. There is good evidence, both from Poland and Hungary, of major participation in private firms by senior members of the *nomenklatura*, their relatives or placemen.

For many people, private economic activity clearly is an alternative to public political activity. A Hungarian professor tells me that there are two quite distinct types among his students: those who wish to go into private enterprise and those who wish to go into oppositional activity—the party of interests, as it were, and the party of values. The sociologist Robert Manchin has found from his research that Hungarians with private sources of income are on

[40] Jacek Rostowski, 'The Decay of Socialism and the Growth of Private Enterprise in Poland', 1988 typescript.

balance less likely to express discontent with the present political system or to articulate conceptions of political change. 'If part-time self-employment is a value-generating strategy at all,' he writes cautiously, 'individual freedom is certainly not one of its core values.'[41] In Poland, I have been told repeatedly by university teachers that private business is now the consuming interest of many of the brightest students. The official politics of 'the reds' (as the Communist authorities are politely called by the disaffected young) are beneath discussion. But the unofficial politics of the opposition also seem to offer few perspectives. What they want is to travel to the West for a year, earn some hard currency, maybe learn some capitalist skills, and then return to set up a small private firm in Poland, whether dealing in video-cassettes, carpentry, decorating, trinkets, toys, or computer software.[42]

There are, however, individuals and groups who connect their advocacy (and practice) of private enterprise with a larger vision of social and political change. If the strategy of the democratic opposition in the 1970s could be described as 'change from below', as opposed to the earlier revisionist hope of change from above, this 1980s vision might crudely be characterized as one of 'change from the side'. In Poland, most advocates of this path would probably be happy with the label liberals—and many use it themselves. In American terms, some might rather be described as neo-liberal or even neo-conservative, but there are significant differences of style

---

[41] Robert Manchin, 'Individual Economic Strategies and Social Consciousness', in the Central and East European special issue of *Social Research*, Vol.55, Nos. 1–2 (Spring/Summer 1988), pp. 77–96, this quotation on p. 93.

[42] Some thirty per cent of entrepreneurs are under thirty-five according to Rostowski, quoting J. Baczyński in *Polityka*, No. 37, 1987. 'Almost ninety per cent of the high school students surveyed in 1987 said they wanted to leave Poland for an extended time in order to earn hard currency' (RFE/RL *Soviet East European Report*, Vol.V, No. 32, August 10, 1988). One other attraction of capitalism was nicely illustrated by an observation made during General Jaruzelski's televised 'meeting with youth' last November. 'My professor,' observed Wojciech Nowakowski, 'used to say that socialism is a beautiful idea but very poor, because it has no economics. And our classes in economics seemed to confirm this, because when we had to learn the principles of capitalist economics these were clear and very easy to remember. But to remember the principles of our economics we really had to sweat' (*Sztandar Młodych*, November 28–29, 1987.)

and philosophy between them. To confuse the Warsaw *Towarzystwo Gospodarcze* (Economic Association) with the Kraków *Towarzystwo Przemysłowe* (Manufacturing Association) is a sin almost as mortal as that of confusing the *New Republic* with *Commentary*. The movement has many intellectual peers,[43] but these two associations, bringing together theorists and practitioners of private enterprise, are probably its most important expressions to date.

The Kraków association began, in true Galician style, as a dining club. Intellectuals and entrepreneurs met for an excellent meal at a private house, in the course of which the intellectuals would explain the theory (out of Hayek by way of Michael Novak) and the entrepreneurs would explain the practice (out of the backyard by way of baksheesh), both sides being suitably fortified with vodka. Not wholly unfrivolous reports of these proceedings were published in the group's underground journal, *13*. Having overcome, as Mirosław Dzielski, an academic and leading figure in the association, explains, the opposition of 'the two most powerful institutions in Kraków'— the university and the Catholic weekly *Tygodnik Powszechny*—they proceeded to draw up the statutes of their association, for 'propagating citizens' economic activity and the principles of market economy'[44] in the Kraków voivodship, and applied to the authorities in all form for legal registration. This they somewhat surprisingly received at the end of last year, and launched a public lecture course entitled 'How to begin [in business]'. A large turn-out confirmed the impression that there is a great reservoir of public interest in this area, particularly among students, young professionals, and younger skilled workers.

The Warsaw association has not, at the time of writing, received permission for legal registration. Led by, among others, Aleksander Paszyński, a former *Polityka* journalist who resigned from the paper at the time of martial law and went on to build up a highly successful private housing consultancy firm, the *Towarzystwo Gospodarcze* has

---

[43] Among them one should certainly mention the veteran publicist Stefan Kisielewski, a founder of the 'Party of Crazy Liberals'; the economist Stefan Kurowski, who was already urging some of these ideas upon Solidarity in 1981 and is now on the board of the *Towarzystwo Gospodarcze;* and the economist-publicists Janusz Korwin-Mikke and Piotr Wierzbicki.

[44] '*Statut Krakowskiego Towarzystwa Przemysłowego*', paragraph 7 (typescript).

been somewhat more direct and more ambitious in its proclaimed goals: For example, it wants the right to work throughout the country. It is potentially a formidable economic force, since the combined capital of its member firms would probably be counted in hundreds of millions of złotys, or, which is more important, in hundreds of thousands of dollars. When I asked a senior government official why the authorities had not given the go-ahead for registration, he said simply: 'For fear of a camouflaged opposition.'

In fact, the mainstream opposition was initially critical of these initiatives, partly because some of their proponents explicitly presented them as an alternative to the Solidarity struggle. The advocacy of private enterprise was treated as a new version of the nineteenth-century post-insurrectionary strategy of 'organic work'. Mirosław Dzielski himself said that he was interested in those who 'in a socialist state want to make arrangements beside socialism and in spite of socialism.'[45] Their theoretical position is: We are not for the government or against the government; let it give us the tools, and we will get on with the job. Yet when you begin to look in detail at the conditions for a long-term, stable environment for a substantial private sector, you soon appreciate that the demand is, in fact, very radical indeed. The Kraków association's commentary on the government programme for the 'second stage of economic reform' begins by saying that it 'greets with satisfaction' the government's proposals. It ends by suggesting a programme of sound money, 'deregulation', privatization,[46] and tax reform that Margaret Thatcher could sign without a moment's hesitation.

The long-term message of the neo-liberals is ultimately little different from that of a conversation I heard between two lads in a crowded Warsaw tram at the time of the 1987 referendum on economic reform. After laughing about a friend who had gone to vote because he was afraid that otherwise the authorities ('*oni*') wouldn't let him go abroad, one lad said: 'But I suppose we *should* try and reform this economy somehow.' 'Come off it,' said the other. 'This

---

[45] See *Kurs*, No. 27 (1987).
[46] 'Privatisation should consist in the gradual sale into private hands of all industries belonging to the state'! Quoted from '*Opinia Krakowskiego Towarzystwa Przemysłowego na temat Programu Realizacyjnego Drugiego Etapu Reformy Gospodarczej*', typescript (Kraków: October 1987), p. 15 and *passim*.

reform hasn't a chance. The only thing is to do it like in America.'[47] An entirely rational position, though hardly one the authorities are likely to adopt. In the short term, however, there are good selfish reasons for the authorities to permit an expansion of the private sector.

In Hungary, the politico-philosophical theory is not so highly elaborated, but the entrepreneurial practice is much more so. Here there are already well-organized associations of entrepreneurs, with which the government is dealing directly. The main organ of entrepreneurial and free-market discussion is not a *samizdat* journal but an entirely official weekly, *HVG*, which might very loosely be described as the Hungarian *Economist*. Thick with advertisments from private and co-operative firms, it brings excellent reports of economic and political developments in Hungary and elsewhere, and prints the most radical reform proposals this side of *samizdat*. Sooner or later, an analysis of this fourth dimension of social emancipation inevitably becomes also a discussion of official proposals for economic and political reform.

Reform

The word 'reform' has been devalued by overuse, both in the writing of Western journalists and scholars and in the rhetoric of Communist leaders. In Lenin's day, 'reformism' was the ultimate transgression for communists; now it is their saving grace. In Western usage, the term has been pressed into service to describe everything from a mere adjustment of economic policy to a fundamental transformation of the system, political as well as economic.

[47]But has not the pope criticized American capitalism? There does seem to be a certain tension between the pope's social teaching and the neoliberals' talk of 'imparting a moral ethos to capitalism' (Mirosław Dzielski in *Kurs*, No.27, 1987). However, his 1988 encyclical, 'Solicitudo Rei Socialis', has a significant passage about the evils that flow from the suppression of individual economic initiative 'in the name of an alleged "equality",' which 'provokes a sense of frustration or desperation and predisposes people to opt out of national life, impelling them to emigrate,' etc. The communiqué of the Polish episcopate immediately after the publication of this encyclical declared roundly that 'in the light of Catholic social teaching, it is essential to extend considerably the role of the private sector in the national economy' (26 February, 1988).

What are reformers in Poland and Hungary today trying to reform, and why are they trying to reform it? A rather clear answer is given in the remarkable private memorandum by Mieczysław F. Rakowski, who became prime minister of Poland in autumn 1988.[48] Poland, he says, has been living through an economic, social, and political 'crisis' (another devalued word!) since 1980, and arguably since 1976. The Polish crisis is *sui generis*, but 'we should not forget that basically symptoms of crisis are becoming apparent in all socialist countries.' 'Not only Poland,' he writes,

> But most socialist countries are threatened with relegation to the position of countries incapable of keeping up with the revolution of technological development in capitalism.

And again,

> If one could transport a capitalist society into our everyday reality, it would very soon rise up in a revolutionary struggle.

But not only a capitalist society. For 'due to the development of the mass media, the societies of our countries can "peer into" the everyday life of the masses under capitalism.' The conclusion is drawn a few pages later. If the socialist 'formation' does not find the strength to reform itself, Rakowski writes, 'the further history of our formation will be marked by shocks and revolutionary explosions, initiated by an increasingly enlightened people.'

Well, exactly. Allowing for some slight differences of terminology, this could almost be an academic analysis for the CIA. Yet this is a text by a man who is not only a politburo member but who, according to informed rumour, became a politburo member on the strength of this text. Private statements by Hungarian politburo members reflect an equally striking realism in the diagnosis of the disease—although neither they nor Rakowski are half as realistic in prescribing the cure. In other words, some men in power see the reality of decay and the prospect of growing relative backwardness, which I sketched above. They also see that if they do not do something drastic to modernize their economies, their own people will unkindly invite them to leave the stage. A younger generation, better educated, better informed, relatively unafraid, looking to

---

[48] See footnote 27 above.

Gorbachev in the East and the European Community in the West, will just not be kidded by fatuous ideology, paper patriotism, or more promises of jam tomorrow.

What the reformers want to reform is thus, in the first place, the economy. Now there is, of course, a more than thirty-year history of attempts at economic reform in Eastern Europe. But as Włodzimierz Brus, the doyen of this subject, wrote recently, 'with a single exception' these attempts 'have failed even in the sense of institutionalizing a new system, let alone in exercising a real impact on performance.'[49] The single exception is Hungary, yet virtually all Hungarian economists now agree that twenty years of the 'new economic mechanism' have not effected a real transformation from the command economy to market socialism. Interference by the central political bureaucracy has remained all-pervasive, with loss-making state enterprises consistently bailed out by huge arbitrary tax breaks or subsidies, and with a vast grey area of managerial-bureaucratic 'bargaining' instead of the free play of market forces.[50]

The task of economic reform becomes more difficult with every passing year. The gap with the West grows wider. The list of the deferred tasks of modernization grows ever longer—not only closing outdated plants and opening modern ones, but also all that neglected investment in infrastructure, not to mention such luxuries as elementary environmental protection. The inevitable social cost of reform therefore continues to grow, while the regimes' popular credit continues to dwindle. They recognize that a 'radical' economic reform is necessary. Those great model enterprises of the heroic phase of Stalinist modernization—the Lenin shipyards, the Lenin steelworks, the Lenin mines—have been making losses and devouring subsidies as huge as their façades. They should have been closed long ago: they must be closed now. Subsidizing the production of basic commodities is a great burden on the state

[49] Quoted from W. Brus, 'The Experience of Economic Reforms: 1956–1987', typescript, p. 3. See also his contribution to Volume 2 of the *Economic History of Eastern Europe*, edited by M.C. Kaser (Oxford: Oxford University Press, 1987).

[50] See János Kornai, 'The Hungarian Reform Process: Visions, Hopes, and Reality', in the *Journal of Economic Literature*, Vol. XXIV (December 1986), pp. 1687–1737.

budget. Many official prices are wholly unrealistic in relation to domestic, let alone Western, markets. The subsidies must therefore come down and the prices—up. People will only work better if they can earn more money by doing so. Some people must therefore earn more than others.

What does this perspective of reform imply for a socialist state? Socialism's proudest boast has been full employment. Reform requires unemployment. Socialism promised equality. Reform means more inequality: a second pyramid of inequality, superimposed on the existing pyramid that has the *nomenklatura* sprawled across its peak.[51] Socialism said 'from each according to his ability, to each according to his need.' It is precisely the unskilled workers, the old, the weak, and the needy who will do worst out of a radical market reform. What is more—according to the sociologists in Poland, at least—those who are likely to do badly out of the reform are precisely those who are at present more inclined to give the government their confidence; whereas those who support the idea of reform are least likely to support the government. And anyway, why should anyone believe that this agonizing wrench will actually produce the goods? How many times already has the regime promised jam tomorrow! Where are the guarantees?

Seeing both the social cost of economic reform and the political credibility gap, the reformers in both Hungary and Poland are now saying that political reform is the indispensable concomitant of economic reform. Indeed, the new leadership in Hungary declares that political reform is the most important side of the equation. This is in diametric contrast to reforms carried out under János Kádár, whose attraction to neighbouring rulers was precisely that they seemed to demonstrate the possibility of successful economic reform without political reform. What is more, the political reforms are at least partly conceived of as what the Polish politburo member Marian Orzechowski recently called 'conscious self-limitation of the Party's

---

[51] For the image of the intersecting pyramids see George Kolankiewicz and Paul Lewis, *Poland: Politics, Economics and Society* (London: Frances Pinter, 1988), figure 2.1, p. 64, drawing on the work of Iván Szelényi.

power.'[52] The more usual euphemistic terminology is 'redefining the leading role of the Party.' The 'strategy of retreat' is the oldest trick in the book of communist attempts at economic reform. It dates back to Lenin's New Economic Policy (NEP). But as a conscious political strategy, an NPP so to speak, it is more novel. Gorbachev's example has, of course, greatly facilitated this part of the discussion.

What would be 'success' for these reforms? A minimal definition of success is easily given: to have averted revolution. A maximal definition is more difficult. For communist reformers like Rakowski or Grósz, it is a fair assumption that maximal success means fulfilling the forty-year-old promise of modernization, making their states respected, competitive members of a larger European community (small *c*), *while at the same time retaining the maximum possible amount of power in their own hands.* They want, in other words, to have their cake and eat it. The Party's retreat, if retreat there must be, is tactical or at best strategic. There is a strong element of *reculer pour mieux sauter.* Lower down the Party apparatus, the selfish motive of preserving your own power and privileges may easily outweigh any larger concern about the future of the country. (This is not to imply that those at the top are any less selfish, just that they are less immediately threatened.) All this is human, all too human. There are very few universally valid laws of history, but one of them is: Men cling to power.

Yet many of those outside the Party who support the reforms, and whose active participation is essential to their success—economists, journalists, academics, lawyers, some managers, entrepreneurs, private or co-operative farmers, skilled workers—have a different maximal definition of success. This is that reform should become transformation. The Party's retreat should be permanent. The courts really should be courts. Parliament really should be parliament. Unions really should be unions. Reform begun at the behest of Party leaders (out of insight into necessity) would march ineluctably beyond those leaders' maximal goals. The forces of change from above, change from below, and what I have called 'change from the side' would somehow combine in the process of transformation: in part willingly, in part unwillingly, but none the less combine. The energies of social emancipation would somehow be harnessed to

[52] See *Trybuna Ludu* (6 September, 1988).

halt, or even reverse, the awful process of economic and social decay. Reform would indeed avert violent revolution. But it would effect a peaceful revolution instead.

The state would reacquire what one might call 'internal sovereignty', in the sense well described by an outstanding Polish political scientist currently living in Rome. 'The state is firmly sovereign when it governs society and also serves society, and allows the nation to realize its own subjectivity', writes this author. 'Queen of Poland!' he continues. 'Queen of Poland, I also wish to entrust you with the difficult task of those who wield authority on Polish soil. The state gains its strength first of all from the support of society.' This may not be the language we usually expect from political science, but the words of Pope John Paul II, addressed as it were directly to the icon of the Black Madonna in the monastery of Jasna Góra, none the less express an analytical truth.[53]

Now, it is obviously germane to ask how the recovery of 'internal sovereignty' might relate to the expansion of 'external sovereignty' or, to revert to the central metaphor of Ottomanization, how the emancipation of societies from states relates to the emancipation of states from the imperial centre. Western analysts have paid considerable attention to the cautious manifestation of verbal autonomy in foreign policy by Hungary, the GDR and, to some extent, Bulgaria, in the years 1983–1985. This might fairly be described as a positive assertion of these states' limited sovereignty. Under Gorbachev, such daring has not been necessary in foreign policy. At the same time, the external limits on sovereignty for East European states have widened, at least in practice and for the time being. This should facilitate the task of recovering a larger measure of internal sovereignty, but there is absolutely no guarantee that individual states, or states and societies together, will be able to take the opportunity. The widening of the external bounds is a necessary but by no means a sufficient condition.

The causal connections in the other direction are even less clear. One might argue, theoretically, that a state that can stand on its own two feet, by its own achievements, will have less need of the threat of force and the imperial centre. The more a state can depend on its own people, the less it need depend on Moscow. But does it follow that the

[53] This was on his 1983 visit. See 'The Pope in Poland'. above, p. 42. For the quotation see *Więz*, Nos. 8–10 (August-October, 1983), p. 52.

imperial centre will have less need of, or hold over, it? The peaceful transformation, so fervently desired by most supporters of reform outside the inner power élites, might indeed reasonably be expected to increase the external autonomy and the 'strength' of the state, as the pope suggests. But that is very far from being the primary goal of the political leaders who are currently initiating 'reform'. Yet before dwelling any more on these putative 'problems of success', one is bound to ask what chance, in practice, the Polish or Hungarian reform experiments have of achieving even minimal success, let alone maximal success or peaceful transformation.

Poland

Clearly, the preconditions are worse in Poland, given the depth of the economic crisis, the inconsistency of the economic reform programme and its implementation, the mixture of popular apathy and desperation, and above all, the continued gulf between the authorities and the most active and organized parts of society. National product per capita is still thirteen per cent lower than in 1978, and real wages are one fifth lower than in 1980. Inflation has been estimated at twenty per cent for August alone and will probably exceed one hundred per cent for the year. Increasingly, the dollar has supplanted the złoty as the Polish currency. Consumer supplies have got worse rather than better. And these are seen by the population to be the fruits of the much vaunted 'second stage of the economic reform', launched in the autumn of 1987.

This is, of course, less than wholly fair. Fault can certainly be found with the technical conception of the reform. Its chief architect, Zdzisław Sadowski, is both an able and reputable reform economist. In the tradition of Oskar Lange and Włodzimierz Brus, he has produced a design for a 'socialist market economy'. Radical as this is by the standards of most previous reform plans, one might well argue, on the basis of Hungarian experience over the last twenty years, that even in conception it is not radical enough. Sadowski talks in general terms about 'equal treatment of the public and private sectors and . . . market resource allocation,'[54] but the detail of the

[54] The quotation is from a speech delivered by Sadowski to the Royal Institute of International Affairs (Chatham House) in London on 21 June, 1988.

plan, let alone the bureaucratic practice, does not begin to amount to equal treatment for the private sector. The neo-liberals would say that just because there is a strong, authentic Polish tradition of design for 'market socialism', the importance of purely private enterprise—of capitalism blue in tooth and claw—is consistently underrated, not just by Sadowski and his team but also by some economic advisers to Solidarity who come from the same tradition.

Of more immediate importance than these faults in design, however, is the failure to execute even the existing design. The official 'Realization Programme of the Second Stage of Economic Reform' of October 1987 is a hastily prepared and cumbersome document, containing a theoretical timetable of 130 'tasks' to be performed over the four years to December 1991, when, it says, all manner of things will be well. The definition of the tasks is often vague, but almost a year later one can go down the list and see what has not been done that ought to have been done.

The failure is the result of external and internal obstacles. The external obstacles are of two kinds. First, there are the Western obstacles, having to do particularly with the country's desperate hard-currency shortage, the dependence of much of Polish industry and agriculture on components or materials that can only be bought for hard currency, the 39 billion dollar debt, and the conditions imposed by Western banks, governments, and the IMF for continuing at least to 'turn over' this debt. According to Sadowski, the government considers balancing the current account with the West to be one of its 'main policy objectives' and aims to achieve it by 1991.[55] Most independent economists consider this to be quite unrealistic. Secondly, there are the 'Eastern' obstacles, having to do with the need to improve trade balances with the Soviet Union, the direct involvement of the Soviet Union in parts of Polish industry, and the problem of existing commitments inside Comecon.

The internal obstacles are also of two general kinds. First, there is the passive or active resistance of large parts of the ruling class: the Party apparatus, the industry ministries, the political bureaucracy at provincial and local levels, many managers. Secondly, there is the passive or active resistance of large parts of the working class. The attempt to restore a degree of domestic market equilibrium

[55] From Sadowski's speech to the Royal Institute of International Affairs.

by sharply increasing the prices of consumer goods while holding down wages can be criticized on purely technical grounds. But the plain fact is that this strategy has also been vitiated by the active resistance of workers who, particularly in the very large factories which were Solidarity strongholds, have easily won large compensatory wage rises by striking or merely threatening to strike.

Besides this active resistance, moreover, there is a deep and almost universal popular disbelief in the possibility of Jaruzelski's leadership's realizing any reform programme. If anyone was prepared to give the Jaruzelski team the benefit of the doubt after 13 December, 1981—and not many were—it has squandered that confidence by the self-confessed failure of what is now called the 'first stage of economic reform', which was supposed to be pushed through under the protective carapace of martial law. These two internal obstacles, the popular and the political-bureaucratic, are, moreover, mutually reinforcing. As two leading Solidarity advisors soberly observe, political leaders who do not enjoy social support 'become prisoners of their own conservative apparatus, and cannot therefore be consistent promoters of reform.'[56]

For eight years now, Solidarity, the Church, and Western politicians have said that the only way to secure popular support for such painful but indispensable economic reform is a dialogue leading to a historic compromise between the self-organized and self-limiting Communist power. Society might be represented in different ways, but somehow, in some form, Solidarity must be included in the compromise. For nearly seven years now, the Communist authorities have done almost everything *except* talk to Solidarity. Any number of consultative bodies, extraordinary concessions to the Church, remarkably liberal censorship, almost free travel to the West, private enterprise, wage rises—anything,

[56] This quotation comes from a penetrating critique of the authorities' reform programme and practice by Ryszard Bugaj and Andrzej Wielowieyski, whose arguments were discussed at a meeting of the 'Group of Sixty' intellectual counsellors of Solidarity in the crypt of a Warsaw church during the strikes last May. (The same group was summoned by Wałęsa to Gdańsk in September, along with the old and new workers' leaders, to help prepare his negotiating strategy.) The Bugaj and Wielowieyski text was subsequently published, after complicated negotiations, in *Tygodnik Powszechny* of 19 June, 1988, but with no less than eighteen censor's cuts. The quotation was among the victims.

everything, except Solidarity. And after nearly seven years, the workers in the country's great industrial strongholds stand up and say: Solidarity! So the authorities do what they have so often said they would never do: they start talking to Lech Wałęsa. Wałęsa in return manages, with difficulty, to end the last strikes.

A landscape that has seemed increasingly complex and obscure suddenly looks very simple and very familiar. There is an iron gate. On one side there are police; behind the police, the army; behind the army, Jaruzelski; behind Jaruzelski, Moscow. On the other side, there are workers; behind the workers, Wałęsa; behind Wałęsa, the pope. It looks simple and familiar, but it is not. Two crucial differences between the situation now and that in 1980 were neatly expressed by a worker in the Lenin Shipyard during the strike in May. Today, he said, the external conditions are better but the internal conditions are worse. In 1980 there was a real fear of Soviet invasion. With Gorbachev, that has greatly diminished. On the other hand, in 1980 there was still some real trust in the capacity of those in power to keep their word, to speak 'as Pole talks to Pole'. Where is that trust today?

The impossible keeps happening in Poland. It would therefore be more than foolish to make any firm prediction about the outcome of the promised round table talks between the authorities and independent representatives of 'society', including Lech Wałęsa. Mieczysław F. Rakowski, the new prime minister, is both a realist and a Party reformist, as the memorandum quoted above makes clear. He continues to enjoy a certain reputation as a 'liberal' in the West. But in Poland he is seen as the man who deceived and abused Solidarity while negotiating with it as a deputy minister in 1981 and who has passionately, even obsessively, defended the imposition of martial law. His appointment is thus turning over an old rather than a new leaf. In any case, the general prognosis can hardly be optimistic. There is a deep mistrust of the authorities on the Solidarity side, and a perhaps even deeper fear among those in power of a restored Solidarity. Moreover, it is very difficult to imagine what a restored— or new—Solidarity would look like and how it could be married to the common goal of economic reform.

If Solidarity were allowed back only on the shop-floor in individual factories, then it would have to work as a trade union, fighting for the workers' jobs and wages. As a democratic organization, and competing with the official trade unions for members, it would be almost bound to oppose factory closings and wage squeezes that its own national economic advisers regard as essential. Moreover, no one can seriously believe that it would remain without a national network for long. The alternative is that Solidarity should return in different guise: as the independent watchdog and guarantor of the whole society's interests at the highest levels of the state.

Thus Solidarity might be represented in parliament, together with Catholic and other independent groups. Its experts might participate in a body empowered to oversee the implementation of economic reform. Its representatives or associates might even hold government office. As an independent, legal, national institution, it could then 'sell' the painful economic reform programme to society as a genuine programme for national recovery, supporting measures that as a local trade union it would be bound to oppose. Like Churchill in 1940, Wałęsa would say, 'I have nothing to offer but blood, sweat and tears . . .' and the nation would rally round. In effect, this is what Lech Wałęsa and his senior advisors have been proposing to the authorities ever since July 1981.[57]

If it was not possible then, why should it be possible now? Because Gorbachev is not Brezhnev? Because the West wants it, and Poland more than ever needs economic help from the West? But the internal obstacles remain formidable. There is absolutely no blueprint for such an arrangement of power sharing. The coalitions of 1945–1948 in East Central Europe are hardly an encouraging example. One could just conceivably imagine its working if there were to be a clear, simple, legally defined division of powers between the parties, enforceable by an independent judiciary. But that is out of the question. One might just imagine its working if there were a large amount of mutual confidence between the parties: as in an all-party wartime cabinet. But there is not.

[57]See chapter 6 in my *Polish Revolution: Solidarity* (London: Jonathan Cape, 1983), where I describe their abortive negotiations with Rakowski. According to the sociological survey 'Poles 88', no less than 84.3 per cent of those asked were of the opinion that 'fundamental change for the better can be introduced only when the authorities come to an understanding with society.' Quoted in a brief report by the team who conducted the survey (Władysław Adamski, et al.) in *Polityka*, 23 July, 1988.

What remains is the compromise of two boxers who recognize that neither can knock the other out and that the ring is collapsing around them. But whence comes the boxers' staying power? Jaruzelski's staying power still derives from the military and the police (more than the Party apparatus), and ultimately from the Soviet leadership continuing to back him, as Gorbachev did demonstratively during his visit to Poland in July. Wałęsa's power rests to some extent (as the government spokesman Jerzy Urban claims) on support from the West and to some extent on his symbolic importance to the whole of Polish society. But his real muscle still comes, as it has all along, from the workers in a score of giant enterprises: from the miners of Silesia, the shipyard workers of Gdańsk, Gdynia, and Szczecin, the steelworkers of Kraków and Warsaw, the engineering workers of Poznań and Wrocław. If you ask, 'Why is Wałęsa back at the table?' the basic answer is: Because those workers put him there.

Now, the corollary of this is that Solidarity leaders simply cannot afford to risk losing the confidence of these, their grenadiers, unless they have cast-iron guarantees of a permanent independent role in the country's national political life. Even this time around, it was only with difficulty that Wałęsa persuaded the angry young men in the Lenin Shipyard and the slow stubborn miners of Jastrzębie to return to work. But the interests of the workers in these industrial strongholds are by no means identical with those of the economy as a whole. During the May strike at the Lenin Shipyard, the workers chanted, 'There is no freedom without Solidarity', while loudspeakers broadcast a message from the management saying that the yard would have to be closed altogether. In the pure interest of national economic recovery, however, the Solidarity troops should probably have chanted, 'Close the yards! Open a stock exchange!' But no one can seriously expect Solidarity to cut off the branch upon which it sits unless it has another very solid branch to go to.

One might speculate that for Poland now to break through the immense barriers of alienation and decay, the authorities would have to take not one but two radical steps: restore Solidarity and restore capitalism. An expanded private sector and new mixed forms of ownership in the public sector might generate economic dynamism and harness the energies of the skilled, the young, and the rich, but it would also exacerbate social tensions, and the private sector could never be guaranteed a stable future without political representation (or at least protection) at the highest level. Solidarity, restored as a national political force, might just conceivably mediate (or at least alleviate) that social conflict and provide that guarantee, but it could hardly leap over its own Christian-social trade-union shadow to become the cutting edge of radical economic change. One might say half in jest (and half in mourning) than when a Solidarity branch declares a legal strike against a private employer, Poland will be on the right course.[58]

The most probable outcome, however, remains a continued muddling through: or, rather, a muddling down. On all Polish precedents, the result is likely, sooner or later, to be another explosion of popular protest. The result of that explosion would, in turn, depend crucially on the circumstances in the Soviet Union, but if present trends in the Soviet Union continue (and if developments elsewhere in Eastern Europe do not contribute to reversing those trends), it is not completely inconceivable that the historic compromise that could not be achieved by reform might yet be achieved by revolution. In an extraordinary passage of his memorandum, Mieczysław F. Rakowski writes that some people in power in Poland may still be thinking that if it comes to another revolt, 'we call in aid our *raison d'état* and remind people that after all somebody might intervene in our international affairs. But what,' Rakowski goes on, 'if that *somebody*, bearing in mind his own interests, does not *want* to intervene?'[59] A thought to concentrate the functionary's mind wonderfully. Of course, it would be morally indefensible for anyone in the West to encourage such a terrible gamble, yet equally, no one in the West can prevent it. And in the long run of Ottomanization, even a failed revolution is not the last word.

[58] An alternative approach, still quite popular in Poland, is that of promoting workers' self-management. But the Yugoslav experience suggests that this would be economically disastrous in present Polish circumstances.

[59] Rakowski, 'Reflections . . .' p. 18.

Hungary

In Hungary, the preconditions are somewhat better. The economic crisis is still not as deep and, although individual alienation is profound, there is no comparable gulf between 'society' and 'the authorities'. One of the many reform manifestos to bloom in the Budapest spring was that of a group describing itself as the March Front. Its twenty signatories range from Rezsö Nyers, who in May became a member of the politburo, to Miklós Vásárhelyi, who was Imre Nagy's press secretary in 1956 and might now be described as the Nestor of the democratic opposition. The March Front has not actually done anything, but in Poland it would not even be possible to get the names on the same piece of paper.

The continuum between critical intelligentsia and reformists-in-government is more substantially exemplified by the present economic reform project. In 1986 a group of reform economists working under the auspices of Imre Pozsgay's Patriotic People's Front produced a radical reform document entitled 'Turning Point and Reform'. In January 1988, several authors of this document moved into cramped offices in the parliament building, as part of an economic kitchen cabinet working for the deputy prime minister, Péter Medgyessy. In mid-July, the new central committee was offered two variants of economic reform, the radical Plan A and the more cautious Plan B. Plan A, for which the central committee voted, was essentially based on the kitchen cabinet's design, which in turn was based on the original document.

Miklós Németh, the central committee secretary for economic affairs, has defined the goal of Plan A as 'a genuine market economy, without any qualifying adjectives.'[60] It has been officially stated that the private sector could account for as much as thirty per cent of this mixed economy. There is to be a real stock exchange. Western majority shareholding should be equally possible in firms from the private, co-operative, and state sectors. The change in forms of ownership inside the socialized sector, vaguely discussed in Poland, is here a detailed plan. The Hungarian reform economists (than whom no one on earth is more ingenious) have worked out a scheme whereby the net worth of a state enterprise would be converted into

[60] In a radio interview quoted in SWB-EE (3 June, 1988), B/3–4.

stocks, which would be given by the state to local councils, pension funds, and the like. These councils or pension funds would then have to live (in part, at least) off the dividends from these stocks rather than the direct state subsidies they currently receive. They would thus acquire at least a quasi-shareholder's interest in the profitability of the enterprise. Irredeemable loss-makers should go bankrupt, with estimated unemployment of 100,000 over the next two to three years. A sharp devaluation should bring at least partial convertibility of the forint within sight. 'What is socialism?' asks the joke of the year. Answer: 'The longest and most painful road from capitalism to capitalism.'

Political reform is seen as indispensable for two reasons. First, to ensure that the political bureaucracy does not continue to vitiate the theoretical autonomy of enterprises, as it has for the last twenty years. What a leading member of the economic think tank laughingly calls the 'invisible hand' of the centre should be reduced to an invisible finger. The Party 'should be removed from economic life.' Economic policy should be the province of the government, supervised and controlled by the parliament. The new company law should provide precise, legally binding definitions of previously political 'negotiable' relationships.

Secondly, political reform must sugar the bitter pill of austerity and win popular support. New courts and new laws delimiting the freedoms of association and speech are one path to this end. An increased role for parliament and local councils, with liberalized election laws, is another. At present the Hungarian parliament meets for just eight days a year. 'We want to abolish the Party-state,' a leading reformist politburo member said to me. 'We want to reintroduce the principles of Montesquieu in modern form.' This is interesting talk from a politburo member, albeit in a private, background conversation. But as we have seen, words are cheap in the new deideologized climate. The deeds have yet to follow. The main economic measures are supposed to be in place by the end of 1988; the constitutional changes, perhaps by 1990.

What are the chances? Even if there were no political, bureaucratic, or social hindrances whatsoever to implementing radical economic reform in its purest form, Hungary would still be running to keep up with an increasingly dynamic European

Community, and with the 'newly industrialized countries'. In purely technical terms, it is not easy to turn a Lada into a Mercedes while continuing to drive down the motorway. Ingenious as the proposals for new forms of ownership are, one cannot imagine their having half the impact of the pure, raw, brutal reprivatization by Thatcherism (so eloquently advocated by the *Towarzystwo Gospodarcze* in Kraków). Radical as the reintroduction of market forces is meant to be, even in design it seems unlikely to reproduce the Schumpeterian 'creative gale of destruction'. Two per cent unemployment is a lot for a socialist country, but Thatcherism in Britain brought—and perhaps required—twelve per cent unemployment to revitalize a much less decrepit economy.

The hard-currency debt is a goad to reform, but if the debt-service ratio becomes too steep, it can be a major impediment to further reform (witness Poland). The Hungarians reckon they have a breathing space until 1991, when loan repayments to Western banks are due to increase sharply. This is not long. Moreover, while their putative West European competitors have the opportunity of the Common Market, they still have the burden of Comecon. To adjust your domestic market to Western markets is one thing. To adjust Comecon to your own needs is quite another. So far as I can gather, Hungary's economic policymakers have more or less given up any hope of turning Comecon into a common market and are merely looking for more realistic bilateral trade with individual countries, including the Soviet Union.[61]

Yet for political reasons, the reform package is most unlikely to be fully implemented. For a start, Károly Grósz is not, by all accounts, comparable to Gorbachev, let alone to Mrs Thatcher. He is a clever, forceful opportunistic politician, but there is no evidence that his present endorsement of radical reform flows from any deep conviction. His politburo contains only three people who one could clearly categorize as reformists (Nyers, Pozsgay, and Németh), and in János Berecz he has (*mutatis mutandis*) his Ligachev. The higher ranks of the Party apparatus contain some intelligent, realistic, reform-minded men. But no one really has the first idea how the new

[61] According to a report in the *Financial Times* (9 August, 1988), 'Hungary's iron and steel producers have threatened to consider halting unprofitable exports to other Comecon countries after the Government's withdrawal of subsidies for metal exports.' A nice illustration in miniature.

separation of powers, or division of roles, between Party and state, central committee, parliament, and courts is going to work. If the Party is not to make economic policy, then what on earth is it to do? Men cling to power: surely here, too. I asked an energetic, realistic, and reform-minded new member of the central committee secretariat what he was actually going to do there. 'Well,' he replied, 'we work out the broad strategic lines of policy, and then we pass them on to Party members in the state apparatus.' This sounded vaguely familiar.

Then there are the corrupt local oligarchies that flourished under late Kádárism. Can their grip really be broken? On a much smaller scale, Grósz has the problem that Gorbachev faces in the Soviet Union. In theory, he wants to decentralize. But before decentralizing, he has to re-establish central control. And then there is the great unknown of social reaction. The leadership has stated clearly that in the short run, reform means that most Hungarians will get poorer. The responsible politburo member, Miklós Németh, told the central committee that Plan A would initially mean lower or even negative growth and 'a lower level of consumption by the population',[62] not to mention the 100,000 unemployed. Hungarian society is too divided for a Polish-style Solidarity movement to seem at all likely, but there has already been one strike in the mines. Repeated local strikes—as in Yugoslavia—and even the founding of independent unions seems possible. Any one of these levels of resistance is probably enough to pre-empt economic take-off in a highly competitive world. Together, they seem almost insuperable.

Except, perhaps by democracy. But democracy is not on offer. Hungary's communist rulers quite understandably want to enjoy the benefits of democracy without paying the price of sharing or being obliged to compete for power. Legal definitions of rights can also be ways of restricting rights. 'An up-to-date practice of jurisdiction can be an even more efficient means of political regulation than direct administrative instructions,' the new head of central committee's

[62] SWB-EE (15 July, 1988), C1/1–5

agit-prop department rather revealingly observed.[63] What Mr Grósz still calls opposition is not what we would call opposition, and what we call opposition Mr Grósz still calls the enemy—a nasty verbal throwback to darker days. While the authorities allowed the populist demonstration for Transylvania, the police broke up a much smaller democratic oppositon demonstration on the anniversary of the judicial execution of Imre Nagy, with some brutality.

The liveliest, but also in a way the saddest, meeting I had in Budapest this June was with a group of law students in their early twenties who have been instrumental in setting up the new democratic youth union (FIDESZ). They have a brilliant programme. It can be summed up in two words: liberal democracy. As we talked, I felt, as I have done so often before, a simple anger. Why should they, who are every bit as civilized, deserving, brave, and clever as their exact contemporaries up the river in Vienna, have to put up with any more half-measures and half-truths. For God's sake, let them have it—*now!* After all, we know, that liberal democracy works: not perfectly, of course, nothing ever does, but in all its West European variants better than any of the East European variants of anything else. If Spain can pass peacefully from dictatorship to democracy, why should not Hungary? In morality and ideology, the ruling party has no answer. Yet no one, not even as a joke, told me that socialism is the longest and most painful road from autocracy to democracy.

The sad fact is that socialism has created in all the East European states an array of *domestic* barriers against the transformation to liberal-democracy-cum-mixed-economy quite as formidable as those that existed in recent West or south European dictatorships, such as Spain, Portugal or Greece. These barriers lie not only in the system of politbureaucratic dictatorship (to use Rudolf Bahro's apt term) and not merely in the character and interests of the *nomenklatura* ruling class, but also in the interests, attitudes, and fears of many of the ruled. Of course, in conditions of full external sovereignty, with liberal democracies on all frontiers, these obstacles would simply be swept aside as they were, gloriously, in Spain, Portugal, and Greece. But those are not the conditions. The Polish revisionist Władysław Bieńkowski once wrote a famous text called

---

[63] *Magyar Hirlap*, 24 June, 1988.

'The Engines and Brakes of Socialism'. We have been discussing the engines and brakes of the transition from socialism. The conclusion is, alas, that even in Hungary, even in the Gorbachev era, the brakes look more powerful than the engines.

One is bound to hope against hope. The Hungarian reformists enter this experiment with that cheerful pessimism that is one of the more attractive features of Hungarian intellectual life. One of the very architects of the entire reform project told me he gives it only a thirty to forty per cent chance of success. It seems reasonable to suggest that the reform has a rather higher chance of *minimal* success—that is, of averting revolution—if only because of the further diversification of social interests that it will promote. The freeing of the private sector, in particular, means that Hungary might yet have an entrepreneurial bourgeoisie that will go to the barricades—against the revolting workers. Capitalists and communists shoulder to shoulder against the proletariat: a suitably Central European outcome to socialism. To estimate the percentage chance of peaceful transformation, by contrast, requires only the fingers of one hand.

Back to Central Europe?

'To Generalize is to be an Idiot. To Particularize is the alone Distinction of Merit.' We may not go quite so far as William Blake, but virtually all general writing about 'Eastern Europe' is either a catalogue or, if analytically more ambitious, extrapolates from the one or two countries the author knows best. The above has something of both faults. To concentrate on Poland and Hungary is, in the autumn of 1988, justified by the fact that these are the two countries of East Central Europe in which fundamental reform experiments are under way. Even here, what has been said is fragmentary and tentative. Yet there are many common features as well as differences. I would venture to predict that when the fundamental reform experiment does get under way in Czechoslovakia, there, too, one will recognize many of the features that I have singled out in Poland and Hungary.

In the case of East Germany, the differences will perhaps be greater than the similarities. A state whose annual transfers of hard currency from West Germany cover the total interest burden on its hard-currency debt—but a state, also, whose citizens learn about their own country every night from West German television—is in a different position from its East Central European neighbours, a position both better and worse. I have not attempted to include Romania or Bulgaria in my analysis.

For the heartlands of contemporary East Central Europe, however, for the more than 60 million Europeans living in the present territories of Czechoslovakia, Hungary, and Poland, there are certainly the contours of a common fate. The oldest of Central European tales has a German general saying to his Austrian ally: 'The situation is serious but not tragic,' to which the Austrian general replies: 'No, mein Lieber, the situation is tragic but not serious.' One might say that the situation of East Central Europe today is tragic but not hopeless.

It is tragic because a half-century of immense struggle, upheaval, work, and suffering has produced so little lasting progress. It is fashionable to talk, as Zbigniew Brzezinski does in the title of his 1988 Seton-Watson Memorial Lecture, of Eastern Europe's being on its way 'back to Central Europe'. Polite reference is made to the positive ideal of Central Europe revived by Milan Kundera, Czesław Miłosz, Václav Havel, György Konrád, and many others.[64] But there can be a 'return to Central Europe' in a negative as well as a positive sense. The dream of emancipatory modernization, by no means only the property of communists in 1945, may yet end in a reality, all too familiar from Central European history, of growing relative backwardness *vis-à-vis* Western, 'modern' Europe. It may end in a new version of Giselher Wirsing's *Zwischeneuropa* or the intermediate zone identified by Hungarian writers and historians, its economies exporting tin saucepans, bottled fruit, cheap shoes, and cheap labour, importing German tourists and Japanese capital. A zone, that is, of weak states, national prejudice, inequality, poverty and *Schlammassel*. It is almost already true to talk, in the case of Hungary and Poland, of a double dependency—on the great powers to the West as well as to the East.

This situation is tragic because of its toll in avoidable human suffering. At times it seems tragic, too, in the sense of classical tragedy: that is, having a relentless logic quite beyond and in spite of the will of the participants. For the petty functionaries defending their privileges are not really evil; and far less are the unskilled

[64]See my essay 'Does Central Europe Exist?' above, p. 161.

workers defending their jobs in factories that should long since have been shut. The more enlightened leaders in Hungary and Poland today are personally little worse than most politicians in the West. Some genuinely care about their countries as well as themselves. But good or evil, they can no more avoid entanglement in the web of internal contradictions that socialism has created than Oedipus could avoid marrying his mother.

So entirely hopeless it is not. It is not hopeless, because, within the setting of overall decay, there are possibilities of individual and group emancipation, of free speech, learning, worship, travel, productive work, and self-help that simply did not exist when I first travelled to Eastern Europe ten years ago. It is not hopeless because these states do, in theory, possess room for manoeuvre in which they might restore a larger degree of internal sovereignty. It is not hopeless because the great power to the East is itself convulsed with change whose outcome no one can predict. It is not hopeless, finally, because the great powers to the West form a more open, successful, attractive, and benign constellation for East Central Europe than at any time in modern history. This is true of the United States, of Western Europe as a whole, and particularly of (West) Germany, on whose approach the future shape of this region once again significantly depends.

To discuss what we in the West can do directly to encourage desirable change in East Central Europe would require another essay, indeed a book.[65] But if present trends continue, it is not unreasonable to look ahead to a time when the West will be not, as since Yalta, a tertiary actor in East Central Europe (after the Soviet Union and the countries themselves) but a secondary actor—as important as the Soviet Union, though in different ways. If we are to play this role wisely, however, the first imperative is to see East Central Europe as it really is and not as a projection of our own fantasies or as a subcategory of Soviet politics. The metaphor of Finlandization and the terms *glasnost* and *perestroika* are of limited use in analysing recent developments in East Central Europe. The

---

[65] Two excellent volumes are Lincoln Gordon, ed., *Eroding Empire: Western Relations with Eastern Europe* (Washington, D.C.: Brookings, 1987) and William E. Griffith, ed., *Central and Eastern Europe and the West* (Boulder, Colorado: Westview Press, 1989). I am working on a book about the contemporary German role in this region.

impact of Gorbachev and the 'new détente' in East-West relations has been great but also complex, indirect, and ambiguous. Terms like *crisis*, *reform*, or *stability* are useless without closer definition.

I have offered the crude metaphor of Ottomanization as at least marginally more illuminating than that of Finlandization. The two faces of Ottomanization, emancipation and decay, both have many dimensions: imperial, regional, and domestic; economic, social, ideological, and political; the emancipation of states from the imperial centre; the emancipation of societies from states, in the overlapping spheres of religion, national articulation, civil society, and private enterprise, and the more or less consciously oppositional variants of each. Revolution, ending in partial failure, is as likely as reform, ending in partial success (i.e., averting revolution). On balance, the former seems more likely in Poland, the latter in Hungary. A maximal success for reform seems scarcely more probable than a maximal success for revolution. Each national case must be studied historically, and for itself. 'Every thing is what it is and not another thing,' as the great Bishop Butler unshallowly remarked.

As these countries are rediscovering their own histories, so also is history the discipline most urgently called for, if we in the West are to understand their present and peer into their future. History, calling in aid economics, sociology, political science, and even security studies, but above all: history. Czechs, Hungarians, and Poles are rediscovering their own history; and they are making it again. To adapt a German philosopher, whose influence on East Central Europe future historians will record as baneful but transient, confined only to a few decades in the second half of the twentieth century: the peoples of East Central Europe make their own history, although they do not make it just as they please.

(SEPTEMBER 1988)

Notebook

'A.M. for ZL?' says my tattered Polish notebook, in a deliberately illegible scrawl. 'Berlin-Berdayev.' 'Lordly invite for K.B. & E.K.?' And beside another scrawled initial: 'Where unpublished novel "The Heritage"?'

During the war, Jurek had another name, false identity papers and a beard. As we talked, a short-wave receiver crackled on the police wavelengths. Mozart for conspirators.

If you want to transport *samizdat* you must strengthen the rear springs. Otherwise the pigs will notice the headlamps' high beam.

'Why are they chanting "Gestapo"?' asks an elderly bystander at the demonstration. 'It should be "SS".'

Underground groups are called 'structures'. Some people offer friends the service of their 'structures'. This makes them important. Then it turns out the structures don't exist. Such men are 'structuralists'.

I flew in from London the day Felek came out of hiding. After two years. 'We're waiting for the police,' they said. We drank. We listened to ancient music. Bob Dylan. Pink Floyd. Felek and Spot swapped tales from internment, conspiracy, occupation: this one, the last, the last but two. We waited. And I watched the pretty, bright-eyed daughter, strangely trembling. For Daddy had come home from the war.

I flew British Airways: just two and a half hours from peace to war. Departure: 1983. Arrival: 1945.

'She'll eat her words,' says the English phrase. And so she did. Mind you, they were written on cigarette paper. We sat on the park bench. She read off the cryptic message. Then she popped it into her mouth. Just like that. Mmmm, finger-licking good. Care for another?

At home you never say anything important. You write it down. Names particularly. Then you burn the paper in the candle. Unless you're hungry, of course.

Underground publishers of my acquaintance thought they had a police spy in the firm. So they sent to him a pretty girl. With a mission. She made love to him. He confessed to her. He is no longer a publisher. As was said of a lady in the Maquis: *'Elle a couché pour la France.'*

Here's a brilliant new writer: Dawid Warszawski. Let's profile him on the features page. Let's get him writing for *Granta*. Except that nobody knows who he is. The pseudonym is inviolate. Early in the war, he tells me, he received a letter from a group of professors via one of the *samizdat* journals. They admired his writing. They would like to meet him in person. He replied, by the same circuitous route, that this was alas impossible 'for conspiratorial reasons'. Back came a frosty little note from the professors. They couldn't understand what he was talking about, they wrote, since they had already met Dawid Warszawski, not once but several times. These conversations had been most stimulating. Somewhere out there was a prize structuralist. Or a laughing policeman.

A cat jumps on to my lap. His name? 'Offset'. A kitten of martial law, when his owners' dream was an offset machine for producing *samizdat*.

Laughing matter. Yet this war had real victims too. There are fresh graves in the Powązki.

Now 1988 was a 'watershed year', 'a year of peace', they tell us. The Cold War has ended. The division of Europe will be overcome. The eagle shall lie down with the bear and all shall be well and all manner of things shall be well.

I read it in the newspapers so it must be true. But I shall believe it

when cigarette papers are for rolling cigarettes
when kittens are called Figaro and radios are for Mozart
when ZL can be there and A.M. here
when my notebook has only real names and full addresses.

(JANUARY 1989)

Refolution

In Poland and Hungary this has been a fantastic spring. As I travel through those countries, attending an opposition fête in Budapest, a triumphal mass in Gdańsk, a Solidarity election meeting in a Silesian coal mine, I have to pinch myself to make sure I'm not dreaming. Walking around Budapest's equivalent of Oxford Circus I pass a stall openly selling *samizdat* publications. Casting an eye over the titles I suddenly notice my own name, on what turns out to be a slim volume of essays hastily translated from *The New York Review*. Next day I am signing copies for people attending the opposition fête. 'Incredible' and 'surreal' are the words that punctuate every conversation about politics, though not about economics, for which the leitmotifs are, rather, 'disastrous' and 'hopeless'.

Last year, I posed the question of political change in these two countries as the historic choice 'reform or revolution?'[1] But what is happening just now is a singular mixture of both reform and revolution: a 'revorm', if you will, or perhaps a 'refolution'. There is, in both places, a strong and essential element of voluntary, deliberate reform led by an enlightened minority (but only a minority) in the still ruling Communist parties, and, in the Polish case, at the top of the military and the police. Their advance consists of an unprecedented retreat: undertaking to share power, and even—*mirabile dictu*—talk of giving it up altogether if they lose an election.[2]

Yet one is bound to ask how far the retreat is voluntary, how far involuntary, and whether it might not become a rout. For if one talks to the intelligentsia in both countries, then the comparison that

[1]See 'Reform or Revolution?', above p. 218.
[2]Both the Hungarian Party leader, Károly Grósz, and the leading Party reformist, Imre Pozsgay, have reportedly made statements to this effect, though without a deadline.

comes to mind is less with 1968 than with 1848, less with the Prague Spring than with the Springtime of Nations. The greatest opposition demonstrations in Budapest have been held on the 1848 anniversary: 15 March. Among other rites, symbolic tribute is traditionally paid before the statue of Józef Bem, who commanded the Hungarian insurrectionary army in 1848. Józef Bem was a Pole.

Polish-Hungarian co-operation has not got quite that far again, but certainly the Poles and the Hungarians, governments as well as oppositions, are now looking to each other for examples, precedents, and even direct support. For they are still alone in Eastern Europe. So far, this is the springtime of just two nations. What they are doing would be quite impossible without Gorbachev's tolerance, his example, and the processes he has, wittingly or unwittingly, set in motion. Unlike in 1848, they can also count on benign (if ineffectual) support rather than resistance from the major powers to their west. But around them are still the frightened, hidebound, or openly repressive regimes of East Germany, Czechoslovakia, Bulgaria, and indescribable Romania: the 'gang of four', as one American specialist has nicely put it.[3]

In the race for freedom of speech and freedom of enterprise, the Hungarians are currently in the lead, although Poland is coming up fast. In the political stakes, Hungary leads in words but Poland in deeds.

In early May, Poland got its first legal, independent, opposition daily paper, the *Gazeta Wyborcza*.[4] Its editor-in-chief is Adam Michnik, and the paper is organized by Helena Łuczywo, for the last seven years editor of Poland's leading underground weekly, *Tygodnik Mazowsze*, and an unsung heroine of the Polish opposition. But this and the revived Solidarity weekly, *Tygodnik Solidarność*, are both subject to formal censorship. Further liberalization of censorship is promised, but *samizdat* publishers and editors still agonize over whether or not to 'surface from underground' and legalize their publications.

---

[3]See Charles Gati, 'Eastern Europe on Its Own', in *Foreign Affairs*, Vol. 68, No. 1, 1988/1989.
[4]The title has been translated in the Western press as 'Election Gazette', which sounds a bit archaic. Actually *Gazeta* just means newspaper, so a closer translation might be 'The Election Paper'.

In Hungary, by contrast, there is no formal censorship, and the once effective conventions of informal (self-)censorship have simply broken down.[5] Independent publishers and periodicals bloom like crocuses. There is almost riotous competition to publish everything and anything—Imre Nagy, Orwell, Solzhenitsyn, the more outrageous the better. And while the Polish official press is now interesting, the Hungarian official press and, what is more, journalists on official radio and television are in the vanguard of emancipation.

In liberating private enterprise, and attracting Western capital, Hungary is also ahead, although the Rakowski government in Poland is in some ways even more shameless. Its message, symbolized by the industry minister, Mieczysław Wilczek, himself at once a millionaire private entrepreneur and Party member, is: *'enrichissez vouz!'* But the message is directed as much—or more—to members of the existing ruling class, the *nomenklatura*, and to Western (especially German and Austrian) investors[6] as it is to the man in the street, who does not have their options or connections. In both Poland and Hungary, the process whereby members of the *nomenklatura* advance into private enterprise, using the power and connections that go with their official positions, proceeds apace.

There have been many suggestions as to how communism might be turned back into capitalism. But this is the simplest of all: communist bosses become capitalist bosses! The simplest, although hardly the most attractive. The Solidarity-opposition election programme (formally, the Election Programme of the Citizens' Committee 'Solidarity') specifically warns against the danger of the *'uwłaszczenie nomenklatury'*, that is, of the *nomenklatura* becoming

[5]On the once effective conventions see my 'The Hungarian Lesson', above, p. 130. One of the most surreal conversations I had in Budapest was with Mr György Aczél, for thirty years the Kádár of Hungarian cultural life. I asked him if he did not think, on looking back, that censorship might have been relaxed sooner. There was no censorship, he said. The decision was up to individual publishers and editors. But surely he would not deny that he himself had exercised political control? Oh no, not control. He had merely, he said, had 'a sort of influence'.
[6]For the invitation to the West see, for example, Wilczek's interview in *Der Spiegel*. No. 3, 1989, under the title 'Labour in Poland is Exceptionally Cheap'.

owners. But others, in both Hungary and Poland, argue that this process also has advantages; compensating some members of the *nomenklatura* for their loss of political power, and dividing it between those who stand to lose and those who stand to gain. One might call this the *'nomenklatura* buy-out' theory.

In politics, Poland takes the lead, with the hectic and sometimes hilarious drama of its first half-way genuine election in fifty years. This is, of course, only a half-free election, the product of a remarkable but risky deal made during two months of negotiations, from early February to early April, at the so-called Round Table meetings—actually many tables, and each with just two sides, authorities and Solidarity-opposition.[7] The Round Table deal is a compromise, but an open-ended compromise. The Solidarity-opposition side secured the restoration of both the workers' and the farmers' Solidarity as fully independent organizations, and the promise of legalization for an independent students' union. It also secured completely free elections to a newly created upper house of parliament, the Senate, and free competition for thirty-five per cent of the seats in the existing lower house, the Sejm.

[7]The statement about two sides must be qualified in at least two respects. First, toward the end of the proceedings it was not at all clear whether the official trade unions (OPZZ) were working with the party of dialogue around Generals Jaruzelski and Kiszczak, or against them. Secondly, at the economic table the divisions ran almost as much within the two delegations as between them, with, crudely speaking, social democrats on both sides and neo-liberals on both sides. Someone should write a short history of this extraordinary negotiation. Stenographic protocols of the main discussions exist, although, as usual, some crucial decisions were taken elsewhere, notably at smaller meetings between Lech Wałęsa, General Kiszczak, and their top advisors.

There is a new genre of opposition anecdote in Warsaw these days, the 'corridor stories'. They tell of fantastic encounters between oppositionists and their former persecutors, in the corridors of the council of ministers, during the two months of the Round Table. One (true) example: Dawid Warszawski, pseudonymous editor of a leading underground journal, KOS, conducted a video interview with the interior minister, General Kiszczak, head of the police apparatus responsible for seven years' struggle with the underground. The general politely observed that he had much enjoyed reading Mr Warszawski's articles over the years. Mr Warszawski, now using his real name, Konstanty Gebert, responded by asking the general to give an interview to KOS— an offence for which the general should then, presumably, punish himself. The general hesitates for a moment. 'Do you offer a large coffee?' he says.

The authorities secured a guaranteed majority in the Sejm, although the Polish United Workers' party as such has only thirty-eight per cent of seats guaranteed, with the rest going to its (until now) compliant 'coalition' parties and collaborationist Catholic organizations. They also got Solidarity's agreement to an early election (first round, 4 June; second round, 18 June), thus giving the opposition virtually no time to organize a campaign from less than scratch. In addition, the constitution now includes a powerful new office of president, which most participants at the round table expect to go to General Jaruzelski.

Around this basic political deal there is wound a large fabric of more detailed agreements—or agreements to disagree—on everything from the economy to censorship and from the judiciary to coal mining. At the Round Table, the opposition had to settle for rather less than half a loaf on most of these issues—but Lech Wałęsa's key political adviser, Bronisław Geremek, argues that 'a dynamic process has been set in motion', and everything is up for transformation in that process. The authorities have agreed, in black and white, that this is 'the beginning of the road to parliamentary democracy.' (No qualifying adjectives, although according to a fly on the wall, the government side at one point tried to introduce a parenthesis after this sentence with words to the effect that 'the government-coalition side regard parliamentary democracy as socialist democracy.' The Solidarity-opposition side then proposed a further sentence to the effect that this was 'the beginning of the building of a sovereign, independent Poland.' Just the beginning! Each then abandoned its provocative formulation. So much for the word 'socialism'.)[8] There are to be free elections in four years' time. Neither side knows what will happen in those four years.

The workers' and farmers' Solidarity unions are slowly being rebuilt, although with none of the euphoric surge of autumn 1980. The rebuilding of the unions and the election campaign are, say most

[8]This and the other main agreements can be found in *Rzeczpospolita*, 7 April, 1989. See also the interesting article by Adam Krzemiński and Wiesław Władyka ('Revolution Step by Step') in the official weekly *Polityka*, 29 April, 1989. This begins by talking of 'the creation of parliamentary democracy in socialism' but ends by describing the goal simply as 'the metamorphosis of a Stalinist system into a parliamentary democracy.' Period.

activists, complementary and mutually reinforcing. Last spring, Lech Wałęsa sat in the Lenin Shipyard in Gdańsk, besieged by riot police, with a thousand angry young workers chanting 'there is no freedom without Solidarity'. This spring, he sits in the Lenin Shipyard, at a calm, wholly legal, meeting with the 261 Solidarity-opposition candidates for parliament. The meeting is filmed under the direction of Andrzej Wajda, himself running for the Senate. The candidates have gathered in the very same hall where it all began with the birth of Solidarity in August 1980. There are the same model ships, the same white eagle on the wall, even the same bust of Lenin.[9] As Wałęsa walks up onto the platform he gives that Lenin a laughing glance, as if to say, 'So *who whom* to you, old chum.'

Interestingly, this Polish deal—a calculated gamble for both sides— has been held up as a positive example by Hungarian party officials, but as a negative example by most independent Hungarian intellectuals and the opposition. They want free elections, with no handicaps, no quotas, and no new upper house. After free elections the one sovereign parliament should form the new government and promulgate a new constitution. 'After the election,' says a senior official in the justice ministry, 'the Hungarian Socialist Workers' party will have the same position as other parties.' It is rather like one of those weary old East European jokes: the Hungarians are behaving like Poles and the Poles are behaving like Hungarians.

Yet some basic elements are the same. There is a government and an opposition. The government is not like any Western government: it is both stronger (with the whole extensive apparatus of the Party-police-military-nationalized industry-state) and weaker (no legitimacy, deeply divided). The opposition is not like any Western opposition. These two heterogeneous, indeed fissiparous partners are talking about how to transform their countries into what they call 'normal' countries, by the end of the twentieth century. When they say 'normal' they mean Western, European, liberal, democratic, with a market economy based on property rights, a freely elected parliament, and an independent judiciary. Something between Switzerland and Sweden. 'Return Kraków to Europe' says a sign in the window of the students' union on Kraków's medieval market

[9] See chapter one in my *The Polish Revolution: Solidarity* (London: Jonathan Cape, 1983).

square, and that is the theme that recurs, again and again, in every programme, speech, and conversation, official as well as unofficial: the return to something called 'Europe'.

They may not arrive. Beside that old favourite, the Spanish model of transition from dictatorship to democracy, excited intellectuals talk of the recent Chilean model, the South Korean, even the Iranian . . . But whatever happens, this is an ineradicable moment. It might be an important moment, too, for the West, and especially for the Western left. For one message of Poland and Hungary today was summed up for me by a leading activist of Hungary's opposition Free Democrats: 'We say there is no third way. There is no credible alternative between Western capitalism and Eastern socialism.'[10] Between the opposition fête in Budapest and the smoke-filled rooms of the British Labour party, with its leadership busy trying to turn a socialist programme into a social democratic one, there is, perhaps, the trace of an historical connection.

Future historians will have to explain how Poland and Hungary, starting from such very different circumstances at the beginning of the 1980s, came to such relatively similar positions at the end of the decade. Among the general causes of these extraordinary developments, they will surely mention the impact of Gorbachev, the economic crisis, relations with the West, Solidarity and other forms of 'pressure from below', and perhaps also the intellectual crisis of the left in the rest of Europe. But to assess the relative importance and complex interaction of these major causes will require greater distance, tranquil reflection, and more sources.

In the meantime, we are condemned to reconstruct the story from a tissue of direct observation, official and unofficial publications, anecdote, and informed guesswork. In Poland, the story is one of a remarkable coming-together: for almost no one imagined that the great gulf between 'the power' and 'the society', between Jaruzelski

[10]In the Hungarian context this remark is directed specifically against the 'populists' of the Hungarian Democratic Forum, many of whom do maintain that there can be a specifically Hungarian 'third way'. And of course there are still some oppositionists in both Hungary and Poland who would firmly identify themselves as being on the left. Yet the general point may stand.

and Wałęsa, could be so swiftly bridged. Many details of this Polish bridge building are still obscure. But two things are clear. First, it would not have been possible without permission from Gorbachev. Secondly, the essential domestic impulse was given by two waves of strikes in May and August of 1988, with the second wave larger than the first, and the strikers putting the restoration of Solidarity at the top of their demands.

Markers on the path to the Round Table included a fraught and tentative debate about a possible 'anti-crisis pact', in the first half of 1988; a Byzantine sequence of private talks about talks; direct talks between Lech Wałęsa and the interior minister, General Kiszczak, which were literally precipitated by the second wave of strikes; a dramatic television debate between Wałęsa and Alfred Miodowicz, the leader of the official trade unions (OPZZ) at the end of November; and, last but by no means least, two stormy meetings of the central committee in which General Jaruzelski even threatened to resign in order to push through the direct dialogue with Solidarity.[11].

The role of Prime Minister Rakowski in all this is murky. The opening seems to have been led rather by General Kiszczak, who as interior minister presumably drew on police intelligence reports about rising popular discontent and the danger of an explosion; by a group of Party reformists including the former foreign minister, Józef Czyrek, and the former labour minister, Stanisław Ciosek; and by some top military men.[12] Rakowski, whose personal grudges against Solidarity go very deep, and who came into office in October 1988 proclaiming his own capacity to save the country without it, was not a major direct actor in the negotiations. The record may one day show this to be a grave underestimation of Mr Rakowski's capacity for duplicity. What is clear is that the conversion of Jaruzelski was

[11]The crucial Tenth Plenum meeting was on 16–18 January 1989. As a preliminary account of the path to the Round Table, by a leading participant, is Bronisław Geremek's article in *Tygodnik Powszechny*, 23 April, 1989.
[12]Among those who threatened to resign at this meeting, alongside Jaruzelski, Kiszczak, and Rakowski, was the defence minister, General Florian Siwicki. Ciosek was minister for trade union affairs in the first period of Solidarity's legal existence.

pivotal.[13] How and by whom that was done is still unknown (at least to this writer). But without question the personal role and authority of General Jaruzelski on this side is as crucial as that of Lech Wałęsa on the other.

The bridge is still of rope rather than steel. Seven years of bitter conflict are not easily forgotten. On both sides there are fierce and vociferous opponents of compromise. Alfred Miodowicz of the official trade unions is the most visible leader of reaction inside the Party. He has strong support from Prague and East Berlin (although that is not much use against Moscow!), a large constituency among the Party bureaucracy and *nomenklatura*, and even the chance of appealing to a significant part of the working class by a populist demagogy directed against the cost and injustice of economic reform. On the opposition side, teenagers still take to the streets shouting the angry chants of martial-law Poland, and Wałęsa's leadership is rejected by groups ranging from the right-wing nationalist Confederation for an Independent Poland (KPN) to the crypto-Trotskyite 'revolutionary' faction of the refounded Polish Socialist party (PPS-RD), as well as by his old comrade in the original Gdańsk strike, Andrzej Gwiazda. Polish politics today are anything but simple.

In the discussions of the Solidarity National Executive Commission (KKW), the lessons of 1980–1981 are constantly being drawn anew. One might almost say that both sides have learned politics. If in 1980 it was workers against apparatchiks, in 1989 it is politicians against politicians. In the long hours and days at the Round Table, the top leaders on both sides do seem to have come to understand each other better, and in part to have found a common language, or at least to have resolved to adhere to some basic rules of self-restraint in a period of political transition. This is still an 'understanding of

[13]This is perhaps the moment to recall the (apocryphal?) story about Jaruzelski and Professor Janusz Reykowski, a psychologist and now politburo member who also headed the government delegation in the Round Table group on political reform. The story concerns a conversation in the summer of 1982, at the height of Jaruzelski's attempt to destroy Solidarity under martial law. 'Is it true that myths never die?' asks Jaruzelski. 'That is correct, General,' replies the professor. Jaruzelski: 'But you have written that Solidarity has become a myth!' (The story is recounted by Dawid Warszawski in *Uncensored Poland News Bulletin*, No. 1, 1989.)

élites.'[14] It can be destroyed from below. In the provinces, things look very different. But the coming-together at the top remains staggering. Just one example: toward the end of the Round Table, Adam Michnik gave an interview in which he excoriated the obstructionism of the official trade unions, comparing them to the hated Zomo riot police. A few days later he was personally congratulated on this interview by... General Jaruzelski. Michnik, for his part, has subsequently gone out of his way to praise General Jaruzelski, publicly, for his political courage in deciding to reverse the course of the last seven years and reach an agreement with Solidarity.

In Hungary, by contrast, the story of the last few years is that of a remarkable coming-apart: the coming-apart of the Kádárite consensus, so that from one apparently seamless (although seamy) web there have suddenly emerged both real opposition parties and very distinct factions within the Hungarian Socialist Workers' party. Even six months ago no one would have imagined that at a fête held be the Alliance of Democratic Youth (FIDESZ) ‗ ‗ dapest youth park, the platform would b   an seven political groupings, with the m   rty just one among many, and seated near   roups represented were FIDESZ, itself, fou   ng[15]; the Alliance of Free Democrats (SZDS   arlier 'democratic opposition'; the Hunga   MDF), an important but inchoate 'pop   alled 'nostalgic' parties, the Social Dem   ers, whose predecessors received, respec   y-seven per cent of the vote in Hungary's la   November 1945; the People's party, an a   n vote, partly initiated by people from v   structures; and the Hungarian Socialist Wo ‗‗ party, that is, the Communist party as effectively refounded after its predecessor disintegrated during the 1956 revolution. Next to the Party representative there was an

[14]See the interview with Bronisław Geremek, *Polityka*, 22 April, 1989, in which he argues that the two sides found a common language, but angrily rejects the charge of an 'understanding of elites'. Yet this is a charge made not just by the journalists of an official weekly, but by many opposition activists, especially in the provinces.
[15]See above, pp. 245 and 269.

empty seat, which was meant to be taken by a spokesman for the Ferenc Münnich Society, a group of disaffected Stalinists. The ghost at the feast.

Not surprisingly at a FIDESZ rally the spokesman for FIDESZ, a forceful and charismatic activist called Viktor Orbán, and the spokesman for the Free Democrats, an eloquent sociologist called Bálint Magyar, earned the warmest applause. Yet as striking as the eloquence of the opposition speeches is the relative weakness of all their organizations. To be sure, most of them are very new. To be sure, as Poland has shown the real prospect of an election concentrates the mind wonderfully. Following the success of this year's 15 March demonstration, most of them got together with surprising alacrity and ease to form a so-called Opposition Round Table, with which it seems the authorities will now have to negotiate the terms of the next parliamentary election. Yet the rough membership figures given to me in April were remarkably small: a claimed (but dubious) 20,000 for the two 'nostalgic' parties, Social Democrats and Smallholders; some 14,000 for the Hungarian Democratic Forum; some 3,000 for the Free Democrats and 2,000 for FIDESZ. Solidarity has more than that in one factory. So far this really is, as Lewis Namier famously wrote of 1848, a 'revolution of the intellectuals'—or at most, of the intelligentsia.

Yet the Hungarian leadership seems to be retreating faster in front of this small, intelligentsia-based opposition than the Polish leadership has in front of their much more formidable, worker- and farmer- as well as intelligentsia-based opposition. Why? One partial answer might be: 'They can't think of any reason not to.' Heavily influenced by contact with the West, long unaccustomed to treating ideology as anything but a veil, fig leaf, or smoke screen, they really cannot think of any good reason why they should *not* give up power! A second, more contingent reason is the indecision of the Party leader, Károly Grósz. Hailed as an opportunistic, but tough and decisive leader when he took over from János Kádár in May 1988, he has proved surprisingly weak and indecisive.

A third, related reason may have to do with the continued struggle for power at the top of the Party. For in that contest, it has increasingly seemed that 'who dares, wins.' Throughout this year, one of Grósz's chief rivals and by now Hungary's most popular Party politician, Imre Pozsgay, has continually forced the pace of the Party's retreat: first, in February, securing a formal (albeit fudged) reassessment of the 1956 revolution and an explicit commitment to the multi-party system: then, in April, holding what was virtually a reformist factional meeting in the town of Kecskemet, and securing a ceremonial Politburo renunciation of the key Leninist principle of 'democratic centralism'; then, in May, winning a commitment to hold an early, special national Party conference in the autumn, with the prospect of further 'personnel changes'.

The pace is dizzy, speculation risks being confounded between the day of writing and the day of publication. At this moment it does look as if Pozsgay reckons that the best form of advance is retreat; that he hopes, perhaps, to transform the Party into something more like the Italian Communist party, and thereby to win not only the highest office for himself but also some twenty-five to thirty-five per cent of the vote in a genuinely free election, thus opening the way to a new coalition government (although perhaps reserving responsibility for foreign policy and defence to a new-style presidency). What is more, some independent opinion polls suggest that if Hungarians were to vote tomorrow he just might have a chance of winning such a percentage. But the Hungarians, unlike the Poles, are not going to vote tomorrow, or for several months, and these sentences already contain far too many 'ifs'.

Prediction is now, more than ever, impossible. The best and brightest people on both sides in Poland and Hungary have launched into a great and perilous adventure. 'You know,' one of the more intelligent Polish Party leaders said to one of the most intelligent of Polish opposition leaders during a coffee break at the Round Table, 'all the textbooks tell us how difficult it is to seize power. But no one has described how difficult it is to relinquish power.'

In this great adventure, there is, of course, one very large unknown. At the moment, the bounds of Soviet tolerance—or benign neglect— seem wide enough for almost anything. But opposition demands for transforming or leaving the Warsaw Pact, and for Austrian-style neutrality will surely test them to the very limit. More important, all the most acute observers in Poland and Hungary, whether in power or in opposition, share the prevailing Anglo-American scepticism about Gorbachev's chances of continued progress in his perestroika. A check or reversal there could not be without consequences here.

But even if there is no Soviet check or reversal, Polish and Hungarian politics over the next five years are likely to be, at best, an almighty muddle. A period of political turmoil and transition is no recipe for clear, consistent economic policy, and least of all for a policy that demands great material sacrifice from those for whose votes you are competing. Yet such a policy is, sooner or later, almost inevitable. In the absence of a currency reform, prices will have to go still higher. Factories will have to be shut, jobs lost. There will be more inequality as well as poverty. Beside the impoverished majority there is already a nouveau-riche minority, Polish and Hungarian yuppies driving around in Mercedes or BMWs.

A Thatcher government in Britain could sustain harsh measures only because it had clear democratic legitimacy, courts whose independence was unquestioned and an unusually strong executive: the 'elective dictatorship' of Lord Hailsham's famous phrase. The measures needed in Poland and Hungary are almost certainly much harsher, but no such strong, democratically and juridically legitimated government is in prospect for several years, if at all.

In the short term, the economic situation will get worse before it (perhaps) gets better. Inflation continues to soar in both countries. There are deep, latent conflicts in these societies—for example, between the interests of manual workers in nationalized industries and those of would-be capitalists, between the clerical and the secular—that have yet to be clearly articulated through opposition politics. And all the stale food of pre-war Central European politics, the prejudices and petty nationalisms, must be brought out of the totalitarian freezer, and aired a little while, before being thrown into the dustbin; or at least, as in Western Europe, being relegated to the political margins. Or so one hopes and prays.

'It may not be better,' says Lech Wałęsa, 'but at least it will be more fun.' He was always an optimist.

(MAY 1989)

INDEX